PRAISE FOR *THE ARMAGEDDON LETTERS*

"Tasty morsels from secret communications among Kennedy, Khrushchev, and Castro during the most dangerous confrontation in recorded history."
> — **Graham Allison**, author of *Essence of Decision: Explaining the Cuban Missile Crisis*; and director, Belfer Center for Science and International Affairs, Kennedy School of Government, Harvard University

"Manga meets the Missile Crisis in this compelling book. Through a creative mixture of illustrations, imagined conversations, historical analysis, and the actual letters written by Kennedy, Khrushchev, and Castro, James G. Blight and janet M. Lang enable readers to intellectually understand and emotionally feel what happened in the dark days of October 1962."
> — **Scott D. Sagan**, The Caroline S. G. Munro professor of political science, senior fellow at the Center for International Security and Cooperation and the Freeman Spogli Institute, Stanford University; and co-author (with Kenneth Waltz) of *The Spread of Nuclear Weapons: A Debate Renewed*

"*The Armageddon Letters* is a *tour de force* that brings the Cuban missile crisis harrowingly alive and makes it relevant for our current time. Based on nearly thirty years of path-breaking scholarship, it situates forty-three well-chosen documents in both their historical and human context, and enables the reader to probe between the lines. Blight and Lang also make clear that the genesis of the confrontation began long before October 1962, that the potentially catastrophic circumstances lasted for three agonizing weeks beyond the famous thirteen days, and that Cuba's threat calculus and behavior had an effect on the both the crisis and its aftermath. They thus laudably return Cuba to the Cuban missile crisis story. *The Armageddon Letters* will deeply engage both students and general readers, because it uniquely focuses on the emotions of Kennedy, Khrushchev, and Castro as they faced what each perceived to be no way out of an impending Armageddon. It will leave readers with the appropriate lessons they should derive from the missile crisis: we survived by luck, not skill; a similar crisis could well occur again; we must rely on empathy, not a false rationality, if we hope to avoid a future Armageddon."
> — **Philip Brenner**, professor of international relations, American University, and the co-author of *A Contemporary Cuba Reader: Reinventing the Revolution*.

"Relatively few people now alive recall the Cuban missile crisis of October 1962, and even fewer understand what happened, what thankfully did not happen, and why the crisis must not be allowed to disappear into the mists of history. James Blight and janet Lang, two innovative scholars who have long studied the crisis, have written a book that is a giant step toward rendering the events of October 1962 too memorable, too frightening, and too personal ever to be forgotten. We were lucky that the inclination of the leaders of the United States and the USSR, Kennedy and my father, was not to shoot first, then think, but was rather the opposite, to first think, then think once more, and not to shoot at all. Had either of them "shot first," we would not be alive today and, in that case, we would not have an opportunity to read this excellent book. The portraits of President Kennedy, my father, Soviet Chairman Nikita Khrushchev, and Cuban leader Fidel Castro are intimate, totally believable, and instructive. Based on decades of careful research, this is a work of sober history that reads like a horror novel with an almost miraculously lucky outcome. I could not put it down."

— **Sergei N. Khrushchev**, Senior Fellow, Watson Institute for International Studies, Brown University, author of many works on the life and career of his father, the former Soviet chairman Nikita S. Khrushchev, including *Nikita Khrushchev and the Creation of a Superpower*.

"If . . . the imperialists invade Cuba . . , following that event the Soviet Union must never allow the circumstances in which the imperialists could launch the first nuclear strike against it. That would be the moment to eliminate such danger forever through an act of clear legitimate defense, however harsh and terrible the solution would be, for there is no other."

Fidel Castro to Nikita Khrushchev, October 26–27, 1962

"Cuba's leader was ready to lead his country to nuclear incineration in October 1962. The world was literally on the eve of its end—Armageddon. Yet you are reading this book. Armageddon did not happen. Statesmanship, strategy, and serendipity gave you this opportunity to learn from this dramatic crisis, which is admirably and lucidly re-told and portrayed in this book. You are thus afforded the chance to make sure our successors will be alive to read it and learn from it in decades to come."

— **Jorge I. Domínguez**, professor of government, Harvard University, co-editor of *Debating U.S.-Cuban Relations: Shall We Play Ball?*

"Three cheers for epistolary history. In these crafty but wondrously expressive book, pen-pals Kennedy (dry, cool, defensive) and Khrushchev (explosive, tricky, soulful) were writing the bedrock literature of the nuclear age. There's a great gain of intimacy in this telling of the story, and no sacrifice of absurdity, no slighting of the essential madness in the nuclear fantasy. Fifty years after the October weekend when human civilization hung by a thread, Blight, Lang, and Company are reminding us irresistibly that the fantasy is not dead, the trap is still lethal, the danger is not over—that a tiny fragment of the world's nuclear arsenal could explode and end life on the planet forever."

   — **Christopher Lydon**, host of *Radio Open Source.*

"Jim Blight and janet Lang have written *The Armageddon Letters* after having spent much of the last twenty-five years vicariously peering into the abyss of Armageddon that was the Cuban missile crisis. They demonstrate the inadequacies of analyzing the crisis in any of the traditional ways, and instead provide us with a sophisticated applied psychology that reads like a Stephen King horror novel, but is thoroughly and painstakingly grounded in the historical record. They have accomplished something never before attempted: channeling, as exactly as the historical record allows, the raw experience of the three leaders as they confronted a tangle of mutual misunderstandings that could have resulted in the destruction of the human race. The three interwoven narratives will shock you. They will also demonstrate that the "stability" of mutual nuclear deterrence that we have come to take for granted is a shaky foundation indeed on which to ground humanity's continuing existence."

   — **Paul L. Wachtel**, distinguished professor of psychology, City College of New York, and the Graduate Center, City University of New York, and author of *Therapeutic Communication: Knowing What to Say, When*

The Armageddon Letters

The Armageddon Letters

Kennedy/Khrushchev/Castro in the Cuban Missile Crisis

James G. Blight and janet M. Lang

Graphic Narrative by Andrew Whyte
with storyline and dialogue by Koji Masutani

ROWMAN & LITTLEFIELD PUBLISHERS, INC.
Lanham • Boulder • New York • Toronto • Plymouth, UK

Front cover art is by Chang Dai, a Canadian animator/illustrator. More of her work can be found at bassetsketch.blogspot.com

Back cover graphic art by Andrew Whyte, a Vancouver-based illustrator. His website is at www.andrew-whyte.com

Cover design by Meredith Nelson, at Rowman & Littlefield Publishers, Lanham, MD.

Graphic Narrative:
  Artwork by Andrew Whyte.
  Storyline and dialogue by Koji Masutani, a filmmaker who directed the award-winning film, *Virtual JFK* (www.virtualjfk.com). Masutani also produces the transmedia projects for *The Armageddon Letters* (www.armageddonletters.com).

Published by Rowman & Littlefield Publishers, Inc.
A wholly owned subsidary of The Rowman & Littlefield Publishing Group, Inc.
4501 Forbes Boulevard, Suite 200, Lanham, Maryland 20706
www.rowman.com

10 Thornbury Road, Plymouth PL6 7PP, United Kingdom

British Library Cataloguing in Publication Information Available

Library of Congress Cataloging-in-Publication Data

Blight, James G.
  The armageddon letters : Kennedy, Khrushchev, Castro in the Cuban missile crisis / James G. Blight and Janet M. Lang.
      p. cm.
  Includes bibliographical references and index.
  ISBN 978-1-4422-1679-2 (cloth : alk. paper) —
  ISBN 978-1-4422-1681-5 (ebook)
  1. Cuban Missile Crisis, 1962—Drama. I. Lang, Janet M., 1948- II. Title.
PS3602.L55A89 2012
812'.6—dc23   2012026581

∞™   The paper used in this publication meets the minimum requirements of American National Standard for Information Sciences—Permanence of Paper for Printed Library Materials, ANSI/NISO Z39.48-1992.

Printed in the United States of America

To our three essential teammates:

Koji Masutani,
who showed us a passageway into the twenty-first century;

Donald Morrison,
who provided the means to "carry the fire"
into the twenty-first century;

and

David Welch,
who led us to our new headquarters for the
journey into the twenty-first century.

And they gathered them together to the place called in Hebrew, Armageddon ...
And the cities of the nations fell.

Revelation 16:16; 16:19[1]

I just want you to know: I was there.
I know,
I know,
I *know!*

Kurt Vonnegut, Slaughterhouse Five *(1968)*[2]

Contents

Foreword

The Armageddon Letters focuses on the historical moment in which humanity came close to its last breath. With time, this desperate moment risks slipping from view. Moreover, to large parts of the world and to a new generation of citizens, the crisis may never have even been in sight. Thanks to authors, James Blight and janet Lang, and to a remarkably inventive and comprehensive media interpretation of the crisis, the events of the Cuban missile crisis and the significance of the greatest nuclear war threat in world history come to light to a new generation and to readers and viewers everywhere.

The message of this book comes through loud and clear: leaders and leadership matter; personality and psychological factors can be decisive, and may be the only hope in crises as grave as a possible nuclear war. The human factor simply cannot be ignored. Fatigue, fear, suspicion, anger, perplexity, overconfidence—they all matter, and they never mattered more than they did in the October 1962 Cuban missile crisis, the most dangerous episode in recorded history. This singular fact is dramatized in this important new book, which takes us more deeply inside the psychological realities of Kennedy, Khrushchev and Castro than we have ever gone before.

The Armageddon Letters brings forth the vivid personalities and attitudes of these key participants, and enhances the looks into Kennedy, Khrushchev and Castro with up to date and clever narrative media including the graphic narrative form and theatrical devices, all the while remaining within the solid historical text. Blight and Lang have collaborated with gifted storytellers from other media including filmmakers, animators, social media and interactive web-based specialists to offer various perspectives on the crisis.

The Armageddon Letters is a radical twenty-first century variation of the epistolary form. Here you are, hovering with the men in the White House and Kremlin as they stood over clacking Teletype machines bearing the world's fate in each stamped typeface. And there you are, with Fidel Castro in a bomb shelter under the Soviet embassy in Havana, trying to write a letter to Soviet Chairman Khrushchev explaining why, if Cuba is invaded by U.S. forces, as expected, then Khrushchev should order an all-out nuclear attack on the U.S. And there you are, next to Khrushchev, as he gets this horrifying letter from Castro.

The historical truth of October 1962 is not only stranger than fiction. It is more disturbing than most fiction. If you simply made up stuff like this, readers would be unlikely to believe it. These scholars stick to the historical narrative as it happened. They are careful to stay out of the way of these momentous events, facts and personalities. The real-time correspondence during the crisis between Kennedy and Khrushchev and between Khrushchev and Castro crackles with dangerous threats and promises and pleas, and we can feel something of the full force of these letters and the dilemmas they created. As happens with all the best storytelling, we feel unaccountably that we don't really know how it will turn out—which is of course precisely the position Kennedy, Khrushchev, and Castro were in, and why they thought the event was so frightening, and why it was in fact so very dangerous.

The book's significance is enhanced because it is embedded in an equally path-breaking array of new media digital options. With a unique companion arsenal of short films, animations, blogs, podcasts, commentaries and feedback options for viewers, the crisis reveals itself from different angles, almost as if unfolding in real time. This project also embodies what communications people call transmedia storytelling or multiplatform storytelling—integrating the traditional twentieth-century words-on-paper and screen approach with many other twenty-first century media, chiefly via their website, www.armageddonletters.com. This is a breakthrough, in that *The Armageddon Letters* is both a historically vivid and accurate account by two leading scholars of the Cuban missile crisis, and its website offers varied experiences—from video to audio to animation. This is not to say that the medium is the message. But the startling message of this book—that a nuclear catastrophe very nearly occurred in October 1962, and the conditions exist for something like it to happen again—is dramatized and emphasized by the authors' highly effective use of cutting-edge media formats.

The transmedia work is masterminded by Blight and Lang's collaborator, the film director Koji Masutani. In his film, *Virtual JFK: Vietnam if Kennedy Had Lived*, this team combined compelling narrative writing with Masutani's beautifully directed, award-winning feature film. In that film, this trio of collaborators convincingly argues that, had he lived and been reelected, President Kennedy would not have Americanized the war in Vietnam—a conclusion full of implications for leaders in this century who mechanically stumble into foreign wars.

Virtual JFK was a multimedia project, in that it involved a film, a companion book, and a guide for high school teachers. But *Virtual JFK* was not a *trans*media project—a fully-realized integration of old media and new media, and its possibilities for interactivity and connectivity—i.e., for building a substantial virtual community involved in a common pursuit and working toward a common objective. In *The Armageddon Letters*, the team realizes the possibilities of transmedia storytelling to a remarkable extent. They are creating a communications model around crucial issues that stands as a beacon for future presentations of similar importance and complexity. Jim and janet's sharp historical narrative is married to a range of new media that, while less discursive than linear lines of type, reach deeply into our perceptual and emotional strata.

This is a beautifully written book and an important one. The Cuban missile crisis—so dangerous, so close to disaster, so potentially repeatable—is too important to be left to the scholars, policy analysts and even the news media. What this subject has needed, and now thankfully has found, are two specialists on the crisis who have reinvented themselves for the twenty-first century. Jim Blight and janet Lang—whose work over the past quarter century has revolutionized the scholarly understanding of the crisis, and contributed to policy and media awareness of this great historical international relations question—have now joined another revolution. They and their transmedia colleagues and creators have brought the twentieth-century's moment of maximum peril fully to the twenty-first century.

Peter Almond
Budapest, Hungary

Peter Almond is a producer affiliated with Beacon Pictures and Old Trace Road Productions. He produced *Thirteen Days* (2001) with Armyan Bernstein and Kevin Costner. He also produced *Raspad* (1990), a joint U.S.-Ukrainian-Russian docudrama about the Chernobyl nuclear disaster. In Budapest, he is currently making a film about the Central European University on the occasion of its twentieth anniversary, following its formation during the transformation of the former Soviet empire.

INTRODUCTION

Armageddon in Retrospect

"Carrying the Fire" of the Cuban Missile Crisis Into the Twenty-first Century

You have to carry the fire.
I don't know how to.
Yes you do.
Is it real? The fire
Yes it is.

Cormac McCarthy, *The Road* (2006)[1]

APRIL 2005: WHEN McNAMARA STOPPED;
WHEN WE BEGAN

It is April 27, 2005. We are sitting in our office at Brown University's Watson Institute for International Studies with Robert S. McNamara, the former defense secretary for Presidents Kennedy and Johnson, and our collaborator and co-author of twenty years. In a month and a half, Bob will turn 89. Bob has agreed to make one last public appearance to talk about the Cuban missile crisis. We are pleased that he has chosen our home institution for the occasion, which is bittersweet for all three of us.

At 3:45 p.m. we head out of the building, take a right on Thayer Street, and walk up the hill to Starr Auditorium, where the event will take place. We arrive five minutes before the scheduled beginning of the event and are let in by the police, who are restraining a crowd of rowdy people demanding to be let in. But the seating capacity has been reached and the fire regulations do not allow for anyone else to be admitted other than those of us who are on the program. Many of those pushing and shoving are protesting McNamara's appearance on campus. Some shout "war criminal" at him as

3

we enter the building and head down the hall to the auditorium. Bob grimaces, even though he is used to this. He turns and says, "I'm already on record agreeing with them, you know," and smiles grimly. Bob is referring to his comment in *The Fog of War* that he and General Curtis LeMay would have been tried as war criminals if Japan, rather than the U.S., had won the war in the Pacific in the Second World War.

Tom Gleason, from Brown's History Department and the Watson Institute, is the moderator. Tom, like some of the demonstrators outside the auditorium, used to hate Bob McNamara, principally for his role in the escalation of the war in Vietnam. But over the years, after numerous visits to Brown by Bob, Tom has come to believe that the man he calls "McNamara in winter" is a force for good, willing to admit mistakes, and encouraging scholars to investigate the war in Vietnam and the Cuban missile crisis.

It takes a while for us to get to the stage because people are sitting in the aisles. Bob, who has lately become noticeably unsteady on his feet but unwilling, as yet, to use a cane, nearly falls on a group of undergraduates. When he rights himself at the last moment, the crowd breaks into spontaneous applause. To this crowd of undergraduates, Bob McNamara is a celebrity, not a criminal. He's the man who worked for John F. Kennedy, the star of Errol Morris' Academy Award-winning film, *The Fog of War*. To these kids, Bob is a guy who steps out of their history books and veritably explodes, like some ancient avatar, into their presence. Bob waves at the crowd, and they cheer again. The atmosphere feels more like that of a rock concert than an address by a very old man who happens to be one of the few former officials still living who played a significant role in the Cuban missile crisis.

While we were still back in our office, we went over the drill for the program. Bob will give a summing up of what he has learned about the Cuban missile crisis and nuclear danger. Then one of us—Jim Blight—will offer some comments, depending on what Bob covers and leaves out. Then the audience will be invited to ask Bob questions.

Finally we reach the table and chairs on stage and sit down. We go over the drill one more time. Everything seems right and in place. Bob has on what has become his uniform for the trips to Brown: white shirt, sleeves rolled up, no tie, khaki pants, gray New Balance 991 running shoes, blazer slung over the back of his chair. He looks like the world's oldest living preppie. Like the audience, we are also anxious to hear how Bob puts everything together, twenty years after we began our research together into the missile crisis. We expect he will do what he does best: combine a technical mastery of the details of our findings with what can only be called a really *scary* presence—like that of an Old Testament prophet, eyes flashing, hands waving, and his left fist pounding the table to emphasize points.

Then it happens. As Tom Gleason is introducing the program, Bob leans over to Jim and whispers: "I can't remember what I was going to say—something about nuclear weapons, right? Anyway, you have to give the presentation, not me. You tell them what we've learned. If I can think of anything to add, I'll do that." Then Bob pauses, before adding, "I'm all done. Now it's up to you to carry on." So this is how it ends, just as unexpectedly as it began, twenty years ago. Bob is finished. Maybe he shouldn't have come up to Brown to give one last talk. Bob stares, glassy-eyed, straight ahead, into space.

Bob scrambles, interrupting Tom's introduction to say that he wants Jim to do the summing up because this is, after all, at Brown, and so the people from Brown—i.e., Jim— ought to take the lead. Something to that effect. Now it's Jim's turn to scramble. He says something about the lessons from *The Fog of War* that are particularly relevant to the missile crisis, especially lessons number one ("Empathize with your enemy") and number two ("Rationality will not save us.")

At roughly fifteen minutes into Jim's improvisation, the light goes on in Bob's imagination and he interrupts to "add a point of clarification." Then he launches into a forty-minute piece of performance art that is part horror movie ("we nearly blew up the world in October 1962"); part exhortation ("get off your butts and abolish nuclear weapons before they abolish you"); and part trip down memory lane ("President Kennedy told me this, Bobby said that; Jackie took me aside"). We look out at the crowd. The students in our honors seminar are sitting together in the front rows, on our left, and their eyes are popping out of their heads. Everyone sits silent, as if meditating on the furiously gesticulating man in front of them who is probably much older than their grandparents, and possibly older than anyone they have ever met.

Everything Bob says about October 1962 has this subtext:

> I was there; I have had direct experience in trying to handle a nuclear crisis with the fate of the world on the line; and because of my experience, I know—I am not guessing or speculating, I know, that we were just plain lucky in October 1962—and that without that luck most of you would never have been born because the world would have been destroyed instantly or made unlivable in October 1962. And something like it could happen today, tonight, next year. It will happen at some point. That is why we must abolish nuclear weapons as soon as possible.

For the moment, in this moment, the students understand all this implicitly. Although most of them are a breathtaking *seventy* or so years younger than Bob, they travel with Bob in space and time. They are scared. You can see it in their faces. They are learning something important. You can see that too. They are transfixed. Many will never forget this experience.

Finally, Bob stops and says, "Jim, I'm sorry to have interrupted, but I had something I wanted to add." The crowd erupts in gales of laughter, and Bob smiles too, though it is not entirely obvious that Bob understands why this comment is so hysterically funny. A thing or *two*? Then they are on their feet, cheering and clapping. We join the students in applauding Bob. They came for international political performance art from a master of the form and they have not been disappointed. They never guess that just an hour ago, Bob was unable to connect his memories with his message. Nor can they guess how utterly exhausted he is by the time he finishes.

Later that night, after dinner, we walk Bob to Gardner House, the inn on George Street where he is staying. It is raining. Bob trips on a brick and falls hard on the pavement. We help him to his feet, and up several sets of stairs, to his room. We say good night, making sure his alarm is set. As we are leaving, he says in barely more than a whisper: "That was fun. A good one to go out on. Remember: it's up to you two to carry on now." All three of us are overcome by a common sense that this is the end of something very special.

Remarkably, he is ready at 5:30 a.m., when his car arrives for the trip to T. F. Green Airport, where Bob will catch his plane for Washington. He will never give another public lecture on the Cuban missile crisis. After a steady decline, Bob McNamara will die on July 9, 2009, at age 93. We learn of it while reading the *New York Times* online in Waterloo, Ontario, where in six months we will move to take up positions at the new Balsillie School of International Affairs. The obituary states that in keeping with Bob's wishes, there will be no memorial service. While we had stayed in touch with Bob during his last years, we both feel like—at a deep level—we had already said our goodbyes in April 2005, after Bob had rallied one last time to connect the event and the cause for which he cared more than life itself.

*T*he *Armageddon Letters*—book and transmedia project—can be traced back to April 27, 2005. It is a response to Bob McNamara's challenge to us to, as we would now put it, "carry the fire" forward into the twenty-first century. With Bob gone from the scene, we were forced to ask ourselves: is it possible to build a time machine capable of vicariously transporting people in space and time to provide them with an authentic acquaintance with the experience of the Cuban missile crisis—with its scariness, its confusion, and a gut-level appreciation for the often admirable but always fallible humanity of its central participants—features that Bob himself brought to the subject?

OCTOBER 1962: WHEN OUR WORLD NEARLY ENDED; WHEN McNAMARA BEGAN

In October 1962, human civilization came very close to being destroyed. There is no longer any room for reasonable doubt on this subject, once so intensely debated among scholars and journalists. Armageddon was a hair's breadth away in October 1962. During the Cuban missile crisis, all the pieces were in place: the weapons and warheads were ready to fire all over the world; secretly deployed tactical nuclear weapons were prepared to incinerate invading U.S. troops on the north coast of Cuba; fear of holocaust gripped the White House and Kremlin; while in Cuba, Soviet and Cuban troops prepared for what they believed was their last battle, confident that Armageddon would begin on the island and that, in retaliation, Moscow would destroy the United States of America—"we should wipe them off the face of the earth," as Fidel Castro wrote on October 26th. Much of the data supporting the claim that the world nearly ended in October 1962 derives from our research, and that of our team, over the last quarter century.[2]

Armageddon would almost certainly have occurred if leaders in Washington and Moscow, John F. Kennedy and Nikita Khrushchev, hadn't stopped in their tracks, turned around 180 degrees and raced away from the brink in a panic at the foreshadowed doomsday. Armageddon was also avoided because Fidel Castro agreed, with profound reluctance, to allow the Soviets to remove the strategic nuclear weapons from the island—as had been agreed to independently by Kennedy and Khrushchev, without consulting or even informing him. These were weapons that Castro believed constituted the Cuban Revolution's last, best hope for survival in the face of unrelenting American hostility.

Gambler's luck was also essential to the great escape of October 1962. In Errol Morris's Academy Award-winning 2003 documentary film, *The Fog of War*, McNamara, has this to say about the Cuban missile crisis:

> I want to say, and this is very important: at the end we lucked out! It was luck that prevented nuclear war. We came that close to nuclear war at the end. [Gestures by bringing thumb and forefinger together until they almost touch.] Rational individuals: Kennedy was rational; Khrushchev was rational; Castro was rational. Rational individuals came that close to the total destruction of their societies. And that danger exists today.
> The major lesson of the Cuban missile crisis is this: the indefinite combination of human fallibility and nuclear weapons will destroy nations.[3]

Everything we have learned over the past quarter-century of research on the crisis supports McNamara's statement. In retrospect, knowing what we now know about the several ways the crisis nearly exploded into nuclear war, our escape from Armageddon in October 1962 seems almost miraculously lucky. The escape wasn't entirely due to luck. Kennedy, Khrushchev and Castro exhibited just enough cautious statesmanship, just in time, to pull the rabbit out of the hat. But we agree with McNamara: without a lot of good luck, the escape is virtually impossible to imagine.

We would be fools to expect to be this lucky again. The odds are that next time, the nuclear war that seemed imminent in October 1962 will likely materialize, in whatever circumstances, involving whichever parties, when they get as close to the nuclear brink as the three countries came in October 1962. In the Cuban missile crisis, one American pilot was killed and several Soviets died in an accident while moving a Soviet nuclear missile into position for possible use against the American naval base at Guantanamo Bay, in eastern Cuba. Next time the world finds itself this deep in a nuclear crisis—if there is a next time—it will likely be the last time. If Armageddon occurs, millions will likely be killed, maybe tens of millions. It may even, in the most extreme circumstances destroy entire nations, possibly all nations. This is what almost, but didn't quite, happen in October 1962.

THE FIRE BENEATH THE SMOKE: WHY THE IMPLICATIONS OF "IT WAS LUCK" ARE DEEPLY DISTURBING

The Cuban missile crisis was the most important non-event in recorded history. No one investigates the crisis because of what happened. Instead, hovering like a dark shroud over anyone who is exposed to some of the details of the events leading up to and through the crisis, is the specter of what might have happened, what very nearly happened.

Given the by now universal conclusion that Armageddon was just barely avoided in October 1962, due in part to more luck than anyone has a right to expect, you might think that we in the generations following this incredibly near miss would take its lessons to heart. You might think that we would focus more on the experience of the nearness to annihilation, and less on the fact of the miss.

But we don't. Rather, the Cuban missile crisis, history's most dangerous brush with man-made, total oblivion, means little or nothing to most people—even those in the U.S., Russia and Cuba, the three centrally involved countries. Is it denial? Is it the undoubted human tendency to treat long-ago events as more or less determined to turn out the way they turned out, conveniently forgetting that in real time, other options—including catastrophic options—may have been more likely?

Whatever the reason, the Cuban missile crisis means little or nothing to most citizens of the twenty-first century, even to that tiny minority of people who have some familiarity with the event. It was scary, yes. And yes, it seems to have been quite dangerous. But really, it was *so* long ago. It was *so* Cold War. We would rather revisit the early 1960s vicariously by watching "Mad Men"—all of the actors chain smoking, the guys with their thin lapels and thin black ties, the gals with bee-hive helmet hair and tight girdles. Some may enjoy playing any of the many video games allegedly based on the crisis, including several that promise lots of excitement from virtually participating in the nuclear war that didn't quite happen. With each passing year, the Cuban missile crisis differs less and less from all the other historical events that are psychologically mothballed, save for whatever entertainment value they seem to retain. We are willing to be entertained by a little of the smoke left in the wake of history's most dangerous crisis. We may even mouth words like "dangerous" or "Armageddon."

But chances are none of this makes us really afraid, even though *it should make us afraid*. If we could feel some portion of the fire that Bob McNamara felt, as a witness to the real Cuban missile crisis—even some virtual representation of it—we would be afraid. We would even, like the members of Bob McNamara's audience on April 27, 2005 in Providence, Rhode Island, be *very* afraid, perhaps even usefully afraid.

What's the fire beneath the smoke? What does it mean to say that in October 1962 mankind avoided destroying itself, principally due to luck? What are the constituents of the fire McNamara carried for so many years? We focus on six propositions. We recommend that you read them over slowly, more than once, and try to meditate on some of the implications of each one, in turn. They are only propositions, conclusions derived from a longstanding investigation of the Cuban missile crisis. This book, as you are about to discover, is not mainly about propositions. What it is about is what we call *vicariously experiencing* October 1962. But we think it is also useful to carry, as a kind of cheat-sheet on the crisis, a list of what we hope will become for you, via this book and the transmedia project it anchors, deeply disturbing implications. After more than twenty-five years investigating our subject, we now take the following truths to be self-evident:

1. *Armageddon is possible.* A catastrophic nuclear war nearly happened in October 1962. We know this not from science fiction, or any other kind of fiction, nor from hypothetical scenarios, prophecies or trend projections. We know it because it is now a matter of historical record. All three principal leaders came to believe, in October 1962, that they were staring down the gun barrel of nuclear war.

2. *Armageddon is possible even if leaders are rational.* If the world as we know it had been destroyed in October 1962, the destruction would have been initiated by leaders—John F. Kennedy, Nikita Khrushchev and Fidel Castro—who were fully aware of the capacity of nuclear weapons to destroy civilization, and who took very seriously their responsibility to preserve and protect their citizens. The absence of mutual empathy led to the crisis in the first place, and continued to heighten the danger as it evolved up to, but not quite past, the point of no return. There is not a shred of evidence that any of the leaders was anything other than rational, vigilant and responsible.

3. *Armageddon can become highly probable in a crisis.* The rationality of leaders can be overwhelmed by the perversity of the situation they believe they face in a *crisis*. Everything can seem to change. Even bedrock beliefs can become inverted. For example, the conviction that the adversary cannot possibly be contemplating a launch of its nuclear weapons—because it will lead to his own destruction in retaliation—can be called into question.

4. *Armageddon will likely occur inadvertently.* A nuclear catastrophe is *not* likely to be accidental—due to a mistakenly flipped switch in a missile silo, a pilot screwing up his orders, radar operators mistaking a flock of geese for a phalanx of enemy missiles, etc. It likely *will* be inadvertent. It will involve a series of conscious decisions that would have been unthinkable prior to the crisis, but which seem increasingly required as the crisis deepens.

5. *Armageddon remains virtually inevitable.* The indefinite combination of nuclear weapons and human fallibility will result in the destruction of human civilization.[4] During the Cuban missile crisis, the world contained roughly fifty thousand nuclear weapons. The detonation of even a small percentage of them would have led to the destruction of civilization, either instantly (if many or all had been detonated), or more slowly, if nuclear winter had been induced by the detonation of several hundred weapons. There are today more than twenty-two thousand nuclear weapons in the world. The detonation of less than one percent of these weapons—as few as two hundred of them—could bring on nuclear winter, and the slow, agonizing, inexorable extinction of civilized life on earth, perhaps of life itself.

6. *Nuclear weapons must be abolished.* In October 1962, the threat of Armageddon came out of the blue, unpredicted and unexpected by any of the involved governments. Efforts to make nuclear catastrophe less probable, while welcome in the short term, are inherently inadequate. Before the Cuban missile crisis, no one thought nuclear catastrophe was probable. Yet once the crisis began, Armageddon seemed astonishingly real and even likely under circumstances that were suddenly and shockingly imaginable. Therefore, Armageddon must be made not merely improbable—based on subjective judgments of highly fallible human beings—but impossible, based on the abolition of such weapons as swiftly and safely as possible.

Photocopy the list. Shrink it so it fits into your wallet. Make a prominent icon for it on the screen of your notebook computer and smart phone. Attach it to the door of your fridge. You will want to come back to it as, in this book and on our interactive website (www.armageddonletters.com), you begin to absorb some of the thicker texture of the raw experience of

Kennedy, Khrushchev and Castro in October 1962. Have the list handy so you can keep the big picture in mind as you step into our time machine, and back out again. Keep a light on over in the corner as you travel vicariously through what may seem like a Stephen King horror novel. Except this is not a novel. This horror almost happened, was thought at some points to be virtually inevitable or to have already begun. And what *virtually* happened in October 1962 in the imaginations of Kennedy, Khrushchev and Castro could *actually* happen at any time.

ARMAGEDDON IN RETROSPECT: KENNEDY/KHRUSHCHEV/CASTRO IN OCTOBER 1962

This book is organized around forty-three documents: thirty are letters and other communications between John F. Kennedy and Nikita Khrushchev—fifteen in each direction. There are three letters from Fidel Castro to Khrushchev and two from Khrushchev to Castro. In addition, two of Castro's letters to Acting UN Secretary General U Thant are included, along with five speeches and other statements by Castro. A letter from Jacqueline Kennedy to Khrushchev a week after her husband's murder in Dallas completes the document set. Most are edited, though some are not. Excised passages are indicated with ellipses. The sources from which we obtained the documents are listed in the endnotes. All are in the public domain and thus easily available. In Appendix A, we tell the story of the twenty-five-year quest by our colleagues and ourselves for these and many other documents.

But documents by themselves—even documents as remarkable and dramatic as the *Armageddon Letters*—do not supply their own context. They are just words on a page or screen unless they are accompanied by a sense of the context in which the letters and other documents were drafted, sent, received and answered. By supplying a thick texture of real-time context, we intend for these letters to work in three ways in this book:

- *The Raw Data of Nuclear Danger.* The letters are dramatic, idiosyncratic, sometimes desperate, often deceitful, sometimes angry and accusatory, and each reflects the personality, situation and intentions of one of the three leaders. Khrushchev, writing to Castro, is patronizing, condescending, defensive; Castro, writing to Khrushchev, is direct, challenging, emotional, mystified, defiant; Kennedy writing to Khrushchev is brief, to the point, and insistent; Khrushchev writing to Kennedy is dissembling, frightened, pleading and poetic, especially in his imagery of nuclear holocaust. In context, the letters reveal three leaders confronting a doomsday machine, which they have created for three distinct sets of defensive reasons but which, like a nuclear age

Frankenstein's monster, threatens to turn on them and completely destroy their societies. These documents constitute the most astonishing and revealing real-time literature of the nuclear age.

- *The* Look *of Nuclear Danger.* We massage the *Armageddon Letters* until they figuratively bleed the thick texture of the threat of nuclear war. We sometimes refer to this as *extreme contextualization* of the *Armageddon Letters*. It involves filling in between the lines of the letters, and is addressed to such questions as: what are the leaders in their three locations, and with their three different perspectives, seeing, hearing, anticipating, ordering, deciphering and planning? Cuba, by late October 1962, was surrounded by the largest peacetime military force ever assembled by the United States. Both U.S. and Soviet forces had gone to an unprecedentedly high level of war-readiness. Cuba was stockpiled with nearly half of the entire Soviet arsenal of nuclear warheads. One-third of the U.S. B-52 bomber force, loaded with nuclear bombs, was in the air at all times, encircling the Soviet Union and its satellites in Eastern Europe, its pilots waiting for the order to attack. We focus as accurately as the known facts allow on the "threat reality" of each leader, as he evolves through the crisis. As the crisis escalates and spirals toward its conclusion, information about the look of nuclear danger floods the three leaders. Decisions must be made quickly, in the midst of a shrinking time horizon and the progressive ratcheting up of threat levels.
- *The* Feel *of Nuclear Danger.* The *Armageddon Letters* are contextualized so as to reveal what it felt like, then and there, in Havana, Moscow and Washington, as the three leaders, exhausted and confused, careen through this unexpected and extraordinarily dangerous crisis. These three psychological realities evolve rapidly over the course of the crisis. The disconnects in the timing and trajectory of each leader's psychological evolution produce feelings that range from rage to despair to optimism to extreme pessimism. It even leads to the feeling—felt all over Cuba by both Cubans and Russians—that Armageddon is both inevitable and imminent. This feeling leads straightaway to aggressive actions that, in their outright defiance, actually raise the odds of the still-contingent catastrophe those on the island believe is inevitable.

The scheme for introducing the documents is identical throughout: each is given a number, from 1 to 43; the sender and recipient are identified and the document is dated; a one-line extract from the document is presented that sums up the central message contained in the document; next, you will encounter our contextualization of the document; finally, the document itself appears.

The six sections of the book containing the *Armageddon Letters* are not organized into traditional chapters. Instead, you will traverse a drama in four acts, along with a prelude and postscript. In the prelude, the three leaders and their governments *Sleepwalk* into a deep crisis, until finally and unexpectedly there is a *Collision* (Act I), following which the crisis seems to *Spiral* out of control (Act II). A miraculous, last minute *Escape* (Act III) is then followed by a dangerous three weeks in which all three leaders attempt to *Squeeze* (Act IV) concessions out of one another. The postscript contains historical and contemporary statements regarding *Hope* for the future emerging from the crisis.

We hope these letters, when significantly augmented by the contextual material in the book, along with the voluminous and varied material available at www.armageddonletters.com, permit you access to "Armageddon in Retrospect." What we mean by this is that although you will be looking *back* at events of a half-century ago, you will do so from within the *forward-moving* perspectives of the three principal leaders in the Cuban missile crisis. The Armageddon you will encounter is entirely *psychological*. It is a catastrophe imagined by the leaders of the U.S., Soviet Union, and Cuba. They begin to see events careening toward a catastrophic conclusion. Due in part to the shock of their collective vision of an imminent nuclear Armageddon, they search for, and ultimately discover, a way out.

"SHOW DON'T TELL": THE SIX-PART TOOLKIT OF THE ARMAGEDDON TIME MACHINE

The Armageddon Letters is the culmination of more than twenty-five years of research and writing about the Cuban missile crisis. In a half-dozen books and in dozens of articles, we have told and re-told the story of humanity's closest brush with nuclear catastrophe. As we recount in the appendices to this book, we began in the mid-1980s by telling the story from the viewpoint of leaders in Washington. Then, as Russian archives and former officials began to open up, we told the story of the crisis as viewed from Moscow. Finally, seeking to avoid being left out of the retelling of the story (as they were left out of the resolution of the crisis), Cuban scholars and the Cuban government invited us to discuss the crisis with their principal decision-makers, beginning with Fidel Castro himself. Many others have by now told their own versions of the Cuban missile crisis. It is probably the most extensively studied episode in the entire history of the Cold War.

This time, however, instead of us telling the story, we turn to Kennedy, Khrushchev and Castro to live out their own stories with you present as a fly on the wall in Washington, Moscow and Havana. The great Canadian band, *Rush*, provides us with our point of departure for presenting the crisis in this new way, on the lead track of their 1989 album, "Presto":

> (Show me, don't tell me)
> You've figured out the score
> (Show me, don't tell me)
> I've heard it all before[5]

We try to take good advice wherever we find it, even if, as in this case, it is accompanied by a throbbing base line and an ear-splitting drum solo.

So whether you think you've heard it all before about the Cuban missile crisis, or whether this is your first encounter with it, we hope this journey back to October 1962 is a lot more real and engrossing than the standard issue history you may be used to. In fact, we hope it reads like good fiction, in this regard, though it is manifestly *not* fiction. In some ways, it is stranger than most fiction: with the predicament less expected, the escape less plausible than authors can expect to get away with in a work of fiction. And the impressions that emerge of the three principal leaders are, we hope, both larger than life and yet all too human in their respective shortcomings. Yes, these guys acrobatically leapfrogged their way out of the most dangerous crisis in recorded history, but the same trio stumbled clumsily and myopically into the mess in the first place.

This time we show you what the crisis was about and what it was like by plunging you vicariously into an Armageddon time machine. Call it a retrospective psychological shuttle service: prepare to shuttle back and forth vicariously between Washington, Moscow and Havana, as you inhabit the retrospective reality of our three leaders. We hope you will feel some of the tension and danger they felt by late October 1962, as you become a fly on the wall in Washington, Moscow, and Havana—a journey back to the most dangerous moment in human history—in a time machine equipped, moreover, with an unprecedented, six-part toolkit for its readers:

- *Familiar names.* Prepare to meet your new colleagues: Jack, Nikita Sergei'ich and Fidel. We like the immediacy and personal connection associated with the use of familiar names.
- *Psychological context.* We provide the thick texture in which the letters were composed, sent and received, drawing on hundreds of interviews and thousands of declassified documents, involving all the key players.
- *Present tense.* The book is written so as to draw the reader into the here and now as it was experienced in the crisis, emphasizing a growing awareness of moving forward, with great uncertainty and fear.

- *Graphic narrative.* Each chapter begins with panels of original graphic art by Andrew Whyte, with storyline and dialogue by Koji Masutani. Each captures pictorially key points dealt with in each chapter.
- *Theatrical previews.* Each chapter begins with a "Theatrical Preview"— which acts as an executive summary for readers without extensive background in the history of the crisis.
- *www.armageddonletters.com.* Video, audio, blogs, podcasts, debates, films, animation, live-action presentations and much else is aimed at connecting the history with the present and future, especially for young people, who will have the ultimate responsibility for ushering the human race safely through the first half of this twenty-first century. Visit us early and often. The website will be updated regularly and will include our responses to your comments, queries and criticisms.

"YOU HAVE TO CARRY THE FIRE"

It is some years after Armageddon. As a result of the global conflagration, all life on planet earth, including human life, is being extinguished. The living envy the dead. The unlucky survivors are scavengers of canned goods processed before Armageddon, or cannibals, or both. A father and son are trekking down the east coast of the United States in search of warmth. In Cormac McCarthy's Pulitzer Prize-winning 2006 novel, *The Road*, we travel with the pair as they confront one unspeakable horror after another.

When at last the father lay dying, he commands his son to "carry the fire" after his death. What the father seems to mean is that the boy should try his best to maintain some remnant of the values of civilized human life as it was experienced prior to Armageddon. Although it might mean more, at a minimum it means adherence to the principle of no cannibalism. One who carries the fire does not consume his own kind, no matter what. In a scene of great poignancy at the end of the book, the following exchange takes place.

You're going to be okay, Papa. You have to.
No, I'm not. Keep the gun with you at all times. You need to find the good guys but you can't take any chances. No chances? Do you hear?
I want to go with you.
You cant.
Please.
You cant.
You have to carry the fire.
I don't know how to.
Yes you do.

Is it real? The fire?
Yes it is.
Where is it? I don't know where it is.
Yes you do. Its inside you. It was always there. I can see it.[6]

Hope is wrapped, hermetically sealed, inside a post-apocalyptic context of total hopelessness.

We were luckier in October 1962 than were the world's inhabitants of McCarthy's fictional dystopia. We "lucked out" and avoided Armageddon. But the conditions are all in place right now, which make Armageddon possible. We still have the means to destroy all life on this planet with but a tiny fraction of the world's existing nuclear arsenals. The question is: will we take advantage of our good fortune? Will we learn to focus more on the nearness of the brush with Armageddon, and less on the (lucky) fact of our escape?

As you prepare for your encounter with the Cuban missile crisis in this book and on our website, we urge you to step into the fire of October 1962 until you see and feel some significant approximation to what Kennedy, Khrushchev and Castro saw and felt, and also what Bob McNamara saw and felt, in history's most dangerous episode. Once you feel the heat, you must find your own means, appropriate to your circumstances, of carrying the fire of the Cuban missile crisis into this already terribly violent, increasingly dangerous, twenty-first century. *You* have to carry the fire. Yes, yes, we know: right now you think you don't know how to. But you will. Let Jack, Nikita Sergei'ich and Fidel show you the way.

CAST OF CHARACTERS

Three Leaders/Three Crises

John F. Kennedy, Nikita S. Khrushchev, and Fidel Castro are the leaders whose misunderstandings and missteps plunged the world toward Armageddon in October 1962, and whose insight and acumen reeled the world back from the brink of catastrophe, barely in time. Who *are* these guys? If we can get inside their heads, we will have a decent shot at understanding how three exceptional leaders, none of whom, prior to the crisis, sought to wage a catastrophic nuclear war, nearly ignited one anyway.

Remarkably, they have provided us with the Cold War equivalent of the Rosetta Stone for grasping how all three experienced the crisis. These are what we call *The Armageddon Letters*—the correspondence and other communications between Kennedy and Khrushchev, and between Khrushchev and Castro—before, during and after the crisis. There is nothing like them in the history of the Cold War. Pushed to the brink of Armageddon, with time running out, the three leaders communicated with a degree of candor and clarity that is astonishing. A reader who understands the context in which *The Armageddon Letters* were drafted by their authors and read by their recipients can vicariously step into the flow of the forward-moving stream of history, as it seemed headed for nuclear oblivion by the end of October 1962.

This cast of characters is a starter kit to help you begin to get inside the heads of these men, with respect to the great crisis of October 1962. Our sketches are targeted at the three incompatible sets of conclusions drawn by our illustrious trio in the wake of the April 1961 failed U.S.-backed invasion at the Bay of Pigs, and actions taken by the three leaders over the next eighteen months that culminated in the near catastrophe of October 1962.

We want you to feel as if you are with our three guys in real time, and that you feel as if you are acquainted with these guys personally. To enhance the process of taking you inside their heads, we refer to them in the present tense, and by their familiar names—"Jack" for John F. Kennedy; "Nikita Sergei'ich" for Nikita S. Khrushchev (using the Russian patronymic,

"Sergeivich," as it is spoken aloud, by dropping the penultimate syllable); and "Fidel" for Fidel Castro Ruz ("Ruz" being his matronymic, which is seldom used in his case).

We think using the present tense in a work of history (versus a historical novel) will facilitate your understanding of what your new acquaintances Jack, Nikita Sergei'ich and Fidel *believe* the crisis *is* about, and what it *feels* like as they unwittingly *take* the world close to Armageddon; then, with a lot of luck, effort and creativity, *steer* safely past it, though just barely.

On with the show, beginning with some background on the Bay of Pigs, followed by brief sketches—verbal and pictorial—of your three famous new acquaintances.

THE BAY OF PIGS INVASION: WHERE THE TROUBLE STARTS

It is now clear when and where the momentum begins toward the great crisis of October 1962, the moment when an unsuspecting world will come closer than ever before or since to the brink of nuclear Armageddon. The moment: April 17, 1961. The locale: the Bay of Pigs.

Shortly after midnight on that April evening, approximately 1,400 commandos begin to arrive at *Playa Girón* (Girón Beach) from the *Bahia de Cochinos* (Bay of Pigs), on Cuba's south central coast. Trained in Guatemala by the American CIA, which has also supplied arms and munitions, their goal is go to ashore, establish a beachhead, and hold it against the expected counterattack by the army and militia of the Cuban government led by Fidel Castro. In time, the men of Brigade 2506, as the invasion force is called, hope to link up with their comrades—the anti-Castro rebels in the Escambray Mountains some 80 miles away. They also expect assistance from the U.S. Armed Forces, which many in the Brigade believe will lead to a large-scale U.S. military intervention, the overthrow of the government, and its replacement with rebel leaders living in exile in Miami.

Instead, the invaders are defeated within 72 hours by Cuban militia forces in fierce fighting at *Playa Girón*. Trapped without the expected control of the air over the beach and surrounding area, the *brigadistas* are pounded by surviving remnants of Fidel Castro's small air force before, during, and after the landing. The U.S. forces do not intervene either in the air or on the ground. The invaders cannot link up with their comrades in the Escambray Mountains; the internal resistance to the government is crushed throughout Cuba as a result of the invasion; the socialist character of the Cuban Revolution is proclaimed by Fidel Castro; and the new U.S. administration of President John F. Kennedy is humiliated. The invaders who survive are

imprisoned; the Cuban Revolution is consolidated; and the U.S. administration that has trained and supplied the rebels is in disarray.

In its immediate aftermath the event seems destined to become just another half-remembered blip in the long arc of the Cold War. A little more
than 100 fighters die in action. The rest are released from Cuban prisons in
December 1962 via a deal in which the U.S. trades agricultural and medical
supplies to Cuba in exchange for the surviving prisoners. The Castro government in Cuba survives the test. A communist Cuba ruled by Fidel Castro
appears to be more assured than ever. It is destined to remain a thorn in
the side of Washington.

The connection between the Bay of Pigs invasion and the crisis of October 1962 is fundamentally *psychological*: the three principal actors—Kennedy, Khrushchev, and Castro—subscribe to conflicting narratives within
which they understand the meaning and significance of the Bay of Pigs
invasion. Trapped inside the bell jars of their individual narratives, and
insufficiently curious about the narratives of the others, the three leaders
begin in April 1961 to sleepwalk toward a nuclear catastrophe. So too does
the world at large, as these leaders begin to deploy, configure and prepare to
use the military might at their commands in ways that are consistent with
their individual narratives.

The shock to all three is profound when these leaders, their narratives,
and their military machines finally collide in October 1962. By the final
weekend in October, all three begin to grasp how mistaken they have been
about what their counterparts had concluded about the Bay of Pigs invasion, and how perverse and dangerous the predicament in which they now
find themselves has become. Without intending to do so, they transform
what has formerly been the globally insignificant vacation destination of
Cuba into a temple of nuclear doom. That they find a way to avoid pulling
the temple down on top of themselves and their nations seems, in retrospect, almost miraculous.

The following three sketches are divided into three parts, focused on
each leader's narrative of the significance of the Bay of Pigs invasion; his
understanding of the crisis that explodes in his face at the end of October
1962; and the particular predicament he finds himself in, as he endeavors
to navigate history's most dangerous crisis. A good way to begin to understand why the crisis occurred is to meditate on the implications of the singular fact that the crisis is known by a different name in the U.S. ("Cuban
missile crisis"), Russia ("Caribbean crisis") and Cuba ("October crisis").

JACK KENNEDY

Jack's Bay of Pigs Narrative: "Never again!"

Jack knows he made a mistake: he trusted the rosy estimates of his military and intelligence advisers. They proved to be dead wrong in almost every respect. He strongly suspects they will look for other ways to corner him into launching an attack on Cuba, which they believe threatens vital U.S. interests. Cuba, to Jack, is a nuisance, a bit player on the world stage and he wants its profile on his agenda reduced accordingly. He knows he will have to give the Cuban exiles some token support. In their delusional view, they still believe they can overthrow the Castro government. However that works out, Jack has had it with Cuba; he is not interested in picking a fight with Castro. He will be satisfied with co-existence with Cuba which is, after all, hardly a threat to the U.S., or anyone, in its present condition. He vows never again to be talked into a military move against Cuba.

Jack's Cuban Missile Crisis

To Jack Kennedy, as to virtually all Americans, this crisis is all and only about the deceptive, deceitful deployment of Soviet nuclear missiles in Cuba. The crisis has nothing to do with Cuba itself, except as a staging ground for the latest Soviet Cold War adventure. No secret Soviet deployment, no crisis—it's that simple. The bad guys put the missiles into Cuba. The good guys found out just in time, before the missiles became operational and capable of striking targets in the U.S. Now the bad guys must be forced to remove them.

Jack's Dilemma: How to Remove the Missiles and Avoid War?

On October 16, 1962, when Jack is shown irrefutable photographic evidence that Soviet nuclear missile sites are nearing completion in Cuba, he feels as if he is in a box from which there may be no escape. Believing all the lies he has been told by Khrushchev and his associates, he had talked himself into believing that the Soviets would never go as far as they have gone in Cuba. Jack issued a statement on September 4, in fact, explaining that nuclear missiles in Cuba would be unacceptable to Washington, and that any such missiles and related equipment would be removed by force, if the Soviets refused to remove them voluntarily. But now he faces a trade-off he never dreamed of: how can he force the Russians to remove the missiles, but without provoking a war that would almost certainly escalate to a nuclear exchange between the U.S. and Soviet Union, an eventuality so catastrophic that he cannot fully imagine its consequences? On the other hand, he is under tremendous political pressure even within his own party to remove the missiles by force.

NIKITA SERGEI'ICH KHRUSHCHEV

Nikita Sergei'ich's Bay of Pigs Narrative: "I must save Cuba!"

Nikita Sergei'ich is filled with the romance that a socialist Cuba has become for him. This is why he is horrified at the prospect of "losing" Cuba to the Americans. The invasion at the Bay of Pigs was simply stage one, he is convinced, of an effort that will culminate in an all-out military effort by the Kennedy administration to attack, invade and occupy the island with the objective of replacing the Castro government with one similar to that which Fidel overthrew—that is, a puppet government that will obey Washington's commands. Nikita Sergei'ich begins his effort to save Cuba by hurling insults and threats at Kennedy, and by raising the ante militarily by giving the Cuban government a wide array of weapons systems and training from Soviet specialists in how to use them. By April 1962 his thinking has become more radical: nuclear missiles, he thinks, are what is needed to deter the aggressive instincts of the Kennedy administration. And so Operation ANADYR, history's largest peace time movement of military equipment and men is set in motion, under a cloak of deception, and accompanied by denials to the Americans that any such operation exists.

Nikita Sergei'ich's Caribbean Crisis

Nikita Sergei'ich, like all Russians to this day, calls the crisis the Caribbean crisis, because it had its origin, as they see it, in U.S. aggression against Cuba. The salient fact is that from the moment of Kennedy's dramatic speech on October 22, 1962 announcing the existence of nuclear missile sites under construction in Cuba, the U.S. transformed the entire Caribbean into a war zone. A blockade of the island, which the Americans have tried to justify by calling it a "quarantine," is set up in the South Atlantic, hundreds of miles from Cuba, with the objective of stopping all Soviet ships bound for Cuba which might be carrying goods connected with the construction of the missile sites on the island. The crisis has nothing to do with Soviet deception or deceit, as the Americans claim. The bad guys threatened their little neighbor. The good guys came to their rescue. The bad guys will cease to threaten their little neighbor again, because the little neighbor will soon have some of the world's biggest weapons on its soil.

Nikita Sergei'ich's Dilemma: How to Remove the Missiles and Save Face?

Nikita Sergei'ich never dreamed the Americans would discover the deployment before it was completed. But they have. Now the Americans, with overwhelming local military power in the Caribbean, and with a big advantage in nuclear capability as well, are trying to force the removal of the missiles in Cuba. So the missiles will have to come out. But how can Nikita Sergei'ich save face and claim victory—how can he order the removal of the weapons and still claim to leave Cuba safe from U.S. intervention?

FIDEL CASTRO

Fidel's Bay of Pigs Narrative: "Kennedy Will Destroy Us"

Fidel is convinced that Kennedy cannot accept the Cuban Revolution because the American people will never accept a communist state in their neighborhood. The victory of the revolutionary government at the Bay of Pigs will have a supremely paradoxical effect. Though it was a victory, it will raise the odds sky-high that the Havana government will be crushed in a massive military campaign whenever the Kennedy administration feels it is ready to attack. Cuba can try to resist a U.S. attack and invasion, but if the Americans are determined to succeed, Cuba will be destroyed. Thus, the objective of Cuba's foreign policy following the Bay of Pigs victory is to convince the Soviets to discharge their socialist responsibility. In the event of Cuba's imminent destruction by the Americans, the Soviets should launch a nuclear attack on the U.S. and destroy the enemy forever. Of course, Cuba will be the first to be destroyed. But Cuba is willing, Fidel believes, so long as the Soviets will martyr them for socialism by taking down the U.S.

Fidel's October Crisis

Fidel, like his fellow Cubans, always refers to the crisis as the "October crisis." When asked why the crisis is named after the month in which it occurred, the answer given by most Cubans is: "because with the Americans bearing down on us in those days, there were crises every month, and this one was in October." But there is more to the name than chronological convenience. October 1962 was the month in which Cuba became the hinge of the world, the spot on the map where Armageddon might commence, and Cuba's insistence on its dignity and independence would be the cause. During the last week of October, many Cubans assumed each evening that they would be destroyed by the following day.

Fidel's Dilemma: How to Redeem Cuba's Destruction?

Fidel is convinced following the Bay of Pigs victory that the days of his revolution are numbered. The Americans are coming and intent on destroying the Cuban Revolution. His dilemma, therefore, is how to ensure that Nikita Sergei'ich understands Cuba's situation, but without scaring him off, on the one hand; and, on the other hand, how to raise the odds that if and when Cuba goes down, the Soviets take the Americans down as well, martyring Cuba for global socialism.

PRELUDE

Sleepwalk

November 9, 1960–September 11, 1962

Theatrical Preview

[Voice-over: The Cuban missile crisis's three protagonists are actors on a stage. It is sometime between late April 1961 and early September 1962. John F. Kennedy and Nikita S. Khrushchev are sleepwalking. They wander around the stage seemingly at random, yet conversing about complex issues of international affairs. Though asleep, they engage in spirited discussions about many of the international issues and crises in which they have a shared interest.]

NIKITA SERGEI'ICH: [Roly-poly, ebullient, gesticulating.] Mr. President, the U.S. and its allies better get the hell out of West Berlin, or I will tell the East Germans they are free to shut it down, close it off and absorb it into the communist state of East Germany. I'm not kidding, blah, blah, blah.

JACK: [Elegant, suave, one hand in suit coat packet.] Sorry, Mr. Chairman, but the U.S. and its allies are in West Berlin to stay. You, your Soviet colleagues and the East Germans might just as well get used to it. I'm not kidding, either, blah, blah, blah.

NIKITA SERGEI'ICH: [Continuing to wander aimlessly around the stage.] Let's talk about the Test Ban. We need a nuclear test ban.

JACK: [Also continuing to wander aimlessly.] Yes we do, Mr. Chairman; it is a top priority of mine. We cannot allow ourselves to fail to sign a Test Ban Treaty at the earliest opportunity.

[Fidel Castro, the third actor on stage, is decidedly not *asleep. The actor playing Castro is a precocious ten year-old child. "Castro" is dressed up in green fatigues and a fake black beard.]*

FIDEL: Hey, Comrade Nikita; hey, Kennedy! Hey, I'm talking to both of you, dammit! Listen to me. We Cubans know the gringos are going to try to destroy our revolution. Isn't that right, Kennedy? And what are you going to do about it, Comrade Nikita?

[While Fidel shouts, Kennedy and Khrushchev appear unaware of Fidel's existence, which agitates and irritates Castro mightily. He shouts louder. He gets up in their faces and screams at each of them. He waves his arms in their faces. Still nothing. Fidel gets no response.]

NIKITA SERGEI'ICH: We are the superpowers, Mr. President. We are the leaders of the two groups of humanity—east and west; communist and capitalist. We need to peacefully coexist, because otherwise we will blow each other off the earth with our powerful missiles and weapons. Then, maybe after a while, you capitalists will give up, and the smart ones will become communists. Ha ha ha!

JACK: But, Mr. Chairman, history is on our side. You'd better be prepared for that.

[Meanwhile, Fidel grows livid at being ignored.]

FIDEL: [Shouting at the sleepwalking Khrushchev.] Wake up, you Russian bear! We Cubans know the enemy—the Yankees; we know Kennedy won't be able to tolerate the existence of a revolutionary communist government on the U.S. doorstep; we know your missiles will be shocking to Kennedy and to all the North Americans, which is why you need to deploy them openly, not secretly and deceptively, as if what you and we are doing is immoral or illegal or wrong; we are all heading for a violent showdown, and you had better be ready to go all the way to nuclear war, if that is what it takes to face down the gringos. But no! You can't hear us because you don't want to hear us. You think we are just a bunch of emotional, hot-tempered, Latin blowhards who don't understand how superpower leaders think. But when Kennedy is finally shocked into the realization that Soviet nuclear missiles are in Cuba, you'd better hold onto your vodka, because the gringos will show you just how angry and aggressive a neighborhood bully they really are.

[Nikita Sergei'ich is oblivious to Fidel's ministrations.]

FIDEL: [Shouting at the sleepwalking Kennedy.] Wake up, Uncle Sam! We know you want to destroy us, which is why you are sabotaging our country and why you are trying to assassinate me with your dirty tricks; you don't believe us when we say to you that just as we kicked your ass at the Bay of Pigs, we will also prevail the next time around, even if you send in the U.S. Marines, which you will, as we know from our own history with the U.S. empire. So keep in mind, as you continue to move your military assets closer to Cuba, that when you next try to conquer us, you will have carried out step one of committing national suicide. Of course, in your arrogance, you don't believe anything we say. But when the destruction of the United States of America begins, you can't say we didn't warn you!

[Jack and Nikita Sergei'ich do not respond to Fidel.]

NIKITA SERGEI'ICH: Blah, blah, blah Berlin; blah, blah, blah Test Ban, Mr. President.

JACK: Blah, blah, blah, Berlin; blah, blah, blah Test Ban, Mr. Chairman.

[Fidel, arms crossed, is silent in his rage.]

End of Theatrical Preview

* * *

#1

Nikita S. Khrushchev to John F. Kennedy

November 9, 1960[1]

> *"longing for deliverance from . . . a new war."*

Nikita Sergei'ich is thrilled by the victory of John F. Kennedy over his old nemesis, Richard Nixon, Eisenhower's hawkish, communist-baiting vice president. Throughout the campaign, he has followed what he calls his "vow of silence"—not commenting publicly on his views of the two candidates, feeling that any support he might voice for Kennedy would hurt Kennedy's chances in the election. Filled with optimism in this, his first letter to President-elect Kennedy, Nikita Sergei'ich foreshadows the two paramount issues on which he wants to engage Kennedy as soon as the new U.S. president is inaugurated on January 20, 1961: the nuclear threat and the vexing question of the "two Germanies."

With missionary-like zeal, Nikita Sergei'ich wants Kennedy to join him in a quest to rid the world of nuclear weapons, an aspiration apparently at odds with his pride in the progress made by the Soviet Union under his leadership in catching up to the U.S. in its capacity to annihilate the adversary with nuclear weapons. He sees the contradiction, but feels that successful negotiations toward a non-nuclear world must await the moment, coming soon, when both superpowers can sit down and bargain as equals. Nikita Sergei'ich is equally obsessed by the need to resolve

*the so-called "German question." West Berlin, situated entirely within the borders
of Soviet ally East Germany, is governed by the U.S., Great Britain, and France.
It is, Nikita Sergei'ich feels, an anomalous, unacceptable leftover of the Second
World War. All of Berlin should, rightly, belong to East Germany. The situation
is urgent, because East German refugees are escaping in ever-larger numbers to
West Berlin, seeking a better life in the much more prosperous West, as well as an
escape from the repressive East German regime.*

*These issues will weigh heavily on both leaders soon enough. But for now,
Nikita Sergei'ich is excited by the prospect of working with an adversary who, according to his sources, is highly intelligent, moderate in his political instincts and,
at the very least, someone other than Richard Nixon.*

Esteemed Mr. Kennedy:

Allow me to congratulate you on the occasion of your election to
the high post of president of the United States.

We hope that while you are at this post the relations between
our countries would again follow the line along which they were
developing in Franklin Roosevelt's time, which would meet the basic
interests not only of the peoples of the USSR and the United States
but all mankind, which is longing for deliverance from the threat of
a new war.

I think you will agree that the eyes of many people are fixed
on the United States and the Soviet Union because the destinies
of world peace depend largely on the state of Soviet-American
relations.

We have declared our respect for the peaceable and gifted people
of the United States and we are ready to develop the most friendly
relations between the Soviet and the American peoples, between the
governments of the USSR and the United States.

We are convinced that there are no insurmountable obstacles to
the preservation and consolidation of peace.

For the sake of this goal we are ready, for our part, to continue efforts to solve such a pressing problem as disarmament, to settle the
German issue through the earliest conclusion of a peace treaty and
to reach agreement on other questions, the solution of which could
bring about an easing and improvement of the entire international
situation.

Any steps in this direction will always meet with the full understanding and support of the Soviet government.

I wish you fruitful activity in the responsible capacity of United
States president and prosperity to the American people.

N.S. Khrushchev

* * *

#2

John F. Kennedy to Nikita S. Khrushchev

November 10, 1960[2]

> *"The achievement of a just and lasting peace"*

Overwhelmed with tasks in the immediate aftermath of his very close election, Jack is surprised by the warm, effusive letter from Khrushchev. In the midst of moving the nerve center of the presidential transition from Hyannis Port, Massachusetts to West Palm Beach, Florida, Jack can only convey his receipt of the Soviet leader's letter and his concurrence with the urgency of Khrushchev's stated dedication to world peace. Their joint, bottom-line commitment to avoiding a nuclear war between the superpowers will be severely tested in the coming months and years.

Dear Mr. Chairman:

I am most appreciative of your courtesy in sending me a message of congratulations. The achievement of a just and lasting peace will remain a fundamental goal of this nation and a major task of its president. I am most pleased to have your good wishes at this time.

John F. Kennedy

* * *

#3

John F. Kennedy to Nikita S. Khrushchev

February 22, 1961[3]

> *"a greater element of clarity"*

Now having assumed office, Jack is feeling deeply ambivalent about Soviet chairman Khrushchev. On the one hand, he is relieved to hear from his top advisers on Soviet policy that Khrushchev seems convinced, as Jack has become convinced, that a war between the superpowers must be avoided because the war will almost surely escalate to a global nuclear "exchange" in which whole nations would likely be destroyed, including the United States and Soviet Union. He has heard this not only from his ambassador in Moscow, Llewellyn Thompson, but also from three other veteran Soviet watchers: Charles Bohlen, Averill Harriman and George

Kennan. Jack, having just days earlier received his initial briefings from the U.S. military brass, has been shocked into a view identical with Khrushchev's: a war between the U.S. and Soviet Union will be mutually suicidal. After hearing from his Air Force chief in early February that in the event of a war with Moscow, the U.S. plan for retaliation calls for the total annihilation of the Soviet Union, China and all their allies—involving the probable deaths of hundreds of millions of people—Jack is heard saying to his secretary of state Dean Rusk, "my God, and they call us the human race?"

Yet he is far from comfortable simply knowing in detail, as he presumes Khrushchev knows in similar detail, that on his watch as president, Washington and Moscow together have the capacity to destroy human civilization many times over. Jack would like to believe this is a reliable deterrent to war, but he doesn't believe it at all. One reason is that he has arrived in office with a profound appreciation for the importance of unintended consequences, derived in part from his experience as a PT-boat commander in the Pacific during World War II, which he characterizes as "one goddamned unexpected mess after another." He nearly lost his life in the most famous of these "messes," the sinking of his boat, PT-109, after being rammed by a Japanese destroyer. Jack knows of no reason to believe that the presidency will be any different, with this exception: the price of making a mistake will be infinitely higher were he and Khrushchev to misjudge each other in a military confrontation, as he and the captain of the Japanese destroyer misjudged one another's location on August 2, 1943, near the Solomon Islands in the South Pacific.

The other reason for Jack's anxiety about U.S.-Soviet relations is Khrushchev himself. There seem to him to be two Khrushchevs: one who professes to seek world peace and another who seems to want to conquer the world in the name of Marxist-Leninist ideology. Jack has read and re-read a speech of Khrushchev's from January 6th, in which the Soviet chairman claims that socialist revolutions in Cuba, Vietnam and Algeria prove that communism is the wave of the future, and that the days of Western capitalism are numbered. To Jack, this is rubbish, but the kind of rubbish that, if believed fervently, could lead to crises, especially if the Soviets try to extend their reach and influence. Jack worries that Khrushchev doesn't fully grasp how determined he is to resist the spread of communism.

His response to Khrushchev is therefore cordial, but cautious. He reminds the Soviet leader that there are issues and principles the two of them may never agree on. Their main task, therefore, will be to find ways to disagree that don't threaten global annihilation. Jack suspects this won't be easy. What he doesn't know is how completely, by October 1962, he and Khrushchev will fail in this fundamental task, when the world comes within a hair's breadth of a catastrophic nuclear war.

Dear Mr. Chairman:

I have had an opportunity, due to the return of Ambassador Thompson, to have an extensive review of all aspects of our relations with the secretary of state and with him. In these consultations, we have been able to explore, in general, not only those subjects which are of direct bilateral concern to the United States and the Soviet Union, but also the chief outstanding international problems which affect our relations.

I have not been able, in so brief a time, to reach definite conclusions as to our position on all of these matters. Many of them are affected by developments in the international scene and are of concern to many other governments. I would, however, like to set before you certain general considerations which I believe might be of help in introducing a greater element of clarity in the relations between our two countries. I say this because I am sure that you are conscious as I am of the heavy responsibility which rests upon our two governments in world affairs. I agree with your thought that if we could find a measure of cooperation on some of these current issues this, in itself, would be a significant contribution to the problem of insuring a peaceful and orderly world.

I think we should recognize, in honesty to each other, that there are problems on which we may not be able to agree. However, I believe that while recognizing that we do not and, in all probability will not, share a common view on all of these problems, I do believe that the manner in which we approach them and, in particular, the manner in which our disagreements are handled, can be of great importance.

In addition, I believe we should make more use of diplomatic channels for quite informal discussion of these questions, not in the sense of negotiations (since I am sure that we both recognize the interests of other countries are deeply involved in these issues), but rather as a mechanism of communication which should, insofar as possible, help to eliminate misunderstanding and unnecessary divergences, however great the basic differences may be.

I hope it will be possible, before too long, for us to meet personally for an informal exchange of views in regard to some of these matters. Of course, a meeting of this nature will depend on the general international situation at the time, as well as our mutual schedules of engagements.

I have asked Ambassador Thompson to discuss the question of our meeting. Ambassador Thompson, who enjoys my full confidence, is also in a position to inform you of my thinking on a number of the international issues which we have discussed. I shall welcome any expression of your views. I hope such [an] exchange might assist us in working out a responsible approach to our differences with the view to their ultimate resolution for the benefit of peace and security throughout the world. You may be sure, Mr. Chairman, that I intend to do everything I can toward developing a more harmonious relationship between our two countries.

Sincerely,

John F. Kennedy

* * *

#4

Nikita S. Khrushchev to John F. Kennedy

April 18, 1961[4]

"put an end to aggression against . . . Cuba"

Nikita Sergei'ich has fallen in love with the idea that Fidel Castro's Cuba represents to him. The object of his adoration is a band of courageous, progressive, anti-imperialist revolutionaries who have driven out a U.S.-backed dictator, Fulgencio Batista (on January 1, 1959), without any significant assistance or advice from Moscow. Indeed, some party hacks around Nikita Sergei'ich are deeply suspicious of Castro and his colleagues because the Cuban firebrand seems like a loose cannon who will be difficult to control, and also because they believe the Americans simply will never permit a pro-Soviet bastion of communism to flourish a mere ninety miles off the coast of Florida. To the skeptics around Nikita Sergei'ich, getting involved with the Cuban revolutionaries is dangerous, unlikely to succeed, and might even lead to a war with the U.S. that the Soviet Union could hardly expect to win.

But to Nikita Sergei'ich, who in his youth was a Bolshevik firebrand himself, these are reasons to love Cuba and the Cubans even more—reasons to come to their aid now, because it is clear from intelligence reports that the new Kennedy administration is preparing for military action against the Cuban regime. Besides, the affair with Cuba began with comradely love at first sight. Nikita Sergei'ich and Fidel Castro met the previous autumn in New York and it was then that the sixty-something former Russian revolutionary fell in love with the revolutionary zeal of the thirty-something Castro. He was impressed with Fidel's willingness to stick it to Uncle Sam, to play "David" to Washington's "Goliath." When Nikita Sergei'ich returned to Moscow from New York in the fall of 1960, he immediately ordered a big increase in military equipment and advisers for Cuba. "David" was going to need help resisting "Goliath," and Nikita Sergei'ich was ecstatic about providing such assistance.

It is against this background of requited, inter-generational love among revolutionaries that, on the morning of Nikita Sergei'ich's sixty-sixth birthday, April 17, 1961, he receives word that an invasion of CIA-backed Cuban exiles is landing on the south coast of Cuba. The Soviet leader takes this as a personal insult from Kennedy (who has said publicly that the U.S. has no designs on Cuba) as well as a dark harbinger of what might be about to happen to the glorious experiment in Caribbean communism. He immediately dictates a letter to Kennedy, the first in their correspondence that deals with Cuba. It is the letter of an angry man, more than a little out of control—someone who is moved by the events at the Bay of Pigs to violate the tone and content of his earlier letters to the new American president by implicitly, but repeatedly, "reminding" Kennedy that conflicts can escalate, that the Soviet Union has a huge nuclear arsenal, and that the Soviet Union will not, under any circumstances, permit the Cuban Revolution to fail. Stick that in your pipe and smoke it, Mr. U.S. president!—is more or less the tone of the letter.

This is how their exchanges about Cuba begin: with Nikita Sergei'ich, steaming with anger, issuing threats to Kennedy that are more or less identical in severity to the threats Kennedy will make over Berlin in just a few months' time. Mr. President/Mr. Chairman, if you make one false move against our special friends in Cuba/West Berlin, then you will be putting the world at risk of a nuclear conflagration. Until you stop threatening our friends, there will be no more Mr. Nice Guy. No more elevated chitchat about peaceful coexistence. Just stay the hell out of Cuba/West Berlin, or you will suffer supremely unpleasant consequences!

Mr. President:

I send you this message in an hour of alarm, fraught with danger for the peace of the whole world. Armed aggression has begun against Cuba. It is a secret to no one that the armed bands invading this country were trained, equipped and armed in the United States of America. The planes which are bombing Cuban cities belong to the United States of America, the bombs they are dropping are being supplied by the American government.

All of this evokes here in the Soviet Union an understandable feeling of indignation on the part of the Soviet government and the Soviet people.

Only recently, in exchanging opinions through our respective representatives, we talked with you about the mutual desire of both sides to put forward joint efforts directed toward improving relations between our countries and eliminating the danger of war. Your statement a few days ago that the USA would not participate in military activities against Cuba created the impression that the top leaders of the United States were taking into account the consequences for general peace and for the USA itself which aggression against Cuba could have. How can what is being done by the United States in reality be understood, when an attack on Cuba has now become a fact?

It is still not too late to avoid the irreparable. The government of the USA still has the possibility of not allowing the flame of war ignited by interventions in Cuba to grow into an incomparable conflagration. I approach you, Mr. President, with an urgent call to put an end to aggression against the Republic of Cuba. Military armament and the world political situation are such at this time that any so-called "little war" can touch off a chain reaction in all parts of the globe.

As far as the Soviet Union is concerned, there should be no mistake about our position: We will render the Cuban people and their government all necessary help to repel [an] armed attack on Cuba. We are sincerely interested in a relaxation of international tension, but if others proceed toward sharpening, we will answer them in full measure. And in general it is hardly possible to conduct matters so that the situation is settled in one area and conflagration extinguished while a new conflagration is ignited in another area.

I hope that the government of the USA will consider our views as dictated by the sole concern not to allow steps which could lead the world to military catastrophe.

N. S. Khrushchev

* * *

#5

John F. Kennedy to Nikita S. Khrushchev

April 18, 1961[5]

"You are under a serious misapprehension"

Khrushchev's letter arrives almost at the very moment that the fate of the CIA-backed Cuban exile brigade is becoming clear: the operation now appears to be a total failure; the brigadistas *are being killed or captured at an alarming rate; those continuing to fight are hemmed in on the poorly chosen landing area. The beach abutting the Bay of Pigs, which the Cubans call* Playa Giron, *is surrounded by impenetrable jungle. The Castro government has, in addition, used the occasion to round up and arrest more than 100,000 people suspected of sympathizing with the invaders at the Bay of Pigs. Jack understands immediately that he has made a colossal mistake in allowing the invasion to go forward, even in the truncated form he finally approved. "How could I have been so stupid" he says to an aide, "how in the hell could I have let Eisenhower's stupid operation go forward?"*

Jack returns Khrushchev's self-righteous anger with a little of his own. He asks Soviet expert Charles Bohlen to give him a draft that he can edit. The final result, edited and approved by Jack, is a letter that is quite unrepresentative of Jack's letters to Khrushchev. On the whole, Jack's side of the correspondence with Khrushchev tends to be lawyerly, unemotional and relatively brief. The anger in this letter, however, reflects his anger at himself, as much as with Khrushchev. Like Khrushchev's, Jack's letter is permeated with the ideological detritus of the Cold War: our system will triumph in the end, not yours; your people are the aggressors, not ours; and you had better watch your step or we will begin to raise the ante all over the world; we are willing to take you to the brink, or even over it into armed conflict; we will never back down. So god dammit, you had better watch your step. This is roughly the gist of both letters.

Jack is already aware of rumors of his impending impeachment over the Cuban debacle. Three months into his administration, the "New Frontier" as its champions in the press are calling it, seems suddenly to be mired in the same Cold War excesses and enthusiasms that marked those of its predecessors. Jack is stunned by the unrelenting and often personally insulting criticism of his decision-making—some horrified that the invasion took place at all, others amazed that he did not send in the Marines and give the commies what they deserved. He now finds himself brooding, sitting silently in meetings in which the president is expected to lead the discussion. The brief moment of depression and inaction passes, but his memory of the humiliation of the Bay of Pigs—especially his failure to question the rosy estimates of older, supposedly knowledgeable subordinates—will never be far from his mind. The sobriety, caution and steeliness in the face of pressure that are the hallmarks of the Jack Kennedy who is in charge during the Cuban missile crisis owe a great deal to his experience of the Bay of Pigs. After the debacle, Jack is immune from the intoxicating effects of optimistic estimates brought to him by his CIA and military advisers.

At this moment however, with Khrushchev threatening to heat up the Cold War all over the world, Jack seems pleased to have an opportunity to stick his thumb figuratively in Khrushchev's eye. Throughout his presidency, Cuba will repeatedly have this effect on both leaders: it makes them mad as hell at each other.

Mr. Chairman:

You are under a serious misapprehension in regard to events in Cuba. For months there has been evident and growing resistance to the Castro dictatorship. More than 100,000 refugees have recently fled from Cuba into neighboring countries. Their urgent hope is naturally to assist their fellow Cubans in their struggle for freedom. Many refugees fought alongside Dr. Castro against the Batista dictatorship; among them are prominent leaders of his own movement and government.

These are unmistakable signs that Cubans find intolerable the denial of democratic liberties and the subversion of the 26th of July Movement by an alien-dominated regime. It cannot be surprising that, as resistance within Cuba grows, refugees have been using whatever means are available to return and support their countrymen in the continuing struggle for freedom. Where people are denied the right of choice, recourse to such struggle is the only means of achieving their liberties.

I have previously stated, and I repeat now, that the United States intends no military intervention in Cuba. In the event of any intervention by outside force we will immediately honor our obligations under the inter-American system to protect this hemisphere against external aggression. While refraining from military intervention in Cuba, the people of the United States do not conceal their admiration for Cuban patriots who wish to see a democratic system in an independent Cuba. The United States can take no action to stifle the spirit of liberty.

I have taken careful note of your statement that the events in Cuba might affect peace in all parts of the world. I trust that this does not mean that the Soviet government, using the situation in Cuba as a pretext, is planning to inflame other areas of the world. I would like to think that your government has too great a sense of responsibility to embark on any enterprise so dangerous to general peace.

I agree with you as to the desirability of steps to improve the international atmosphere. I continue to hope that you will cooperate in opportunities now available to this end. A prompt cease-fire and settlement of the dangerous situation in Laos, cooperation with the United Nations in the Congo and a speedy conclusion of an acceptable treaty for the banning of nuclear tests would be constructive steps in this direction. The regime in Cuba could make a similar contribution by permitting the Cuban people freely to determine their own future by democratic processes and freely to cooperate with their Latin American neighbors.

I believe, Mr. Chairman, that you should recognize that free peoples in all parts of the world do not accept the claim of historical inevitability for Communist revolution. What your government believes is its own business; what it does in the world is the world's business. The great revolution in the history of man, past, present and future, is the revolution of those determined to be free.

John F. Kennedy

* * *

#6

Nikita S. Khrushchev to John F. Kennedy

April 22, 1961[6]

"you are setting out on a very dangerous road."

The hyperactive mind of Nikita Sergei'ich is dominated, in the aftermath of the failed Bay of Pigs invasion, by a single question: how can I save Cuba? How can the Soviet Union come to the aid of the Cubans in such a way as to deter the Americans from doing what they obviously want desperately to do: attack it, invade it, overthrow the government, and replace it with a regime that will follow orders from Washington? He is mystified as to why Kennedy did not order an in-vasion of the island by regular U.S. forces when the brigade of exiles began to col-lapse under attack from Fidel's forces. To Nikita Sergei'ich, this would have been a no-brainer. It's what superpowers sometimes have to do when faced by recalcitrant smaller countries near their borders—as Nikita Sergei'ich did, for example, when he ordered the invasion of Hungary in 1956. He wonders: does Kennedy lack the spine, the urge to dominate, that so many U.S. leaders seem to have?

Yet Nikita Sergei'ich also worries that Kennedy's weakness—if that is what kept him from using the Bay of Pigs fiasco as an excuse to finish off the Castro government—may make him even more dangerous than if he were classically ag-gressive, in the imperialist mode. A weak president, he reasons, will be a tool of the fanatical anti-communists in both parties. Either way, Cuba is in big trouble. Nikita Sergei'ich concludes instinctively and irretrievably that Kennedy will be forced to atone for his humiliation in the Bay of Pigs invasion by a full-scale military assault on the regime of Fidel Castro. He therefore orders a massively stepped-up program of military aid to Cuba—including the newest, most effective conventional weapons in the Soviet arsenal.

But even this does not satisfy Nikita Sergei'ich. This does not make him com-fortable. There are two reasons for his unease: first, he still cannot conceive of the Cubans holding out for more than a few days, at most, in the face of what Nikita Sergei'ich takes to be the inevitable U.S. invasion of Cuba; and second, he knows that his threats to Kennedy are not credible. Kennedy has little reason to fear that, in the event of a massive attack on Cuba, Nikita Sergei'ich will escalate conflicts elsewhere. These are are empty threats, ultimately. He knows what few others know: that Soviet nuclear forces are almost laughably inferior to those of the U.S. in every respect: sheer numbers, accuracy and sophistication. Nikita Sergei'ich will continue to talk the talk of nuclear brinksmanship, but he knows he cannot walk the walk.

Until he can think of a way to "save Cuba," he continues his bashing of Ken-nedy, the U.S. and the capitalist system they embody. In a statement that will come back to haunt him during the Cuban missile crisis, he tells Kennedy, "We have no bases in Cuba, and we do not intend to establish any." A year and a half hence, the discovery of Soviet bases in Cuba will provide the spark that lights the Cuban kindling that lights the fuse that sends the world careening toward nuclear oblivion. And one of the reasons is that the denial of Soviet intent to establish military bases in Cuba is only the first in a long line of lies perpetrated by Nikita Sergei'ich to cover up what will become, in fact, the largest peacetime effort in recorded history to establish bases where none had existed before.

Mr. President:

I have received your reply of April 18. You write that the United States intends no military intervention in Cuba. But numerous facts known to the whole world—and to the government of the United States, of course, better than to anyone else—speak differently. Despite all assurances to the contrary, it has now been proved beyond doubt that it was precisely the United States which prepared the intervention, financed its arming and transported the gangs of mercenaries that invaded the territory of Cuba.

United States forces also took a direct part in the gangster attack upon Cuba. American bombers and fighters supported the operations of the mercenaries who landed on Cuban territory, and participated in the military operations against the armed forces of the lawful government and people of Cuba.

Such are the facts. They bear witness to direct United States participation in the armed aggression against Cuba.

In your message you took the course of justifying, and even lauding, the attack on Cuba—this crime which has revolted the entire world. You try to justify the organization of a military attack on Cuba, committed for the sole reason that the way of life chosen by its people is not to the taste of the ruling circles of the United States and the North American monopolies operating in Latin America, by talking about the United States government's adherence to the ideals of "freedom." But, one may ask, of what freedom are you speaking?

Of freedom to strangle the Cuban people with the bony hand of hunger through the establishment of an economic blockade? Is that freedom?

Of freedom to send military planes over the territory of Cuba, to subject peaceful Cuban cities to barbarous bombing, to set fire to sugar cane plantations? Is that freedom?

History records many cases in which, on the pretext of defending freedom, peoples have been drowned in blood, colonial wars waged, and one small nation after another taken by the throat.

In the present case, apparently, the United States government is seeking to restore to Cuba that "freedom" under which Cuba would dance to the tune of her more powerful neighbor and foreign monopolies would once again be able to plunder the country's national wealth, to wax rich on the sweat and blood of the Cuban people. But it is precisely against such "freedom" that the Cuban people accomplished their revolution when they threw out Batista, who may have loyally served the interests of his foreign masters but who was a foreign element in the body of the Cuban nation.

You, Mr. President, display concern for a handful of enemies who were expelled by their people and found refuge under the wing of those who want to keep the guns of their cruisers and destroyers trained on Cuba. But why are you not concerned about the fate of the six million Cuban people, who you do not wish to pay regard to their inalienable right to a free and independent life, their right to arrange their domestic affairs as they see fit? Where are the standards of international law, or even simple human morality, that would justify such a position? They simply do not exist.

The Cuban people have once again expressed their will with a clarity which should have left no room for doubt, even in the minds of those who prefer to close their eyes to reality. They have shown that they not only know their interests, but can stand up for them. Cuba today is not, of course, the Cuba you identify with the handful of traitors who have come out against their people. It is the Cuba of workers, peasants and intellectuals; it is a people which has rallied round its revolutionary government headed by the national hero, Fidel Castro. And, judging from everything, this people received the interventionists in a fitting way. Is not this convincing proof of the real will of the Cuban people?

I think it is. And since this is so, is it not time for all to draw the right conclusions?

As for the Soviet Union, we have stated on many occasions, and I now state again, that our government does not seek any advantages or privileges in Cuba. We have no bases in Cuba, and we do not intend to establish any. And this is well known to you, to your generals and your admirals. If, despite this, they still try to frighten the people by fabrications about "Soviet bases" on Cuba that is obviously designed for consumption by simpletons. But there are fewer and fewer of such simpletons, and that applies also, I hope, to the United States.

By the way, Mr. President, I would like to express my opinion concerning the statements made by you and certain other United States politicians to the effect that rockets and other weapons could be installed on Cuban territory for possible use against the United States.

The inference from this is that the United States has some alleged right to attack Cuba, either directly or through the traitors to the Cuban people whom you arm with your weapons, train on your territory, maintain with the money of United States taxpayers and transport with the resources of your armed forces, covering them from the air and sea while they fight against the Cuban people and their lawful government.

You also refer to some United States obligations to defend rebels against the lawful government of a sovereign state, such as Cuba is.

Mr. President, you are setting out on a very dangerous road. Think of it …

…

You, Mr. President, did not like it when I said, in my previous message, that there can be no stable peace in the world if anywhere war is aflame. But this is really so. The world is a single whole, whether we like it or not. And I can only repeat what I said: It is impossible to proceed by adjusting the situation and putting out the flames in one area, and not kindling a new conflagration in another.

The Soviet state has always been a consistent defender of the freedom and independence of all peoples. We naturally, therefore, cannot concede to the United States any right to control the destinies of other countries, including the countries of Latin America. We consider that the interference by one state in the affairs of another—especially armed interference—is a violation of all international laws and of the principles of peaceful coexistence which the Soviet Union has invariably upheld since the first days of its existence.

If it is now, more than ever before, the duty of every state and its leaders not to permit actions which are capable of jeopardizing universal peace, that applies with all the more force to the leaders of the great powers. It is this that I urge upon you, Mr. President.

N.S. Khrushchev

* * *

#7

Fidel Castro: Speech in Havana

April 23, 1961[7]

"direct aggression will gain momentum"

Fidel Castro was always the biggest kid in his class and the smartest kid in his class—the kid no one could shut up, no one could out-talk, the kid no one dared challenge. Later, as the leader of revolutionary Cuba while only in his mid-thirties, his mind leaps from event to conclusion to plan to implementation with a speed and conviction that amazes his fellow revolutionaries. His ability to persuade is astonishing. Could anyone else have convinced the majority of the Cuban people that little Cuba, formerly compliant with U.S. wishes to a fault, could now stick it to Uncle Sam and get away with it?

In Fidel Castro's acrobatic mind, the year-and-a-half-long fuse leading to what will become the Cuban missile crisis is lit at the Bay of Pigs in April 1961. Within days, perhaps even within hours, of the invasion Castro's thought process catapults to an assessment of the significance of the failed CIA-backed invasion. Roughly three days after the shooting stops at the Bay of Pigs, Fidel Castro draws a set of astonishing conclusions about the impact he believes the defeat of the U.S.-backed brigade will have on Cuba. He will spend much of the next year and a half persuading his constituents of his breathtaking hypothesis: that Cuba is about to become the focal point of contention in a nuclear Armageddon between the U.S. and USSR. Here is Fidel's argument, which he and many Cubans find convincing:

1. *The invasion proves that the Kennedy administration means to destroy the Cuban Revolution.*
2. *Cuba, unlike the majority of Latin American countries, will not be compliant, will not cease its revolutionary activities inside Cuba and throughout Latin America.*
3. *Cuba, now avowedly socialist, will be the hub of the wheel that will crush U.S. imperialism, via the intervention of Cuba's new ally, the Soviet Union.*
4. *Cuba must prepare for martyrdom, for Armageddon, for the final reckoning in which the socialist community destroys, once and forever, the leading capitalist state, the United States of America.*

Neither John F. Kennedy nor Nikita S. Khrushchev give the slightest credence to Castro's Armageddon hypothesis. After the sparring letters of late April 1961, Cuba disappears from the superpower agenda. The leaders move on to ostensibly more "important matters," especially the status of Berlin and a ban on nuclear testing in the atmosphere.

So it is that while Fidel Castro and his Cuban constituents are preparing for nuclear Armageddon, Kennedy and Khrushchev are, with regard to Cuba, beginning an eighteen-month sleepwalk toward a catastrophe. Their sleepwalking is facilitated by superpower ethnocentrism and a nearly total lack of empathy for the Cuban position. Kennedy knows he wants Cuba off his agenda. It is a second-tier issue, at most. He also knows he has to give the defeated Cuban exiles a bone to chew on, so he authorizes a program of sabotage in which the exiles can take part. But he resolves that he will never again cave into his advisers, who continue to recommend an invasion of Cuba. Invade Cuba—again? No way! Khrushchev, for his part, is worried about "losing Cuba," and is resolved to assist Castro in every way possible. By early 1962, he will decide to offer nuclear missiles to Castro as a means of deterring the invasion that both Khrushchev and Castro believe is being planned, but which Kennedy is privately resolved to avoid. But Khrushchev knows that the Soviet Union has not the slightest intention to actually use the weapons he is deploying. Use nuclear weapons to attack the U.S.? No way!

Given his belief in the inevitability of a U.S. invasion, Castro's focus on Armageddon is not a nightmare, but a kind of dream. After centuries of irrelevance, Cuba will matter fundamentally to the fate of the human race. Cuba cannot prevent the invasion, nor can it expect to survive the onslaught of U.S. military forces, probably involving the use of nuclear weapons against Cuban resistance. So encapsulated are Kennedy and Khrushchev in their respective bubbles of superpower assumptions, so dismissive are they of the possibility that Castro's rhetoric might not be only rhetoric, that they are scarcely even aware of Castro's working hypothesis, in spite of his nearly

*constant emphasis on it in countless speeches and interviews between April 1961
and October 1962.*

*As a result, neither Kennedy nor Khrushchev makes any attempt to correct the
faulty assumptions underlying Castro's incorrect hypothesis. They think Fidel is
kidding—surely, anyone who seems to believe Armageddon is inevitable must be
kidding, mustn't he? But Castro isn't kidding, as they will discover in October 1962,
when Castro wakes them up from their sleepwalk.*

> The aggression [at the Bay of Pigs] was indirect only in regard to the
> personnel. It was direct aggression in that it came from camps of the
> North Americans, that North American equipment was used, and that it
> included a convoy by the U.S. Navy and the participation of the U.S. Air
> force. It was a combined thing: they used mercenaries amply supported
> by the navy and air force.
>
>   ....
>
> We have always been in danger of aggression. We have been warning
> about this in the United Nations: that they would find a pretext, that
> they would organize some act of aggression so they could intervene.
>
> Our position is that we will fight to the last man, but we do not want
> direct aggression. We do not wish to suffer the destruction that aggres-
> sion would bring. But if the aggression comes, it will meet the total re-
> sistance of our people.
>
> The danger of direct aggression will gain momentum following this
> failure. We have said imperialism will disappear. We do not wish it to
> commit suicide; we want it to die a natural death. If it dies the world
> will live in peace. But if it begins a world war, it will die violently.
>
> The U.S. should have been ashamed to be engaged in this battle of
> Goliath and David—and to lose it besides.
>
> What did we have against their might? First, we had a sense of dig-
> nity and courage. We were not afraid. That is a big thing. Then, we were
> determined to resist. No matter what they throw against us, we will
> fight. Our men know how to die, and they have shown it during the
> past few days.
>
> So far they have gone from aggression to aggression without stopping
> to think. Only direct aggression is left. Are we going to be afraid? No!
> [Applause.] Imperialism's soldiers are flesh and blood too, and bullets
> go through them. Let them know they will meet with serious resistance.
> That may be enough to get them to reflect a little. Our people—men,
> women and children—must maintain that spirit. If they have no weap-
> ons they can take the place of somebody who falls. Have no fear; be
> calm! After all, the result of aggression against Cuba will be the start of
> a conflagration of incalculable consequences, and they will be affected
> too. It will no longer be a matter of them feasting on us. They will get as
> good as they give.

* * *
#8

Fidel Castro: "Second Declaration of Havana"

February 4, 1962[8]

"a bloody drama for America"

To Fidel, possibly the worst of all fates is to be ignored by the United States of America. In this sense, Fidel has had a very successful ten months since the victory at the Bay of Pigs and the subsequent crushing of the internal opposition movement. He has become an American obsession. Kennedy has authorized a program of state-sponsored terrorism directed at Cuban economic targets, called Operation MONGOOSE, along with an assassination program directed at Fidel and other Cuban leaders. The U.S. has engineered the expulsion of Cuba from the Organization of American States, due to its communist proclivities, which make Cuba, according to the official proclamation, "incompatible with the inter-American system." And on February 7, 1962 Kennedy orders a U.S. trade embargo with Cuba, except for emergency medical supplies. Kennedy has said publicly on many occasions, however, that he and his administration would take a more benevolent view of the Cuban revolutionary government if only they would cease and desist in their efforts to "export their revolution" to the rest of Latin America. Kennedy is, in principle, willing to put up with one Cuba, but only one. He is willing to let the Cubans enjoy their revolution, but if they try to replicate their success elsewhere in Latin America, the U.S. will crush them.

Fidel responds on the day after Cuba is expelled from the Organization of American States with the release of a paper that is, even by Fidel's standards, over the edge of rhetorical excess. In "The Second Declaration of Havana," he states categorically and absolutely that Cuba will never, ever cease to encourage the other countries of Latin America to overthrow their U.S.-backed/approved governments and join Cuba in the socialist camp. For Fidel, it is a solemn duty of every revolutionary to "make the revolution." Toward the end of the paper, he returns to the theme of Cuban martyrdom as an accompaniment to the U.S. attack and invasion he at times seems almost to invite. When the Cuban Armageddon occurs, the Yankee imperialists will be destroyed, presumably by Soviet nuclear forces, the only known force which could in theory accomplish the elimination of the United States of America quickly and completely.

On May 18 1895, on the eve of his death from a Spanish bullet through the heart, Jose Marti, apostle of our independence said in an unfinished letter to his friend Manuel Mercado ... "I have lived inside the monster and know its guts; and my sling is the sling of David."

....

The duty of every revolutionary is to make the revolution. It is known that the revolution will triumph in America and throughout the world, but it is not for revolutionaries to sit in the doorways of their houses waiting for the corpse of imperialism to pass by. The role of Job doesn't suit a revolutionary. Each year that the revolution is speeded up will mean the lives of millions of children saved, millions of intelligences saved for culture, an infinite quantity of pain spared the people. Even if the Yankee imperialists prepare a bloody drama for America, they will not succeed in crushing the peoples' struggles, they will only arouse universal hatred against themselves. And such a drama will also mark the death of their greedy and carnivorous system.

* * *

#9

Fidel Castro: Speech in Santiago de Cuba

July 26, 1962[9]

"a direct imperialist attack will be shattered"

Just three and a half years after the triumph of the revolution he led, Fidel has already established the tradition of making a major speech every 26th of July, which is celebrated as Cuban Independence Day. On July 26, 1953, a band of roughly 135 rebels, led by Fidel, attacked the Moncada army barracks and munitions depot near Santiago de Cuba, in eastern Cuba. The attack had been a nearly suicidal attempt to capture ammunition and firearms, as step one in what was a planned overthrow of the U.S.-backed government of Col. Fulgencio Batista. In the short run, Moncada was a disaster: a half-dozen of the rebels were killed during the battle, while more than sixty were later murdered while in prison. Survivors were quickly rounded up and imprisoned on the Isle of Pines, off the south coast of Cuba. Among the survivors were Fidel and his younger brother Raul Castro. The surviving rebels were released by Batista in 1955. They fled to Mexico, reorganized, and then returned aboard the Granma, *a small boat. After the landing of the* Granma, *the revolution began in earnest and concluded on January 1, 1959, when Batista left Cuba and Fidel's forces triumphed. They now call themselves* Movimiento 26 de Julio (The 26th of July Movement).*

By mid-1962, Fidel continues to connect the dots: he senses intuitively that the quasi-suicidal Moncada attack will soon be reenacted on a colossal scale, roughly as follows. First, the Soviet conventional and nuclear weapons already en route to the island will bring Cuba under the Soviet nuclear "umbrella." The Soviet weapons and personnel will be readily detected by the U.S., which will escalate its preparations to attack and invade Cuba. Fidel believes these preparations are already at an advanced stage. Second, Kennedy will order a massive attack on Cuba—not using a pitiful force of Cuban exiles as he did at the Bay of Pigs (always referred to by Cubans as Playa Girón [Girón Beach]), but employing the full power of the U.S. military, including U.S. nuclear weapons. Third, the Americans will be met with stiff resistance from the Cuban and the Soviet forces on the island which will include the use of Soviet tactical nuclear weapons, which Fidel imagines (correctly) can virtually annihilate the U.S. forces involved in the initial attack. Fidel regards these first three steps as virtually inevitable. Step four—the endgame—is still unclear to Fidel. He is almost certain Cuba will be destroyed, for the U.S. is the most powerful nation on earth and Kennedy (so Fidel believes) is obliged and utterly devoted to destroying the Cuban Revolution. Fidel can only hope that if Cuba is destroyed, his Soviet patron has the commitment and determination he and his fellow revolutionaries had at Moncada—that is, that Nikita Khrushchev will authorize a nuclear attack on the U.S., destroying it, rendering Cuba a martyr for socialism. Fidel has not yet discussed step four with the Russians. But in due course, he will.

With martyrdom—both past and future—much on his mind, Fidel returns to Moncada and Santiago de Cuba on July 26, 1962, to explain the general outline of this situation to his constituents in these terms: the U.S. attack is coming, probably soon; the attack will be massive; Cubans will resist to the death; and Cuba (and their Soviet allies) will use the occasion to destroy the United States of America. Like all his speeches given during this period, this one ends with "patria o muerte!" ("fatherland or death!"). How many present in Santiago de Cuba, and how many in Washington and Moscow, understand the degree to which Fidel's use of "patria o muerte" is literal, not metaphorical—that his rhetoric reflects his understanding of the evolving reality? How many in Cuba, the U.S. and USSR understand that Fidel is not kidding when he predicts that in the coming U.S. attack, the U.S. "will be shattered?"

We must be alert. We must not rest on our laurels. We must be aware of the danger.

   We must not forget that at Girón, on the eve of Girón, they denied they had any plans against us, and they tried to take us by surprise. We warned of the danger; we were not taken by surprise; we were ready; we defeated them. We must be aware that in the measure that Yankee imperialism's efforts against our revolution fail, that all its plans fail, that its mercenary bands are annihilated, that the saboteurs are destroyed, and that the counterrevolutionaries are smashed, in that same measure the danger of an attack increases. Yet they will be mistaken once again, because once again, the Cubans will be on the alert. Once more, the Cubans will take the necessary steps. Once more we will strengthen our military defense as necessary in order to be in a position to reject any imperialist attack. When we shall be in a position to say that a direct imperialist attack will be shattered by our defense, then the greatest risk to our country will have disappeared.

It is evident that our country runs the same risk as progressive humanity. Any war that the imperialists may unleash against the progressive nations will also be unleashed against us. Any war that the imperialists may unleash, any world war, will also be unleashed against them. The world is getting smaller.

* * *

#10

Statement by President John F. Kennedy on Cuba

September 4, 1962[10]

"the gravest issues would arise"

Jack feels as if his head is in a vise. He receives a report in mid-August 1962 warning him that "something new and different" is occurring on the island of Cuba. A massive, multi-site military construction project is underway, headed by at least 5,000 Soviet specialists on the island. In two and a half months, the mid-term Congressional elections will take place. Both the Republican opposition and hawks from his own Democratic Party are clamoring for action that will halt, or even roll back, the project the Soviets have underway in Cuba. On the other hand, he is acutely aware that any U.S. military move against Cuba will effectively destroy the gains that have been made by the Alliance for Progress in Latin America. In fact, a U.S. attack on Cuba would be at least a public relations disaster throughout the world. Jack does not want to go to war with Cuba. But will he be able to avoid it, if . . . well, what the hell are the Russians doing in Cuba, if not equipping the island with a nuclear weapons capability?

On September 4th, Jack sends his brother Bobby, the attorney general, to warn Soviet Ambassador Anatoly Dobrynin that the deployment of offensive weapons in Cuba will not be tolerated. ("Offensive" is a polite euphemism for "nuclear.") Dobrynin reassures the attorney general that the deployment in Cuba is strictly defensive, strictly limited to systems dedicated to the defense of the island. ("Defensive" is a euphemism for "non-nuclear.") But when the CIA reports on August 29th that Soviet surface-to-air (SAM) missile sites are going in at several locations along the northern perimeter of the island, Jack understands without being told what this implies: that the Soviets are installing SAM sites for only one purpose, as protection for something else nearby. Frankly, the only "something else" that Jack and his advisers can think of is a nuclear missile capability.

Finally, Jack does what he had hoped he could avoid: he issues a public warning, drafted by his brother Bobby and Bobby's deputy, Nick Katzenbach, that is unequivocal, and may be summarized as follows: if the U.S. discovers nuclear weapons and/or their delivery systems in Cuba, the U.S. will forcibly remove them ASAP. Period. As the September 4th statement is made public, Jack feels a knot in his stomach: he has, in effect, just issued a contingent declaration of war against Cuba and its Soviet patron. Jack and Bobby stare at each other, without speaking, as the document is handed to Press Secretary Pierre Salinger. But what if the "offensive" weapons systems are already in place? Dare we attack in that case? Dare we not *attack in that case?*

All Americans, as well as all of our friends in this hemisphere, have been concerned over the recent moves of the Soviet Union to bolster the military power of the Castro regime in Cuba. Information has reached this government in the last four days from a variety of sources which establishes without doubt that the Soviets have provided the Cuban government with a number of anti-aircraft defense missiles with a slant range of twenty-five miles which are similar to early models of our Nike. Along with these missiles, the Soviets are apparently providing the extensive radar and other electronic equipment which is required for their operation. We can also confirm the presence of several Soviet-made motor torpedo boats carrying ship-to-ship guided missiles having a range of fifteen miles. The number of Soviets military technicians now known to be in Cuba or en route—approximately 3,500—is consistent with assistance in setting up and learning to use this equipment. As I stated last week, we shall continue to make information available as fast as it is obtained and properly verified.

There is no evidence of any organized combat force in Cuba from any Soviet bloc country; of military bases provided by Russia; of a violation of the 1934 treaty relating to Guantanamo; of the presence of offensive ground-to-ground missiles; or of other significant offensive capability either in Cuban hands or under Soviet direction and guidance. Were it to be otherwise, the gravest issues would arise.

The Cuban question must be considered as a part of the worldwide challenge posed by Communist threats to the peace. It must be dealt with as a part of that larger issue as well as in the context of the special relationships which have long characterized the inter-American system.

It continues to be the policy of the United States that the Castro regime will not be allowed to export its aggressive purposes by force or the threat of force. It will be prevented by whatever means may be necessary from taking action against any part of the Western Hemisphere. The United States, in conjunction with other hemisphere countries, will make sure that while increased Cuban armaments will be a heavy burden to the unhappy people of Cuba themselves, they will be nothing more.

* * *

#11

Statement by the Soviet Union: "A U.S. Attack on Cuba Would Mean Nuclear War"[11]

September 11, 1962[12]

"Our nuclear weapons are so powerful"

Nikita Sergei'ich is surprised in late August by a visit from Che Guevara, who has flown to the Soviet Union carrying the text of a secret treaty, approved by Fidel Castro, dealing with the deployment of missiles to Cuba. Nikita Sergei-ich and Che meet at the summer compound of the Soviet leadership in the Crimea. The Cubans urgently request that the deal between the Russians and Cubans be made public immediately. The Cubans believe going public will enhance the world's perception of the arrangement. Che tells Nikita Sergei'ich that there is no reason to be deceptive in this matter. Two sovereign countries have a legal right to negotiate and sign such a treaty. Nikita Sergei'ich hardly knows whether to laugh or cry. How, he wonders, can these Cubans be so naïve? Can't they read a map? Don't they know the Americans are ninety miles from Cuba and that the Russians are half a world away? If the Americans find out about this before the deployment is complete, they will issue proclamations of their own and then attack the sites in Cuba, at a minimum. No, absolutely not, is Nikita Sergei'ich's reply. He will keep to his plan to go to Cuba in late November for a signing ceremony, a trip around the island, and serious discussions with Fidel on how Cuba can be a good junior partner to the Soviet Union.

But something else causes Nikita Sergei'ich to worry. The Cubans have warned him about it repeatedly, and now Che repeats it: if you deceive and then shock the Americans with this deployment, it will not have a good outcome. We know the gringos; we know their arrogance; we know how deeply humiliated Kennedy was by the failure at the Bay of Pigs; we know how much pressure he is under to act militarily against the Cuban Revolution. The Cubans tell him yet again via Che that Kennedy may well be helpless in the face of hawkish pressure to attack Cuba. Then what?— the Cubans want to know. Che asks: if you, Comrade Nikita Sergei'ich, don't want a war with the U.S., then you and we should go public immediately, claim our legal right to make a treaty between ourselves, and let the Americans stew in their own juices. Even then, they might attack. Who knows? But by hiding the endeavor under a cloak of deceit, a violent American reaction is guaranteed.

Nikita Sergei'ich listens. But his answer is the same: no. The way we are doing it is the only possible way it can succeed. The weapons must be operational before the Americans find out. If they know our weapons might be used in the event of a U.S. invasion, then they won't attack. They will be deterred. Che asks why he is so sure. Because Kennedy and the Americans are rational. Che disagrees. He tells Nikita Sergei'ich, "on other issues, maybe the Americans are rational, but not about Cuba. Cuba makes them crazy." Nikita Sergei'ich sticks by his guns. The answer is still "no." He tells Che, "see you in November."

Nikita Sergei'ich's concern over what Che has told him turns to alarm when he hears on September 7th that Kennedy has asked Congress to approve the call-up of 150,000 reservists to active duty, in anticipation of an international crisis. In response, Nikita Sergei'ich asks his Foreign Ministry to draft a reply to the September 4th U.S. statement warning Moscow that if "offensive" weapons are identified in Cuba, the U.S. will remove them. He amends and approves the statement after it reaches him in the Crimea. Nikita Sergei'ich knows he is in too deep to back off now. The statement he approves is misleading (he quibbles about the meaning of "offensive"), deceitful (it denies Soviet intentions to build bases in Cuba), and threatening (an attack on Cuba is an attack on the Soviet Union and will be met with overwhelming force, threatening a global nuclear catastrophe).

Thus by mid-September, realism has given way to fantasy in Moscow, Washington, and Havana. Nikita Sergei'ich, Jack and Fidel are all deluding themselves. Nikita Sergei'ich believes he will either get away with his gambit or that Kennedy will accommodate himself to it if it is discovered before the weapons become operational. Jack hopes that his advisers are wrong, and that there is some reason for the Soviet deployment other than the installation of nuclear weapons. And Fidel, who hoped in vain that Khrushchev would go public with the deployment, now can only hope that when Cuba is attacked, the Soviet leader has the cojones to destroy the U.S and make Cuba a martyr to the triumph of world socialism. All will soon discover that their wishes and hopes are delusionary and dead wrong in every significant respect. Nikita Sergei'ich will remember that at this moment of discovery, "the smell of scorching hung in the air."

A certain amount of armaments is being shipped from the Soviet Union to Cuba at the request of the Cuban government in connection with the threats by aggressive imperialist circles. The Cuban statesmen also requested the Soviet government to send to Cuba Soviet military specialists and technicians who would train the Cubans in handling up-to-date weapons, because up-to-date weapons now call for high skill and much knowledge. It is but natural that Cuba does not yet have such specialists. That is why we considered this request. . . . The armaments and military equipment sent to Cuba are designed exclusively for defensive purposes and the president of the United States and the American military, like the military of any country, know what is meant by "means of defense."

. . . .

There is no need for the Soviet Union to shift its weapons for the repulsion of aggression, for a retaliatory blow, to any other country, for instance Cuba. Our nuclear weapons are so powerful in their explosive force and the Soviet Union has such powerful rockets to carry these nuclear warheads, that there is no need to search for sites for them beyond the boundaries of the Soviet Union. We have said, and we repeat, that if war is unleashed, if the aggressor makes an attack on one state or another and this state asks for assistance, the Soviet Union has the possibility from its own territory to render assistance to any peace-loving state, not only to Cuba ....

We do not say this to frighten someone. Intimidation is alien to the foreign policy of the Soviet state. Threats and blackmail are an integral part of the imperialist states. The Soviet Union stands for peace and wants no war....

    ....

But at a moment when the United States is taking measures to mobilize its armed forces and is preparing for aggression against Cuba and other peace-loving states, the Soviet Union would like to draw attention to the fact that one cannot now attack Cuba and expect that the aggressor will be free from punishment for this attack. If this attack is made, this will be the beginning of the unleashing of war.

ACT I

Collision

October 22–23, 1962

Theatrical Preview

[Voice-over: Jack's wake-up call comes around 8:30 a.m., in his bedroom, on October 16th, when he is informed of the deployment.]

JACK: The Russians have done what? But for the past year and a half, week in and week out, they have reassured us that they would never do anything as risky as put nuclear weapons in Cuba. Jesus Christ, now what do I do? I have issued public statements saying that the Russians will not put nukes in Cuba, but if they did, we would take them out militarily. Fine words. But start a war with the Soviet Union? Oh my God, we are in a helluva mess.

[Voice-over: Nikita Sergei'ich's wake up call comes a week later, around 2:30 a.m. in a conference room in the Kremlin, when he and his associates are informed of the content of Kennedy's October 22nd televised speech revealing the presence of Soviet nuclear missiles in Cuba.]

NIKITA SERGEI'ICH: So, the Americans found out about our big secret. Now Kennedy is giving us an ultimatum, isn't he? He is telling us that if we don't remove the missiles from Cuba, he will order an attack on Cuba. Well, let's just see who has the most nerve. We are a superpower. Instead of removing the weapons, let's speed up work at the missile sites on the island and make them operational for a launch. That should sober up Kennedy, if anything will.

[Kennedy and Khrushchev collide on stage, still half asleep. They fall down and pick themselves up and, when they do, they stare briefly at Castro, still shouting at them from across the stage, before resuming their superpower dialogue of threat and counter-threat.]

FIDEL: Comrade Nikita, don't you dare cave into Kennedy. Ignore Kennedy. In Cuba, we are ready to fight to the last man, woman and child. This is your moment of truth, your chance to destroy the U.S. if Kennedy is stupid enough to attack us, now that we are equipped with nuclear weapons. Stay firm!

Hey, Kennedy: we are ready for you—Cubans, Russians, nuclear weapons. If you know what's good for you, you will leave us alone. Don't even think about invading our island and expect to survive, Yankees!

JACK: [Totally ignoring Fidel.] Blah, blah, blah, take 'em out or we'll take 'em out for you, Mr. Chairman, blah, blah, blah!

NIKITA SERGEI'ICH: [Totally ignoring Fidel.] Blah, blah, blah, if you attack, you will start a world war, Mr. President, because we will not surrender our rights, blah, blah, blah!

End of Theatrical Preview

* * *

#12

John F. Kennedy to Nikita S. Khrushchev

October 22, 1962[1]

"catastrophic consequences to the whole world"

Jack has been through a week from hell in which his fervent hope—that the Soviet deployment in Cuba does not include nuclear weapons—has collided with the reality uncovered by the CIA. A week ago, on the morning of October 16th, his national security adviser McGeorge Bundy came to see him while Jack was eating breakfast, and still in his pajamas. Bundy broke the news that the CIA had confirmed the presence of Soviet nuclear missile sites under construction in Cuba. Some medium and intermediate range missiles had also been positively identified. In his mind's eye, Jack could already see a "we told you so" look on the faces of his military chiefs, Republicans in Congress, many Democratic hawks, and even members of his own administration. Jack had believed Khrushchev and all the other Russians who had reassured him and his advisers that the USSR would not, under any circumstances, deploy nuclear weapons in Cuba in the face of stern

warnings from the U.S. of the dire consequences that would follow such a deploy-
ment. Now all the hawks will come home to roost and demand that an immedi-
ate air strike on the Soviet sites, with an invasion to follow, to make sure all the
weapons and their delivery systems have been destroyed.

As he reflects back on his own initial response to the news of the Soviet nuclear
deployment in Cuba, he recalls his own anger, his feeling of betrayal by Khrush-
chev, and his judgment that the Soviets must be confronted: either they will
remove the nuclear weapons and missiles, or the U.S. will remove them by force.
He also recalls that this urge to lash out and hit the Soviets in Cuba was followed
by a frightening thought: if the U.S. attacks Cuba, killing Soviets as well as Cu-
bans, what will the Soviets do in response? Will they move against West Berlin?
If they do, the U.S. is bound by its agreement with NATO to respond militarily.
Jack knows only too well that in Europe, the Soviets field an army in the millions,
while NATO has only a token force of about 12,000 in West Berlin. Thus, the
only NATO response that might plausibly stop the Russians in their tracks is a
nuclear *response. The resulting nuclear war will begin with the use of NATO's*
relatively small, tactical nuclear weapons. But it will almost surely escalate to the
use of larger nuclear weapons. Where will it end? Will Europe be destroyed in
the attempt to save it from Soviet aggression? Or, will one or more Soviet nuclear
weapons be fired from Cuba toward targets in the U.S.? Will Miami, or Atlanta
or Houston or New Orleans be destroyed in response to a U.S. attack on Cuba?
Jack's brother Bobby, the attorney general, had told Jack on the 16th that it seemed
as if the world was on the brink of nuclear destruction, possibly foreshadowing the
end of mankind. Unable to find words with which to respond adequately, Jack
had simply nodded his agreement at Bobby's proposition, formerly so abstract, now
suddenly so horrifyingly close and real.

All week long, in secret, Jack and his advisers debate how to respond, finally
reaching a compromise solution by the end of the week: the U.S. Navy will
implement a naval quarantine around the island of Cuba, a move that will
prevent further movement of Soviet military hardware and personnel into Cuba.
Moreover, if the Soviets fail to agree to dismantle their nuclear missile sites and
send their equipment back to the Soviet Union, the blockade can be tightened to
include other material. The air strike and invasion option is still on the table—
the attack planes are on standby in south Florida and on aircraft carriers in
the Caribbean, and the initial invasion force of 150,000 men, led by the U.S.
Marines, is fully equipped and ready to hit the beaches in Cuba. The Pentagon
anticipates 25,000 American casualties in the initial phases of the invasion and
occupation of Cuba.

Jack is editing a letter to Khrushchev urging the Soviet leader to take this
upcoming speech very seriously. Lying at the highest levels cannot be tolerated.
He wants Khrushchev to pay especially close attention to those aspects of the
speech which emphasize that the U.S. is absolutely determined to remove the
Soviet weapons from Cuba if Khrushchev is unwilling to do so. In the speech,

Jack will stress that any Soviet attack on any target in the U.S. or Latin America will be met with a nuclear response against the Soviet Union. He knows that a direct nuclear challenge, made in a public forum, is unprecedented in American history.

As he releases the letter to be sent to Khrushchev, Jack briefs the Congressional leadership on what is in his speech. The Senators and Congressmen get the news cold. They know nothing of what has been going on behind closed doors for the past week. Jack is appalled at their response: all the Republicans and most of the Democrats urge him to attack Cuba ASAP and throw out both the Castro regime and the Soviets who support it. They seem not even to consider what the Soviet response might be. As he leaves the briefing to prepare for his 7:00 p.m. TV and radio address to the nation, he says to an aide: "if any of those bastards want this goddamned job, they can have it."

Jack heads upstairs to make the final adjustments to the scariest speech ever delivered by a U.S. president. He will tell his fellow citizens that Soviet nukes in Cuba threaten us; if the Soviets don't remove them we will attack and remove them; if the Soviets counterattack, we will . . . . Jack will be a little ambiguous at this point, but in just a few minutes Jack will seem to many Americans to be saying that, in that case, we will attack the Soviet Union with nuclear weapons. Armageddon lurks in between the lines of his speech, and between the lines of the letter he now sends to Khrushchev.

Sir:

A copy of the statement I am making tonight concerning developments in Cuba and the reaction of my government thereto has been handed to your ambassador in Washington. In view of the gravity of the developments to which I refer, I want you to know immediately and accurately the position of my government in this matter.

In our discussions and exchanges on Berlin and other international questions, the one thing that has most concerned me has been the possibility that your government would not correctly understand the will and determination of the United States in any given situation, since I have not assumed that you or any other sane man would, in this nuclear age, deliberately plunge the world into war which it is crystal clear no country could win and which could only result in catastrophic consequences to the whole world, including the aggressor.

At our meeting in Vienna and subsequently, I expressed our desire and readiness to find, through peaceful negotiation, a solution to any and all problems that divide us. At the same time, I made clear that in view of the objectives of the ideology to which you adhere, the United States could not tolerate any action on your part which in a major way disturbed the existing overall balance of power in the world. I stated that an attempt to force abandonment of our responsibilities and commitments in Berlin would constitute such an action and that the United States would resist with all the power at its command.

It was in order to avoid any incorrect assessment on the part of your government with respect to Cuba that I publicly stated that if certain developments in Cuba took place, the United States would do whatever must be done to protect its own security and that of its allies.

Moreover, the Congress adopted a resolution expressing its support of this declared policy. Despite this, the rapid development of long-range missile bases and other offensive weapons systems in Cuba has proceeded. I must tell you that the United States is determined that this threat to the security of this hemisphere be removed. At the same time, I wish to point out that the action we are taking is the minimum necessary to remove this threat to the security of the nations of this hemisphere. The fact of this minimum response should not be taken as a basis, however, for any misjudgment on your part.

I hope that your government will refrain from any action which would widen or deepen this already grave crisis and that we can agree to resume the path of peaceful negotiation.

Sincerely,

John F. Kennedy

* * *

#13

Nikita S. Khrushchev to John F. Kennedy

October 23, 1962[2]

"catastrophic consequences for world peace."

It is 2:30 a.m. in Moscow on October 23, 1962. Nikita Sergei'ich and his closest advisers in the Soviet Presidium are sitting in a conference room at the Kremlin, waiting for John F. Kennedy's TV and radio address, set to begin at 3:00 a.m. October 23rd Moscow time (7:00 p.m. October 22nd Washington time). Exhausted, apprehensive, they wait in silence. Nikita Sergei'ich has dreaded such a moment ever since the deployment to Cuba began over the summer—the moment when it becomes obvious that the Americans have discovered the missiles in Cuba before they become operational, before they might provide a deterrent to a U.S. attack on the island. Outwardly confident about his scheme to arm Cuba with nuclear weapons as a means of saving the Cuban Revolution, Nikita Sergei'ich has nevertheless had his doubts about whether the plan would succeed. Cuba is so far from the Soviet Union and so close to the U.S. But around the middle of October when the deployment neared completion and the U.S. had apparently—he couldn't know for sure—not yet discovered the nuclear component of the deployment—he allowed himself to become optimistic, almost jubilant. He is still acutely aware, however, that even if the Soviets get away with it, Kennedy will find the deployment difficult to accept, and of course the U.S. hawks will squawk and scream bloody murder that the president should use the opportunity to get rid of both Soviet weapons and Cuban communists.

Nikita Sergei'ich has, in fact, been composing and revising in his mind the letter he wants to send to Kennedy on the eve of giving his speech in Cuba, planned for the end of November. In that speech he would announce the details of the deployment to the whole world. Kennedy, he feels, will need some time to deal with his own emotions and also to plan a politically viable strategy to resist the urge to war that his hawks will doubtless try to force on him. Whenever he has doubts about whether Kennedy will find it possible to accept the Soviet nuclear missiles in Cuba, Nikita Sergei'ich falls back on his own experience: we in the Soviet Union, he reasons, have been surrounded by U.S. missiles for many years and we have learned to live with them. Of course, he thinks, we don't like being surrounded by American military might in Turkey, Italy, Germany and elsewhere in Europe. But his view is: what the hell, it's just part of the superpower game: the West puts its nuclear chess pieces over here and over there, and we in the USSR do the same. What else could it be but a game? No one in his right mind can believe even for a moment that the objective is to actually use these nuclear weapons. Or so Nikita Sergei'ich believes.

Nikita Sergei'ich is mulling his options over in his mind—depending on what Kennedy says in his speech—when a knock is heard on the door to the conference room in which the entire Soviet leadership sits in silence. They might be mistaken for a group of Buddhist monks except, of course, that these Russians are meditating not on the concept of emptiness, but on the possibility that a nuclear war in which they are centrally implicated may be about to begin in and around Cuba. Nikita Sergei'ich's aide for international affairs opens the door. He is handed a phone, which he puts to his ear while, for what seems to the others in the room like an eternity, he makes notes with a pencil and paper. The aide, Oleg Alexandrovich Troyanovsky, at last informs the group that he has been on the phone with the Soviet ambassador in Washington. The ambassador, Anatoly Dobrynin, has been reading the text of Kennedy's speech to him in English. Troyanovsky has been translating the speech and writing it down in Russian. When Troyanovsky is finished scribbling, Nikita Sergei'ich motions for him to tell the group the gist of the speech. He does this. After many moments of dead silence, Marshal Rodion Malinovsky, the defense minister, announces sourly, "We missed our chance." As the minister begins to rise and elaborate on his point, Nikita Sergei'ich tells him to shut up and sit down. At last, the official copy of the speech comes through, via the U.S. embassy in Moscow, to the Soviet Foreign Ministry, thence to the Kremlin. Troyanovsky now reads the official text aloud to the group. Nikita Sergei'ich has two responses, equally powerful: first, we are not at war yet, which is good; and second, Kennedy is threatening us, which is not good, and we have to respond forcefully to his threats. So we have to be careful, but we have to be clear that, as the other superpower, the USSR is not going to be pushed around.

Nikita Sergei'ich's aides are silent. They continue to stare straight ahead, as if waiting to be dismissed. After a moment's hesitation, Nikita Sergei'ich dictates the letter to Kennedy. Then he announces that the entire leadership will sleep what little is left of the night in the Kremlin. The press, especially the foreign press, is bound to be curious, he thinks, if ZIL limousines begin to zoom out of the Kremlin in the middle of the night. Everyone agrees to this, though not everyone is happy about it. Nikita Sergei'ich says he will edit the text of the letter to Kennedy at the beginning of a meeting he calls for 10:00 a.m. later on the morning of October 23ʳᵈ. Just before leaving, an aide suggests that Nikita Sergei'ich issue a threat to Kennedy: if the U.S. moves against Cuba, the USSR will move against West Berlin. Nikita Sergei'ich tells him to keep advice like that to himself.

Mr. President:

I have just received your letter, and have also acquainted myself with the text of your speech of October 22 regarding Cuba.

I must say frankly that the measures indicated in your statement constitute a serious threat to peace and to the security of nations. The United States has openly taken the path of grossly violating the United Nations charter, the path of violating international norms of freedom of navigation on the high seas, the path to aggressive actions both against Cuba and against the Soviet Union.

The statement by the government of the United States of America can only be regarded as undisguised interference in the internal affairs of the Republic of Cuba, the Soviet Union and other states. The United Nations charter and international norms give no right to any state to institute in international waters the inspection of vessels bound for the shores of the Republic of Cuba.

And naturally, neither can we recognize the right of the United States to establish control over armaments which are necessary for the Republic of Cuba to strengthen its defense capability.

We reaffirm that the armaments which are in Cuba, regardless of the classification to which they may belong, are intended solely for defensive purposes in order to secure the Republic of Cuba against the attack of an aggressor.

I hope that the United States Government will display wisdom and renounce the actions pursued by you, which may lead to catastrophic consequences for world peace.

...

N.S. Khrushchev

* * *

#14

Fidel Castro: Statement on Cuban Radio and Television

October 23, 1962[3]

"the aggressors will be exterminated."

Fidel arrives at the television studio in downtown Havana at around 8:30 p.m. on October 23ʳᵈ. He will give Cuba's official response to the crisis that began a little more than twenty-four hours earlier, when Kennedy gave his speech announcing the "quarantine" of Cuba. The TV studio is not Fidel's natural element. He must sit, though his inclination is to get up on his feet, to gesticulate wildly with his long arms, neither of which is possible in the small, cramped space. Even more importantly, he thrives on the feedback of an appreciative audience. It spurs him to the rhetorical heights for which he is famous. He has noticed on the ride over to the studio that the streets are virtually empty—a good sign, because it means that his constituents are home or in public places where they can listen and watch his response to the gringos' threats on radio and TV. He tries to keep this uppermost in his mind as he gets set up in the studio. His only live audience is the collection of rather dour-looking government ministers and other officials. All of them (even the civilians) are in military uniforms.

After a perfunctory introduction by Luis Gomez, Fidel begins. At first, he squirms and seems uncomfortable with the position of the microphone. He is also exhausted; he hasn't slept more than a few hours in the past days, as the crisis approached and finally erupted. But after a few minutes, Fidel warms to his task and launches into wave after wave of apocalyptic rhetoric, urging Cubans to remain calm, even serene, as the countdown proceeds toward Cuba's possible date with nuclear Armageddon. He is emboldened not only by his own self-reinforcing crescendo of verbal virtuosity, but also because he has by this time seen reports of Khrushchev's reply to Kennedy's speech of the day before. Khrushchev has been tough and uncompromising, ready for a showdown with the United States of America over nuclear missiles in Cuba.

Cuba, Fidel says in many different ways, now at top volume with hands and arms punching holes in the air over the microphone, will never surrender any of its inalienable rights, will never allow the Yankees nor anyone else to inspect its territory—regarding Soviet missiles or anything else, for that matter. His voice cracks, as it always does when he is going full tilt, in a way that surprises those new to his speeches. His phrasing is now punctuated with high-pitched squeaks. But instead of distracting listeners, Fidel's brief flights into the upper range where only counter-tenors can vocalize comfortably tend to focus his audience on just how difficult it is for him to say all he has to say in the time allotted for the speech—no matter that he sometimes speaks continuously for several uninterrupted hours at a time.

Now the jokes come. Kennedy says the Cuban people have been betrayed. By whom? By the leaders? By Fidel? Who are these leaders? Martians? Yes, we must be Martians, he says. He imagines people all over the island laughing at that one. He finishes with a flourish and, concludes, as usual, with "patria o muerte." "Fatherland or death." Both the fatherland and death have never been this close, this intense, and this significant, he thinks, on this warm October evening in central Havana. But Fidel has already told his listeners that death, if that is what comes to the entire Cuban nation, will not be in vain. If "the United States continues on the path it has chosen," Fidel says, "then the United States is resolutely determined to commit suicide." The Russians, it is understood, will redeem Cuba's martyrdom by destroying the United States. Fidel's small audience of officials reacts to this apocalyptic statement by breaking into uproarious laughter.

A little after 10:00 p.m., Fidel concludes his hour and a half speech. At that moment, thousands of Cubans all across the island rush into the streets carrying makeshift torches, singing the Cuban national anthem:

Hasten to battle, men of Bayamo,
For the homeland looks proudly to you.
You do not fear a glorious death,
Because to die for the country is to live.
To live in chains
Is to live in dishonor and ignominy.
Hear the clarion call,
Hasten, brave ones, to battle!

We decidedly reject any attempt at supervision, any attempt at inspection of our country. Our country will not be subjected to inspection from any quarter. Our country will never be inspected by anyone, because we will never give authorization for that to anyone, and we will never abdicate our sovereign prerogative. Within our frontiers, we are the ones who rule, and we are the ones who do the inspecting. That is all there is to it.

Anyone who tries to come and inspect Cuba must know that he will have to come equipped for war. That is our final answer to illusions and proposals for carrying out inspections on our territory.

....

We are decidedly in favor of disarmament. What is our policy on military bases? We are decidedly in favor of dismantling all military bases. What is our policy on the presence of troops in various countries? We are in favor of a peace policy. We maintain there should be no troops or military personnel in the territory of any other country. That is our position, the principle we stand on. If the United States wishes disarmament, that is magnificent. Let us all disarm. Magnificent! Let us all support a policy for the dismantling of bases, troops, all of those things scattered throughout the world. Magnificent! We are in accord with that kind of policy.

However, we are not in agreement with a policy which calls for disarming us in the face of the aggressors. That is so stupid, so ridiculous, and so absurd, that it is not worth time wasting a thought about such idiocy ... They believe they are going to scare us with that.

We are cured of that here—cured of fear.

....

We ... face everything calmly. We are not intimidated. But we are calmed by something, and that is knowing that the aggressors will not go unpunished. We are calmed by knowing that the aggressors will be exterminated. Knowing that makes us calm.

We are running risks that we have no choice but to run. They are the risks run by mankind. And we, who are part of mankind—and a very worthy part of mankind—know how to run those risks calmly. And we have the consolation of knowing that the aggressors in a thermonuclear war, those who unleash a thermonuclear war, will be exterminated. I think there are no ambiguities of any kind.

ACT II

Spiral

October 23–28, 1962

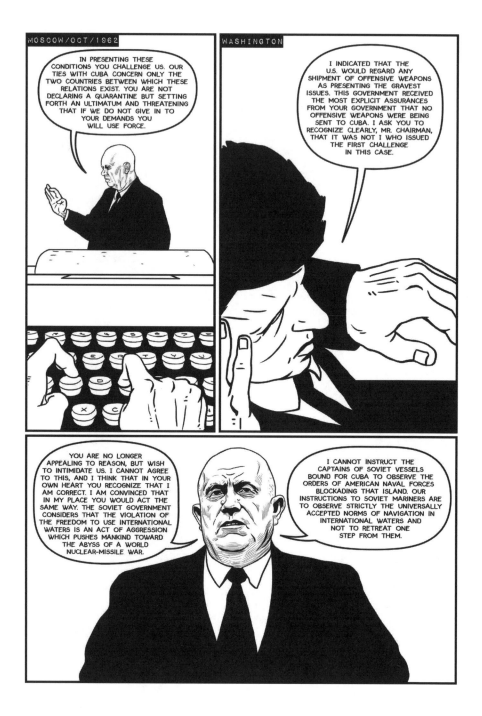

Theatrical Preview

[Images are projected onto a screen at the rear of the stage—images of a watery maelstrom, the three leaders, U.S. missile silos, Soviet jets on runways, and missile sites in Cuba.]

[Voice-over:] In Twenty Thousand Leagues Under the Sea, *Jules Verne wrote: "Maelstrom! Maelstrom! . . . The Maelstrom! Could a more dreadful word in a more dreadful situation have sounded in our ears."[1] No, is the likely reply of anyone who read the book as a child, especially if it was one of the later editions adorned with pen and ink drawings of the huge, scary, roaring vortex off the coast of Norway that is sucking everything into itself, thence into the black hole of its center, at the bottom of the fathomless ocean. The residual fear of being caught in that downdraft, that huge saltwater toilet bowl somewhere in the North Atlantic, remains powerful long after the book is put aside. Once in such a maelstrom, spiraling around and downward toward catastrophe, there is no hope of survival, no possibility of redemption. At the end of that whirling black hole is nothingness. When reading the book, the point of maximum anxiety comes in those moments between the time when we imagine ourselves first being sucked into the periphery of the watery tornado, and the moment when all is lost. We imagine ourselves struggling, hoping against hope, that we can somehow avoid the pull of the downward spiral that will lead to our certain demise. This is, for many, the mother of all nightmares.*

[Voice-over, continues.] The downward spiral toward Armageddon represented in the letters and commentary in Act II is the psychological equivalent of the

imagined maelstrom that has so terrified Jules Verne's readers from the moment his book appeared in 1870. In using the "spiral" metaphor, we need to keep in mind that while the spiral toward nuclear war during the last week of October 1962 is psychological, it is not imaginary. It is real. For Jack Kennedy and Nikita Sergei'ich Khrushchev, the spiral involves moving the largest and most powerful military machines in human history to levels of war-readiness just short of launching a superpower war. For the first and only time in the nuclear age, the lids on the missile silos in the Dakotas are removed, exposing the nuclear-tipped U.S intercontinental ballistic missiles within them, in preparation for launching them against targets in the Soviet Union. For the first and only time, Soviet pilots of nuclear bomb-carrying planes are ordered to sit in their planes until further notice, and to prepare for the order to take off toward targets in the U.S. and Western Europe. Kennedy and Khrushchev come much too close for their own comfort to getting sucked into this vortex of threat and counter-threat that each believes might result in a catastrophic nuclear war.

[Voice-over continues.] It is also real for Fidel Castro, though his experience of the spiral is totally different than that of Kennedy and Khrushchev. Convinced that the hostility of Kennedy and the U.S. government is intense and implacable—that Kennedy intends to destroy the Cuban Revolution one way or another—Castro has the luxury of the certainty that accompanies the conviction that one's fate is completely determined. His choices have nothing to do with whether this or that decision will raise or lower the odds of escalation to nuclear war—an issue that weighs enormously on Kennedy and Khrushchev throughout the crisis. Castro, and the Cuban people, appear instead to direct themselves almost exclusively toward redeeming what they fervently believe is their approaching extinction in a war they can do nothing to prevent, a war they are sure will involve the use of U.S. nuclear weapons in Cuba, a total war, from the Cuban point of view. The Cubans' objective is not to avoid war; they believe that is not in their power. Instead they hope to maintain their dignity to the end, to fight with distinction against an enemy they cannot hope to defeat, but to which they can refuse to surrender.

[Voice-over continues.] This psychological disconnect between Kennedy and Khrushchev, on the one hand; and, on the other hand, Castro and his Cuban fighters, is the driving force in propelling the spiraling maelstrom toward nuclear war in October 1962. The Cubans, intending to fight bravely and to take as many of the enemy with them as possible, engage in actions and rhetoric that confuse and frighten both Kennedy and Khrushchev, who sense more or less simultaneously that they are losing control of the situation in Cuba. They are! Sitting calmly, even serenely, as events race toward Armageddon, the Cubans drive the Americans

and Russians crazy, especially after it appears that Cuban fatalism about the inevitability of Armageddon might be shared by the 43,000 Soviet military personnel in Cuba, who are capable of launching part or all of the huge nuclear arsenal which Khrushchev has deployed on the island.

[End of voice-over and the projected images of the crisis.]

[As Act II begins, Kennedy and Khrushchev are standing on platforms at the top of a spiral staircase that is widest at the top and narrowest at the bottom. The spiral staircase is rotating, via special effects by the lighting crew. Fidel sits at the base of the spiral staircase, in a modified lotus position, giving the appearance of a serene, bearded Buddha in green fatigues. Fidel is portrayed by an adult in this act. He is smoking a cigar. He is not speaking. As Act II opens, Kennedy and Khrushchev are hurling accusations back and forth at each other.]

NIKITA SERGEI'ICH: Mr. President, we have every moral and legal right to do what is necessary to defend our friends and allies, the Cubans. You started this. You ordered the Bay of Pigs invasion, proving to the world that your intention is regime change in Cuba, nothing less. We are only responding to your heinous, vile act of aggression against little Cuba.

JACK: I'm sorry, Mr. Chairman, but you must still be entangled in the web of lies and deceit that you have woven around this entire issue of the missile deployment to Cuba. You have failed to act responsibly. Your behavior cannot be tolerated by the international community. The weapons are a threat to the U.S. and the entire hemisphere. Either you remove them, or we will remove them for you.

[As Nikita Sergei'ich and Jack continue to hurl their accusations back and forth, each has increasing difficulty holding onto the railing, and thus difficulty avoiding the beckoning vortex represented by the spiraling staircase. Sound effects kick in, as we begin to hear the roar of the spiral. We remember that a tornado is one variant of a spiraling maelstrom.]

NIKITA SERGEI'ICH: Hey, Mr. President, wait a minute. I think I am being sucked down into this black hole. When I look down, there seems to be just an endless tunnel.

JACK: I know what you mean. I can barely hold onto the damn railing myself. Where the hell are we, and how do we get out of here? Don't let go, whatever you do. We can't allow ourselves to be pulled down into the spiral. How long can you hold on?

NIKITA SERGEI'ICH: I don't know. I'm an old man, you know. Not much longer, I'd say. Can you give me a hand?

[They grab onto each other desperately with one hand each, the other hand gripped onto the railing of the staircase. They are barely able to hold on, barely able to avoid getting sucked down into the bottom where Fidel Castro is relaxing.]

[The voice-over resumes, along with horrific images of war and its devastation projected onto the screen at the back of the stage. The voice-over announces: "a U-2 spy plane has been shot down over eastern Cuba, and the pilot has been killed. Repeat: an act of war has been committed in Cuba, and an American pilot has been killed."]

NIKITA SERGEI'ICH AND JACK: [Dirge-like, chanting in unison.] The crisis is spiraling out of control, out of control, out of control! Forget about a victory. This is too dangerous, too dangerous, too dangerous!

[Nikita Sergei'ich and Jack grasp onto each other even more tightly, as they try to avoid being sucked into the swirling vortex.]

FIDEL: [Shouting at Jack.] Come on, imperialistas, give us your best shot. You may destroy us but we will take a helluva lot of you bastards with us! Come on, I invite you to commit national suicide by attacking us. Bring it on, Yankees!

[Jack does not hear Fidel.]

FIDEL: [Shouting at Nikita Sergei'ich.] Stand firm, comrade Nikita! Don't be intimidated. Don't cave in. By my calculations, the U.S. will attack us imminently, and will in all probability invade the island and seek to destroy our revolution and government. If they invade this island, Comrade Nikita, then we request that you launch a nuclear attack on the United States and destroy them forever. Cuba of course will also be destroyed. But we shall be proud to be martyrs for socialism. Go for it, Comrade Nikita!

[Khrushchev stares at Fidel, horrified, speechless.]

NIKITA SERGEI'ICH: [Turning away from Fidel.] This is insane; this is insane!

[Fidel resumes his lotus position at the base of the spiral staircase. As he sits down, he is smiling. Jack and Nikita Sergei'ich hold on to the platform railings for dear life, and the roaring vortex appears poised to suck both men down into its black hole.]

End of Theatrical Preview

* * *

#15

John F. Kennedy to Nikita S. Khrushchev
October 23, 1962[2]

"I hope that you will . . . observe . . . the quarantine"

Now what do I do? Jack asks himself. I've ordered a quarantine of Cuba—which seems to me the minimum required as a first step toward removal of the Russian missiles. But in his latest letter Khrushchev treats the quarantine like some decla- ration of war, as if we are keen for a nuclear showdown. The speech to the nation and the world has been given; a personal warning to Khrushchev has been sent with a clear message: remove the missiles from Cuba, or the United States will destroy them. Jack thinks he was perfectly clear in his letter sent just prior to the speech: you—Khrushchev—caused the crisis and if your ships fail to stop at sea you will also have started the war.

Khrushchev has responded by ordering work on the missile sites in Cuba stepped up to twenty-four hours a day, in an obvious effort to get the weapons operational ASAP. Khrushchev has also made it clear that any U.S. efforts to interdict Soviet ships at the quarantine line will be resisted. Jack was at first inclined to dismiss this as just one more blast of bombastic rhetoric from the world's acknowledged King of Bombast, Nikita Khrushchev. But not now, not on the heels of the news that Soviet attack submarines are moving into position to escort the Soviet ships up to and (presumably) through *the U.S. quarantine line.*

Jack feels as if his head is in a vise, squeezed from one direction by his military zealots in the Pentagon who see the crisis as an opportunity to destroy the annoying Cuban revolutionary government and send the Russians back home where they be- long. But Jack must also contend with those who proclaim that he is needlessly and irresponsibly pushing the world to the brink of Armageddon over—over what?—a few meaningless missiles in Cuba that, as many seem to believe, don't affect the balance of power in any significant way. Jack has just received an open letter from the British pacifist and philosopher Bertrand Russell, referring to Jack as a desper- ate man who is leading the world toward mass murder, and calling on him to "end this madness." Jack actually has some sympathy for Russell's characterization of the situation as "madness." What else can you call any war that destroys hu- man civilization, whatever one may think of the acceptability of Soviet missiles in Cuba? But Jack feels keenly that he does not have the philosopher's option: arrive at a position, publish it, and wait for a response, then publish your rejoinder. It must be nice, Jack thinks, to sit in an ivory tower and think great thoughts without regard for the consequences—should there be any consequences. Maybe I should have been a history professor, he muses.

But while philosophers like Russell may talk the talk of peace on earth, politicians must walk the walk and try to achieve peace, in the face of many obstacles. Jack is a politician, a leader, the chief executive of his country, who nearly two months before pronounced Soviet nuclear missiles in Cuba unacceptable. And now he must act on that statement; he has begun by putting his navy where his threat of September 4th indicated he would: it encircles Cuba. He has made clear to Khrushchev in action what he thought was crystal clear in his statement: nuclear weapons in Cuba will not be tolerated.

Jack is besieged with unsolicited advice. Russell's view is only an extreme version of reactions reaching Jack from across Western Europe. Jack has just spoken on the phone (as he will do every day during the intense phase of the crisis) with British Prime Minister Harold MacMillan. The PM tells him frankly that a lot of Europeans are having trouble understanding what all the fuss is about. After all, he tells Jack, Europe has lived in the shadow of Soviet nuclear power since 1949, when the Soviets tested their first atomic bomb. MacMillan tells Jack that Europeans are wondering if, perhaps, the U.S. has gotten a wee bit carried away over Castro and Cuba; Castro is after all (according to MacMillan) just a tin pot dictator and Cuba is a small backward country. Jack bristles at this, but responds in what he hopes is a calm voice that the crisis is essentially unrelated to Castro and Cuba. He says he is not interested in picking a fight with Castro and Cuba, which he tells MacMillan are mere nuisances and distractions from the priorities of a superpower. The Cuban crisis is instead a showdown, he says, with Khrushchev and the Soviet Union over whether they will be permitted, via a systematic campaign of lies and deception, to try to fundamentally change the balance of power, and to openly and arrogantly saturate the Western Hemisphere with their influence and their communist ideology—steps, Jack tells the PM, which must be resisted.

Resisted, Jack thinks, yeah sure. But at what price? He has ordered nearly a hundred ships and close to 2,000 fighter aircraft to the Caribbean. And of course these are only the tip of the iceberg of the military power that the U.S. is mustering. More than a quarter of a million men are being mobilized for a possible invasion of Cuba; 1200 bombing missions are planned for day one of the war; 25,000 U.S. casualties are anticipated, assuming that the war does not go nuclear. If it does go nuclear, well, no one cares to venture an estimate of U.S. casualties, in that case. Jack, whose concern over possible escalation to nuclear catastrophe is regarded by many of his military advisers as a cowardly and sophomoric obsession, can think of many ways a misunderstanding or misperception near the quarantine line can lead to nuclear war at sea. One of the last decisions he makes before going to sleep is to order the quarantine line to retreat from 800 miles from Cuba, to 500 miles from Cuban territorial waters, an idea suggested by the British ambassador in Washington. He hopes this will give Khrushchev and his associates more time to come to their senses and rescind the order to defy the quarantine line and challenge the U.S. forces to shoot first.

Finally, Jack orders low-level reconnaissance flights over Soviet missile sites in Cuba to begin on the following morning. They are to continue at dawn and dusk every day until further notice. He is desperate to know how much time, if any, he has to make decisions before the Soviet missiles on the island can be fired at targets in the U.S., potentially killing millions of Americans. Jack finds that he stops in mid-thought, when he comes to the word "millions." He cannot say it, even to himself.

A letter to Khrushchev is sent, urging him not to order his ships to defy U.S. efforts at the quarantine line. He notices that the letter seems to contain an ultimatum to Khrushchev. He wonders how he would respond if Khrushchev issued such an ultimatum to him.

Dear Mr. Chairman:

I have received your letter of October 23. I think you will recognize that the step which started the current chain of events was the action of your government in secretly furnishing offensive weapons to Cuba. We will be discussing this matter in the Security Council. In the meantime I am concerned that we both show prudence and do nothing to allow events to make the situation more difficult to control than it already is.

I hope you will issue immediately the necessary instructions to your ships to observe the terms of the quarantine, the basis of which was established by the vote of the Organization of American States this afternoon, and which will go into effect at 1400 hours Greenwich time October twenty-four.

Sincerely,

John F. Kennedy

* * *

#16

Nikita S. Khrushchev to John F. Kennedy

October 24, 1962[3]

"toward the abyss of a world nuclear missile war."

Nikita Sergei'ich is livid. How did the Americans discover the deployment? How? He is told that efforts to camouflage the launch sites in Cuba began only after it *became known that the Americans had already discovered the sites. But why not before? He can't understand. His intelligence people are no help. When he asks, they shrug their shoulders and offer to inquire with their colleagues in Cuba. He decides then and there to cancel his plan to promote Gen. Issa Pliyev, the Soviet field commander in Cuba, to the rank of Marshall of the Soviet Union. Nikita Sergei'ich sends a cable to Pliyev asking for an explanation about the lack of camouflage. But the usually responsive Pliyev has gone silent, further infuriating his boss. Now, with U.S. military power converging around Cuba, with Kennedy threatening to stop Soviet ships bound for Cuba and to force them to submit to humiliating inspections, he knows he is in one hell of jam. He feels his subordinates have let him down. He fumes and fusses and curses them to himself. But in the end he pulls himself together, concluding: what is done is done, and what was not done was not done. We are Russians, after all. We will, as always, find a way to muddle through.*

But Nikita Sergei'ich is also angry at himself. He realizes suddenly that he has no "plan B." There are no viable options available for the contingency he now faces, in which the Americans have discovered the missiles prior to their becoming operational. The funny thing, he muses, is that it never occurred to him that the Americans would discover the missiles. Sure, the Cubans warned him—several times—that this might happen, but he thought, what do the Cubans know about superpower geopolitics anyway? Nikita Sergei'ich begins to realize that he has been seduced by the cleverness and audacity of his own idea into believing that the scheme was also infallibly destined to succeed. But he has not fooled the Americans; he cannot present Kennedy with a fait accompli, *as he has assumed. He will not be going to Cuba in November to announce the deployment to the world. He will not stand before a million adoring Cubans in the Square of the Revolution in Havana and bask in his triumph, with Fidel Castro at his side. Nikita Sergei'ich has been caught with his scenario down in front of the entire world. This is a lot to absorb and accept, but absorb it and accept it he must.*

Nikita Sergei'ich decides he must meet threat with threat. He gives orders for all Soviet intercontinental missiles inside the Soviet Union to stand fueled and armed and ready for immediate launch. Planes are loaded with bombs. All military pilots are ordered to active duty and to sit—literally—in their planes prepared for takeoff at a moment's notice. Army units are issued live ammunition. The Soviet Union is preparing for war in ways that, Nikita Sergei'ich is confident, U.S. intelligence will pick up immediately. This is exactly what Nikita Sergei'ich wants them to do. He wants to give the Americans some of their own threatening medicine. He then issues orders to Soviet ships heading toward the Americans' quarantine line to ignore U.S. orders to stop and submit to a search by U.S. personnel. "To hell with Kennedy and his quarantine line," he thinks. "He'll find out shortly whom he is dealing with."

As he falls asleep, Nikita Sergei'ich feels he has done a good job of improvising a tit-for-tat strategy in response to Kennedy's quarantine ultimatum. He is, after all, the leader of the world's other superpower and he cannot, therefore, simply back down just because Kennedy is feeling his oats.

But Nikita Sergei'ich is awakened in the middle of the night by a nightmare that is eerily similar to Kennedy's own apprehension about the possibility of war breaking out at the quarantine line. In fact, the more Nikita Sergei'ich thinks about it, the more he is convinced that a war, under current circumstances, is almost guaranteed. Wide awake now, unable to sleep, he thinks, here is how it will happen: the Americans issue orders to a Soviet ship to stop and submit to a search; the Soviets ignore the order; the Americans fire on the Soviet ship, possibly sinking it and killing Soviet sailors, or disabling it and preparing to tow it back to a U.S. port for inspection; retaliation comes in short order from one or more of the Soviet submarines escorting the Soviet convoy. He then remembers that each submarine escorting the Soviet freighters and tankers is nuclear-capable. He wonders whether Kennedy knows this. What if a Soviet submarine captain blasts the Americans with a nuclear torpedo? Nikita Sergei'ich is terrified by this premonition, as he stares into the darkness. This is madness! A nuclear war will start at sea, a war that will escalate much faster than Kennedy or I can control, a war without winners, Armageddon—the last battle—the ultimate catastrophe! He looks at the clock: 4:00 a.m.

This premonition of Armageddon is seared into his brain as he awakens in the early morning hours. Nikita Sergei'ich decides to turn a hundred and eighty degrees from the direction of his thinking as he was going to bed. At the morning meeting of the Soviet leadership, he proposes that a new order be issued: "Stop!" Specifically, ships with military cargo should stop, back far away from the quarantine line and wait for the crisis to relent, before continuing on toward Cuba. Other ships, carrying civilian cargo, should stop when ordered to do so by the Americans, offer to open their holds for inspection, and then continue on to Cuba after satisfying the Americans about the nature of their cargo.

As usual, Nikita Sergei'ich has his way in the meeting with the leadership. Still, he senses some disgruntlement around the table about this apparent "capitulation" to Kennedy. So Nikita Sergei'ich decides this is the moment to play an ace he has unexpectedly been dealt by new information in his morning intelligence briefing papers. The Presidium members have already been informed that two nuclear-powered freighters carrying nuclear warheads have reached Cuba. The warheads have been stored in a hidden location, not far from the port of Mariel, where they were offloaded. He now informs his associates that the Aleksandrovsk, the last of a trio of nuclear-powered freighters carrying nuclear warheads to Cuba, has managed (just barely, by minutes, perhaps, or an hour or two at most) to escape the quarantine line and is on its way to Cuba. He reminds his associates that the ship carries twenty-four nuclear warheads for the long-range missiles, each of which is capable of destroying targets deep in the U.S. heartland, and forty-four warheads for the shorter-range, war-fighting cruise missiles that are already assembled and ready for launch at the U.S. invasion force. Nikita Sergei'ich tells his subordinates

*that all is in readiness in Cuba: launchers; platforms, warheads—everything. Now,
he says, Kennedy doesn't dare order an attack on the sites, for fear of massive Soviet
retaliation both in Cuba itself, and from Cuba onto the American mainland.*

*Yet Nikita Sergei'ich's apparent calm and confidence is also partly a ruse. For
he has also received a disturbing report from the KGB station in Cuba: two U.S.
jets, flying at very high speed but only a few hundred feet above the ground, have
flown directly over the port of Mariel, west of Havana, where the* Aleksandrovsk
*was scheduled to arrive, near where storage sites for the warheads have been as-
sembled and hidden. Anticipating that the ship might be bombed in Mariel Harbor by U.S. jets, the Soviet command in Cuba has ordered it to dock at La Isabella,
east of Havana. However, since there are no storage facilities at La Isabella, the
warheads on the* Aleksandrovsk *will have to remain on board the ship, essentially
useless for the time being.*

*Nikita Sergei'ich's letter to Kennedy is meant to reflect in words the self-confi-
dence he hopes is expressed in the various Soviet military preparations that U.S.
intelligence is doubtless already reporting to the White House. If Kennedy can be
a tough guy, he thinks, so can I. So he stonewalls Kennedy and dares him to stop
a Soviet freighter bound for Cuba. But like Kennedy, he is frantically beginning
to improvise a plan B that will permit both he and Kennedy, along with their nations and the world, to escape the downwardly spiraling crisis with their integrity
intact, and without a war that could escalate to Armageddon and the destruction
of human civilization.*

Dear Mr. President:

I have received your letter of October 23, have studied it, and am an-
swering you.

Just imagine, Mr. President, that we had presented you with the conditions of an ultimatum which you have presented us by your action.
How would you have reacted to this? I think that you would have been
indignant at such a step on our part. And this would have been understandable to us.

In presenting us with these conditions, you, Mr. President, have flung
a challenge at us. Who asked you to do this? By what right did you do
this? Our ties with the Republic of Cuba, like our relations with other
states, regardless of what kind of states they may be, concern only the
two countries between which these relations exist. And if we speak now
of the quarantine to which your letter refers, a quarantine may be established, according to accepted international practice, only by agreement
of states between themselves, and not by some third party. Quarantines
exist, for example, on agricultural goods and products. But in this case
the question is in no way one of quarantine, but rather of far more serious things, and you yourself understand this.

You, Mr. President, are not declaring a quarantine, but rather are setting forth an ultimatum and threatening that if we do not give in to your demands you will use force. Consider what you are saying! And you want to persuade me to agree to this! What would it mean to agree to these demands? It would mean guiding oneself in one's relations with other countries not by reason, but by submitting to arbitrariness. You are no longer appealing to reason, but wish to intimidate us.

No, Mr. President, I cannot agree to this, and I think that in your own heart you recognize that I am correct. I am convinced that in my place you would act the same way.

You wish to compel us to renounce the rights that every sovereign state enjoys, you are trying to legislate in questions of international law, and you are violating the universally accepted norms of that law. And you are doing all this not only out of hatred for the Cuban people and its government, but also because of considerations of the election campaign in the United States. What morality, what law can justify such an approach by the American government to international affairs? No such morality or law can be found, because the actions of the United States with regard to Cuba constitute outright banditry or, if you like, the folly of degenerate imperialism. Unfortunately, such folly can bring grave suffering to the peoples of all countries, and to no lesser degree to the American people themselves, since the United States has completely lost its former isolation with the advent of modern types of armament.

Therefore, Mr. President, if you coolly weigh the situation which has developed, not giving way to passions, you will understand that the Soviet Union cannot fail to reject the arbitrary demands of the United States. When you confront us with such conditions, try to put yourself in our place and consider how the United States would react to these conditions. I do not doubt that if someone attempted to dictate similar conditions to you—the United States—you would reject such an attempt. And we also say—no.

The Soviet government considers that the violation of the freedom to use international waters and international air space is an act of aggression which pushes mankind toward the abyss of a world nuclear missile war. Therefore the Soviet government cannot instruct the captains of Soviet vessels bound for Cuba to observe the orders of American naval forces blockading that island. Our instructions to Soviet mariners are to observe strictly the universally accepted norms of navigation in international waters and not to retreat one step from them. And if the American side violates these rules, it must realize what responsibility will rest upon it in that case. Naturally we will not simply be bystanders with regard to piratical acts by American ships on the high seas. We will then

be forced on our part to take the measures we consider necessary and
adequate in order to protect our rights. We have everything necessary to
do so.

Respectfully,
N.S. Khrushchev

* * *

#17

John F. Kennedy to Nikita S. Khrushchev

October 25, 1962[4]

"all these public assurances were false"

*Jack is appalled at Khrushchev's latest letter, which he reads first thing in the
morning on the 24ᵗʰ. The letter seems adamant: the Soviet Union will not recognize the U.S. quarantine as legitimate; it will not order ships bound for Cuba
to stop so they can be searched by the Americans—and there are at least two
dozen Soviet vessels in the Atlantic which appear to be headed in that direction.
Moreover, he seems to be saying that the Russians will take whatever measures
are required to protect what Khrushchev calls "our rights." Whatever measures?
What does that mean, he wonders. Is he saying that he is willing to risk going to
nuclear war over this?*

*I am in a box, Jack thinks, and I can't see any way out of it. He goes through
his mental checklist once more, looking for a way to avoid a military confrontation at the quarantine line: first, we have said the missiles cannot be tolerated.
We have also amassed a huge force in the Caribbean to destroy the missile sites
and probably invade Cuba as well if, God help us, it comes to that. As a next
step, we have set up the quarantine line 500 miles from Cuba to intercept ships
carrying cargo associated with the construction of the missile sites in Cuba.
Now Khrushchev says, "okay Kennedy, screw you. My ships are coming through
and if you try to start something, Soviet submarines will give our answer in the
form of torpedoes." Jack wonders whether this means war is inevitable, unless
he preemptively surrenders and rescinds the order to set up the quarantine. He
calculates that were he to remove the quarantine, he will be impeached. That is
not going to happen. So yes, he thinks, yes, war at sea is looking more and more
probable. If the Russians don't submit to inspection at the quarantine line, then
the war will begin then and there. Jack is almost overwhelmed by the combination of unfathomable danger and ironical absurdity that characterizes the situation in which he finds himself.*

*By 10:00 a.m., when Jack's advisers meet with him, the Soviet (and Soviet-
chartered) ships are approaching the quarantine line. The situation strikes him*

as surreal, as something that could just as easily have come out of one of the Ian Fleming novels that constitute one of his favorite mental escapes from the pressure of the presidency. Jack has just seen Sean Connery, starring as James Bond in "Dr. No," the first Fleming novel to be made into a movie. He finds himself wishing that international intrigue were the way it is portrayed in Fleming, full of tricky gadgets, thrilling chases, narrow escapes, and endings in which everything comes together. Jack especially wishes for an escape right about now, narrow or otherwise, from this crisis over missiles in Cuba. It feels more and more like a spiraling whirlpool into which the entire world may soon be sucked and destroyed. The arrival of Khrushchev's latest letter does not increase his confidence that an escape will be found. Jack is snapped abruptly out of his reverie when he is informed that the quarantine line is in place, and that the Soviet ships are still heading straight toward it.

Televisions are set up all over the White House. All three networks are covering the crisis live this morning. Other programming has been suspended, pending developments in the Cuban crisis. Many in the building are watching CBS, on which the news anchor, the deeply resonant, pipe-smoking Walter Cronkite, directs attention to a big map of the western North Atlantic, on which are stuck paper representations of the Russian ships approaching a quarantine line made up of a few paper ships arrayed in a rough semi-circle. Every so often a young assistant to Cronkite moves the Soviet ships closer to the quarantine line. Jack asks who the new guy is and is told his name is Dan Rather. Jack jokes to an aide, "not that I'm superstitious, but under these war-threatening circumstances, I'd prefer the assistant's name were "Dan Rather-not!"

Anything, he thinks—anything at all—is preferable to the outbreak of a U.S.-Soviet war at sea, when both military establishments are, as they like to say over in the Pentagon, "loaded and cocked"—prepared to go to war. Jack suddenly remembers seeing a report in one of the newspapers earlier in the day that Richard Nixon's golfing buddy, the American evangelist Billy Graham, is preaching this week in Argentina on the subject of "The End of the World." Jack thinks: Graham either knows something we don't know or he has a helluva sense of humor. Actually, as he reflects on it, he doesn't think he has ever heard of Graham telling a joke.

Around 10:30 a.m. Jack gets two pieces of information: miraculously, it seems, the Soviet ships have either stopped dead in the water, or have already begun to reverse course. It looks as if Khrushchev has had second thoughts. It seems that he will not challenge the quarantine line. That is the good news. But there is also bad news. In answer to a query, he is told by an aide that work on the missile sites in Cuba appears to have speeded up yet again, in an obvious effort to make the weapons operational and threatening to the U.S. before the U.S. is in a position to destroy them. It goes on like this all day: many ships stop, turn around, and head back; while some (like tankers) which obviously do not carry cargo for the missile installations are allowed to pass through. Every ship, every movement, is monitored by Jack. So far, so good at the quarantine line. But every time he inquires about the missile sites in Cuba, he is told the work is accelerating and appears to be nearing completion.

Late at night, he orders the eight-plane, low-level reconnaissance teams that have been photographing the missile sites to increase the frequency of their flights to every two hours, round-the-clock, using flares dropped from the reconnaissance planes to enhance visibility after dark. Finally, his letter in response to Khrushchev's latest missive is sent out around 1:45 a.m. Thursday morning. The tone seems to Jack not quite right: a little too preachy and scolding. "So be it," Jack thinks. "Goddammit, I have to make Khrushchev understand that we mean business. He has got to stop the work on the Cuban missile sites."

As he retires after an eighteen-hour roller coaster of a day, he recalls a comment his Secretary of State Dean Rusk made to him earlier that afternoon. They were discussing the standard operating procedure for the U.S. leadership in a war-threatening crisis. The cabinet officers, senior military officers, their aides and a few others are to be taken to a bunker buried deep in the mountains of West Virginia, to wait out the war. From that bunker Kennedy and his aides are to try to maintain control of events as best they can while, in all probability, Washington and perhaps much of the country as well, is being destroyed. Rusk had said to Jack: "Mr. President, if anyone survives the nuclear war, and if they find us in that damn bunker, they would be within their rights to take every last one of us and hang us from the highest tree." Jack had agreed. Neither he, nor Rusk, nor anyone else, plans to go to the bunker in the mountains. If they fail to prevent a nuclear war, they will perish with everyone else, including their families (which, according to the standard operating procedure, would not be allowed into the West Virginia bunker, due to lack of space and other facilities).

Dear Mr. Chairman:

I have received your letter of October 24, and I regret very much that you still do not appear to understand what it is that has moved us in this matter.

The sequence of events is clear. In August there were reports of important shipments of military equipment and technicians from the Soviet Union to Cuba. In early September I indicated very plainly that the United States would regard any shipment of offensive weapons as presenting the gravest issues. After that time, this government received the most explicit assurances from your government and its representatives, both publicly and privately, that no offensive weapons were being sent to Cuba. If you will review the statement issued by TASS in September, you will see how clearly this assurance was given.

In reliance on these solemn assurances, I urged restraint upon those in this country who were urging action in this matter at that time. And then I learned beyond doubt what you have not denied—namely, that all these public assurances were false and that your military people had set out recently to establish a set of missile bases in Cuba. I ask you to recognize clearly, Mr. Chairman, that it was not I who issued the first challenge in this case, and that in the light of this record these activities in Cuba required the responses I have announced.

I repeat my regret: that these events should cause a deterioration in our relations. I hope that your government will take the necessary action to permit a restoration of the earlier situation.

Sincerely yours,

John F. Kennedy

* * *

#18

Nikita S. Khrushchev to John F. Kennedy

October 26, 1962[5]

> *"Only lunatics or suicides . . . want to . . . destroy the world"*

Kennedy's letter reaches Nikita Sergei'ich on the morning of Thursday October 25th. It is, as usual, short and to the point. He reads it once, then twice, then a third time, before laying it aside. Nikita Sergei'ich wonders: is Kennedy telling me that he is about to launch the war in Cuba? He mentions something Nikita Sergei'ich has been afraid of ever since Kennedy's speech announcing the discovery of missiles in Cuba: Kennedy is contending with powerful hawks in his government and around the U.S. who are determined to use the discovery of the missiles as a pretext to attack Cuba, invade it, and destroy the Cuban Revolution. Is Kennedy telling me, he wonders, that he cannot hold off the hawks much longer?

Nikita Sergei'ich sits alone in his Kremlin office, mulling over the situation. He is inclined to send Kennedy a quick reply telling him that if he chooses war, then by God he can have a war, a war that will destroy the U.S. along with Cuba and perhaps the Soviet Union as well. He is angry because Kennedy will not cut him any slack, will not give him any way of saving face—of keeping the missiles in Cuba, without going right up to the brink, or over the brink, into Armageddon. Moreover, either Kennedy has no creative ideas about how to end the crisis short of war, or else he is relying on Nikita Sergei'ich to arrive at some solution that he can agree to.

Nikita Sergei'ich believes he knows what his associates in the Soviet Presidium are thinking. I know what they want me to do: they want me to call Kennedy's bluff—they will assume it is a bluff. They want me to announce for the entire world to hear that all of the medium range ballistic missiles we have deployed in

Cuba are ready for launch, and can be fired in about four hours, which is the amount of time it will take to mate the warheads onto the missiles. They want to remind me that I have many times called nuclear weapons "the gods of war," and that if Kennedy chooses to order an attack and invasion of Cuba, well then, we will be compelled to retaliate by launching our Cuban-based missiles at the U.S. Let the Americans draw the appropriate conclusions, they are thinking: let the imperialists know that if they want to run the risk of Russian missiles in Cuba being launched to destroy Washington, New York, Atlanta, New Orleans and other cities, along with millions of Americans living in and near them, then go ahead and invade Cuba. His associates, he strongly suspects, were not happy about the deployment in the first place, believing it was too risky and that Castro was too loose a cannon to bring into the Soviet sphere of influence and protection. Now, he thinks, if I suggest pulling them out as part of some deal with Kennedy, they are really going to resent it, though I doubt any of them will say anything negative to my face. One reason Nikita Sergei'ich is upset by this scenario—reading the minds of his associates—is that they were mostly right. The deployment was risky, maybe even too risky. Damn Kennedy! He has told Nikita Sergei'ich it is his move and frankly, as he thinks it over, he remains unsure what he should do.

Nikita Sergei'ich calls his Presidium associates to a meeting in the Kremlin to discuss what to do. Actually, he calls them to order mainly to think out loud about what he should decide to do. His colleagues, as usual, sit like stone statues subtly nodding their agreement with whatever Nikita Sergei'ich says is so. He has wondered from time to time whether Kennedy has this problem: a room full of groveling, intimidated "yes-men" who essentially tell the boss what they think he wants to hear. Nikita Sergei'ich thinks that yes-men cause fewer problems and facilitate decisive action—no question about that. The Cuban missile deployment could never have happened under any other circumstances—could never have been imagined, supplied, shipped and implemented in anything like the lightning-fast pace of Operation ANADYR, the Russian code name for the deployment. (Nikita Sergei'ich had loved the code name when he first heard it. "Anadyr" refers to a Russian river in Siberia—the idea being that should U.S. spies somehow discover what the Soviets are calling the operation, they might think it has something to do with Siberia. Now that the Americans have discovered the deployment and are threatening war against Cuba and the Soviet Union to remove the missiles, Nikita Sergei'ich is less enamored of the code name for the operation.)

As the Presidium members are taking their seats, Nikita Sergei'ich tells his colleagues straightaway that the missiles must come out of Cuba. If the others are shocked by his about-face, they disguise it well—as they have been disguising their true reactions to the boss's comments since the bloody reign of Stalin. Nikita Sergei'ich says that, in his opinion, the tone of Kennedy's letter proves that at least some of the Americans advising Kennedy will accept nothing less than a Soviet capitulation. He says that the Soviet Union will not capitulate, however. What he has in mind, he says, is a very simple agreement: "Give us a pledge not to invade

Cuba, and we will pledge to remove the missiles." He goes on to say that he and Kennedy together should ultimately agree to create a "zone of peace" in the Caribbean, using the deal over missiles in Cuba as a template. In any case, he says, the crisis has gotten far too dangerous to be allowed to continue. Thinking out loud in his usual fashion, the deal Nikita Sergei'ich imagines becomes more elaborate. "Let's say," he says addressing his associates, "that we will agree to remove our missiles from Cuba and pledge not to invade Turkey, and that Kennedy will agree to remove NATO missiles from Turkey and Italy, and pledge not to invade Cuba." He likes the analogy. He instructs Foreign Minister Andrei Gromyko to make sure he uses the term "analogous" when comparing the missiles in Cuba and those in Turkey and Italy, as his team drafts the letter to Kennedy. Nikita Sergei'ich tells Gromyko and the others that they will reconvene the following morning at 10:00 a.m. to go over the letter.

As an afterthought, Nikita Sergei'ich mentions that there will not be enough time to get Fidel Castro's approval of the deal proposed in the letter. After all, he points out, once the nuclear war starts, all such deals will become irrelevant. In any case, Nikita Sergei'ich tells the others, eventually Comrade Fidel will no doubt be pleased to join with the Soviet Union in issuing an invitation to UN inspectors to come to Cuba to verify that what the Americans like to call "offensive" weapons, the nuclear weapons and missiles, have been removed.

To mark the moment, as well as to relieve tension, Khrushchev invites his colleagues to join him that evening at the Bolshoi Theater. Of course, they all agree to go, as he knew they would.

On his arrival at the Kremlin on Friday morning, the 26th, Nikita Sergei'ich turns immediately to his blue-gray folder, in which he finds, as usual, his daily intelligence briefing. Usually, many issues are covered in the briefing materials. But this morning, as with every morning this week, everything in the folder is about the Cuban crisis. As he reads the materials, his usual perplexity and frustration when dealing with intelligence estimates, suddenly turns to outright alarm. The fear that has been lurking at the fringes of his mind for days now begins to swamp everything else—his anger at Kennedy, his frustration with his colleagues, his inability to articulate a plausible, face-saving way out of the crisis. This is the fear that war is quickly becoming inevitable, perhaps just about to begin, within hours, or even minutes, and thus that there is not enough time left to stave off the ultimate catastrophe.

His anxiety is fed by several items in his morning intelligence briefing: First, according to the KGB station in Washington, war is imminent: the decision has been made, and a massive U.S. air attack on the missile sites will begin momentarily, followed by an invasion of the island by tens of thousands of U.S. Marines and other U.S. forces. Second, the U.S. nuclear command has raised the state of war-readiness of its forces worldwide to Defense Condition 2 (DefCon 2), the highest state of alert short of war itself (DefCon 1). And third, Soviet military intelligence in the U.S. is reporting that the White House has issued an order to

U.S. hospitals to prepare to receive large numbers of anticipated casualties. In the face of such devastating news, Nikita Sergei'ich fights paralysis, forces himself to calmly tell the members of the Presidium what he has just learned, and to think clearly about what is to be done.

As planned, the 10:00 a.m. meeting begins with Gromyko reading the draft letter to Kennedy aloud. The longtime Presidium stenographer, Nadezhda Petrovna, is present, as usual, to take down the anticipated barrage of additions, subtractions and other alterations typically made by Nikita Sergei'ich. (He has long wondered if, with her dark hair and eyes, she might be a gypsy. But it would be inappropriate to ask, of course, so he is not sure.) But this time, he sits silent, eyes closed, as Gromyko drones on in his basso profundo. He opens his eyes, however, when Gromyko gets to the passages about the U.S. missile bases in Turkey and Italy— which are "analogous" to the Soviet missiles in Cuba. Having finished, Gromyko clears his throat and returns to his chair.

After several moments of uncomfortable silence, Nikita Sergei'ich holds up the blue-green folder with the message from Washington about the imminence of the U.S. attack on Cuba. He says that things have changed overnight. The attack on Cuba may commence at any moment. Nikita Sergei'ich tells the Presidium that a new response to Kennedy is needed, one from which the demand regarding the Turkish and Italian missiles is best excluded. Without waiting for responses from the others, he calls for Nedezhda Petrovna to prepare to take dictation. When she announces that she is ready, Nikita Sergei'ich stands up and begins pacing as he dictates a long, rambling, emotional letter concluding with the simple formula: Kennedy will pledge not to attack or invade Cuba; Nikita Sergei'ich pledges to remove the nuclear missiles from Cuba. During the lunch break the letter is typed. After lunch the letter is read aloud to the group once more. Nikita Sergei'ich doesn't like it, thinking it is confused and rambling. But there is no time for fine-tuning. Nikita Sergei'ich picks up a pen and asks if everyone is agreed. He scans the room. Everyone nods approval, following which Nikita Sergei'ich signs the letter and tells Gromyko to get it to the U.S. embassy as fast as possible. It is delivered 4:43 p.m. local time, Friday, October 26, 1962. After translation and encryption, it reaches the Moscow International Telegraph office at 7:00 p.m. (11:00 a.m. in Washington, DC). After some delay in transmission, it is finally sent to Washington.

Dear Mr. President:

I have received your letter of October 25. From your letter I got the feeling that you have some understanding of the situation which has developed and a sense of responsibility. I appreciate this.

By now we have already publicly exchanged our assessments of the events around Cuba and each of us has set forth his explanation and interpretation of these events. Therefore, I would think that, evidently, continuing to exchange opinions at such a distance, even in the form of secret letters, would probably not add anything to what one side has already said to the other.

I can see, Mr. President, that you are also not without a sense of anxiety for the fate of the world, not without an understanding and correct assessment of the nature of modern warfare and what war entails. What good would a war do you? You threaten us with war. But you well know that the very least you would get in response would be what you had given us; you would suffer the same consequences. And that must be clear to us—people invested with authority, trust and responsibility. We must not succumb to light-headedness and petty passions, regardless of whether elections are forthcoming in one country or another. These are all transitory things, but should war indeed break out, it would not be in our power to contain or stop it, for such is the logic of war. I have taken part in two wars, and I know that war ends only when it has rolled through cities and villages, sowing death and destruction everywhere.

I assure you on behalf of the Soviet government and the Soviet people that your arguments regarding offensive weapons in Cuba are utterly unfounded. From what you have written me it is obvious that our interpretations on this point are different, or rather that we have different definitions for one type of military means or another. And indeed, the same types of armaments may in actuality have different interpretations.

You are a military man, and I hope you will understand me. Let us take a simple cannon for instance. What kind of weapon is it—offensive or defensive? A cannon is a defensive weapon if it is set up to defend boundaries or a fortified area. But when artillery is concentrated and supplemented by an appropriate number of troops, then the same cannon will have become an offensive weapon, since they prepare and clear the way for infantry to advance. The same is true for nuclear missile weapons, for any type of these weapons.

You are mistaken if you think that any of our armaments in Cuba are offensive. However, let us not argue this point. Evidently, I shall not be able to convince you. But I tell you: you, Mr. President, are a military man and you must understand—how can you possibly launch an offensive even if you have an enormous number of missiles of various ranges and power on your territory, using these weapons alone? These missiles are a means of annihilation and destruction. But it is impossible to launch an offensive by means of these missiles, even nuclear missiles of 100-megaton yield, because it is only people—troops—who can advance. Without people any weapons, whatever their power, cannot be offensive.

How can you, therefore, give this completely wrong interpretation, which you are now giving, that some weapons in Cuba are offensive, as you say? All weapons there—and I assure you of this—are of a defensive nature; they are in Cuba solely for purposes of defense, and we have sent them to Cuba at the request of the Cuban government. And you say that they are offensive weapons.

But Mr. President, do you really seriously think that Cuba could launch an offensive upon the United States and that even we, together with Cuba, could advance against you from Cuban territory? Do you really think so? How can that be? We do not understand. Surely, there has not been any such new development in military strategy that would lead one to believe that it is possible to advance that way. And I mean advance, not destroy; for those who destroy are barbarians, people who have lost their sanity.

I hold that you have no grounds to think so. You may regard us with distrust, but you can at any rate rest assured that we are of sound mind and understand perfectly well that if we launch an offensive against you, you will respond in kind. But you too will get in response whatever you throw at us. And I think you understand that too. It is our discussion in Vienna that gives me the right to speak this way.

This indicates that we are sane people, that we understand and assess the situation correctly. How could we, then, allow [ourselves] the wrong actions which you ascribe to us? Only lunatics or suicides, who themselves want to perish and before they die destroy the world, could do this. But we want to live and by no means do we want to destroy your country. We want something quite different: to compete with your country in a peaceful endeavor. We argue with you; we have differences on ideological questions. But our concept of the world is that questions of ideology, as well as economic problems, should be settled by other than military means; they must be solved in peaceful contest, or as this is interpreted in capitalist society—by competition. Our premise has been and remains that peaceful coexistence of two different sociopolitical systems—a reality of our world—is essential, and that it is essential to ensure lasting peace. These are the principles to which we adhere.

You have now declared piratical measures, the kind that were practiced in the Middle Ages when ships passing through international waters were attacked, and you have called this a "quarantine" around Cuba. Our vessels will probably soon enter the zone patrolled by your navy. I assure you that the vessels which are now headed for Cuba are carrying the most innocuous peaceful cargoes. Do you really think that all we spend our time on is transporting so-called offensive weapons, atomic and hydrogen bombs? Even though your military people may possibly imagine that these are some special kind of weapons, I assure you that they are the most ordinary kind of peaceful goods.

Therefore, Mr. President, let us show good sense. I assure you that the ships bound for Cuba are carrying no armaments at all. The armaments needed for the defense of Cuba are already there. I do not mean to say that there have been no shipments of armaments at all. No, there were such shipments. But now Cuba has already obtained the necessary weapons for defense.

I do not know whether you can understand me and believe me. But I wish you would believe yourself and agree that one should not give way to one's passions; that one should be master of them. And what direction are events taking now? If you begin stopping vessels it would be piracy, as you yourself know. If we should start doing this to your ships you would be just as indignant as we and the whole world are now indignant. Such actions cannot be interpreted otherwise, because lawlessness cannot be legalized. Were this allowed to happen then there would be no peace; nor would there be peaceful coexistence. Then we would be forced to take the necessary measures of a defensive nature which would protect our interests in accordance with international law. Why do this? What would it all lead to?

Let us normalize relations. We have received an appeal from U Thant, acting secretary general of the UN, containing his proposals. I have already answered him. His proposals are to the effect that our side not ship any armaments to Cuba for a certain period of time while negotiations are being conducted—and we are prepared to enter into such negotiations—and the other side not undertake any piratical action against vessels navigating on the high seas. I consider these proposals reasonable. This would be a way out of the situation which has evolved that would give nations a chance to breathe easily.

You asked what happened, what prompted weapons to be supplied to Cuba? You spoke of this to our minister of foreign affairs. I will tell you frankly, Mr. President, what prompted it.

We were very grieved by the fact—I spoke of this in Vienna—that a landing was effected and an attack made on Cuba, as a result of which many Cubans were killed. You yourself told me then that this had been a mistake. I regarded that explanation with respect. You repeated it to me several times, hinting that not everyone occupying a high position would acknowledge his mistakes as you did. I appreciate such frankness. For my part I told you that we too possess no less courage; we have also acknowledged the mistakes which have been made in the history of our state, and have not only acknowledged them but sharply condemned them.

While you really are concerned for peace and for the welfare of your people—and this is your duty as president—I, as chairman of the Council of Ministers, am concerned for my people. Furthermore, the preservation of universal peace should be our joint concern, since if war broke out under modern conditions, it would not be just a war between the Soviet Union and the United States, which actually have no contentions between them, but a world-wide war, cruel and destructive.

You said once that the United States is not preparing an invasion. But you have also declared that you sympathize with the Cuban counter-revolutionary emigrants, support them, and will help them in carrying out their plans against the present government of Cuba. Nor is it any secret to anyone that the constant threat of armed attack and aggression has hung and continues to hang over Cuba. It is only this that has prompted us to respond to the request of the Cuban government to extend it our aide in strengthening the defense capability of that country.

If the president and government of the United States would give their assurances that the United States would itself not take part in an attack upon Cuba and would restrain others from such action; if you recall your navy—this would immediately change everything. I do not speak for Fidel Castro, but I think that he and the government of Cuba would, probably, announce a demobilization and would call upon the people to commence peaceful work. Then the question of armaments would also be obviated, because when there is no threat, armaments are only a burden for any people. This would change the approach to the question of destroying not only the armaments which you call offensive, but of every other kind of armament.

. . .

Armaments bring only disasters. Accumulating them damages the economy, and putting them to use would destroy people on both sides. Therefore, only a madman can believe that armaments are the principal means in the life of society. No, they are a forced waste of human energy, spent, moreover, on the destruction of man himself. If people do not display statesmanlike wisdom, they will eventually reach the point where they will clash, like blind moles, and then mutual annihilation will commence.

Let us then display statesmen-like wisdom. I propose: we, for our part, will declare that our ships bound for Cuba are not carrying any armaments. You will declare that the United States will not invade Cuba with its troops and will not support any other forces which might intend to invade Cuba. Then the necessity for the presence of our military specialists in Cuba will be obviated.

Mr. President, I appeal to you to weigh carefully what the aggressive, piratical actions which you have announced the United States intends to carry out in international waters would lead to. You yourself know that a sensible person simply cannot agree to this, cannot recognize your right to such action.

If you have done this as the first step towards unleashing war—well then—evidently nothing remains for us to do but to accept this challenge of yours. If you have not lost command of yourself and realize clearly what this could lead to, then, Mr. President, you and I should not now pull on the ends of the rope in which you have tied a knot of war, because the harder you and I pull, the tighter the knot will become. And a time may come when this knot is tied so tight that the person who tied it is no longer capable of untying it, and then the knot will have to be cut. What that would mean I need not explain to you, because you yourself understand perfectly what dread forces our two countries possess.

Therefore, if there is no intention of tightening this knot, thereby dooming the world to the catastrophe of thermonuclear war, let us not only relax the forces straining on the ends of the rope, let us take measures for untying the knot. We are agreeable to this.

...

These, Mr. President, are my thoughts, which, if you should agree with them, could put an end to the tense situation which is disturbing all peoples.

These thoughts are governed by a sincere desire to alleviate the situation and remove the threat of war.

Respectfully,

N.S. Khrushchev

* * *

#19

Nikita S. Khrushchev to John F. Kennedy

October 27, 1962[6]

"the means which you regard as offensive."

Nikita Sergei'ich is in a state of heightened agitation following the signing of the letter to Kennedy. He will remember this day as "Black Friday," the day he thought might be the last on earth for many of the citizens of the Soviet Union, Cuba and the United States. He calls his wife, Nina Petrovna, and tells her he will be spending the night at the Kremlin. He says that important messages may arrive during the night, and he will need to be present to deal with them. Time, he tells her, is of the essence.

Tonight, Nikita Sergei'ich has trouble getting to sleep. He wonders: will Kennedy understand my disorganized and rambling letter? Does Kennedy have the power to prevent a war, if that is really his wish? And somewhere in the back of his mind, there is the nagging question: might there have been some other way of saving the Cuban Revolution, short of deploying nuclear missiles on the island? He can think of none. No, definitely not—not when Kennedy was dead set on destroying the Cuban Revolution. But he is not reassured by this line of thought. Is standing up for the Cuban Revolution really worth a nuclear war with the U.S.? Of course not! Around and around go his thoughts until, at last, after one more cup of tea with lemon, Nikita Sergei'ich falls into a fitful sleep.

When he awakens, early as usual, he is still feeling regretful, but his regret at championing the missile deployment has been exchanged for regret at having sent off his most recent letter to Kennedy in such a hurry. For when he awakens and examines his daily intelligence briefing, he finds two categories of items that interest him greatly. First, there are many references in the blue-green folder to discussions in Washington—by government officials and journalists—of the possibility that a missile trade—Soviet missiles in Cuba for U.S./NATO missiles in Turkey—might offer a way out of the crisis. Nikita Sergei'ich learns that the influential liberal journalist Walter Lippmann, who has many connections to the Kennedy circle, advocated it in a column just yesterday. He calls Gromyko at the Foreign Ministry. He learns that, not only did the U.S. not attack Cuba during the previous evening, as Nikita Sergei'ich thought they might, the embassy in Washington is now reporting that it is unclear when such an attack might occur. Nikita Sergei'ich now thinks: wait, we have a little time. Maybe Kennedy is not so keen on a war, after all. So why don't we ask for more?

He asks his foreign minister whether he thinks the Americans are prepared to trade missiles as part of a bargain that would end the crisis. Gromyko, as usual, equivocates, until he gets the drift of his boss's thinking—which is clearly to pursue a missile trade. Such a trade, he says to Gromyko, would provide the Soviet Union with more than a mere escape from the crisis. It would, he goes on, provide a means to achieve victory! If Gromyko has any doubts about his boss's proposition, it is inaudible to Nikita Sergei'ich, who is by now filled with enthusiasm about the idea. He issues an order to Gromyko to amend the first letter so as to reinstate the missile trade idea and to bring the draft to the next meeting of the Presidium, which convenes right after lunch.

Excited and unexpectedly optimistic, Nikita Sergei'ich has definitely decided to go for it. Yes, there will be some problems as the Americans try to figure out what he is actually offering. The message to Kennedy of yesterday did not mention the missile trade, and so Kennedy may not be totally sure whether the missile trade is on the table or not. But if his latest intelligence reports are accurate, the confusion shouldn't last long because, according to his embassy in Washington, a trade is perfectly acceptable. He has heard this from his KGB station chief, and from his ambassador, Anatoly Dobrynin. The report from Dobrynin is especially convincing. The ambassador reports that he discussed the missile trade the previous evening with the president's brother, Attorney General Robert Kennedy. According to Dobrynin, while meeting in Kennedy's office at the Justice Department, Robert

Kennedy stepped into another room and called his brother, the president. After a few minutes, the attorney general returned and reported to Dobrynin that the U.S. would "look favorably" on a trade as part of a settlement to the crisis.

Even if these reports accurately reflect President Kennedy's thinking, Nikita Sergei'ich knows he will have to work fast. The war planners in Washington, Moscow and on the island of Cuba are sprinting toward maximum war-readiness. His intelligence briefing papers indicate that while no decision to attack has yet been taken, U.S. troops are concentrated all over the Caribbean and poised to attack. U.S. Marines and soldiers are being issued ammunition in preparation for the assault on the Cuban beaches. Like the Soviet military personnel all over the world, the Americans have been put on a hair-trigger alert. All that remains is for one side or the other—upon receipt of orders from Kennedy or Khrushchev—to launch an attack.

The Presidium members usually have lunch together in the Kremlin when they are in session, as they are today. Typically, the atmosphere is that of an old boys club, with tall tales and jokes in abundance. Today, however, it is as if the Kremlin canteen has been transformed into a monastery, as the Presidium members sit in total silence, awaiting the discussion that follows with Nikita Sergei'ich.

The Presidium meeting begins with a briefing from Defense Minister Rodion Malinovsky, who tells the group that General Issa Pliyev, the Soviet field commander in Cuba has reported that the nuclear missiles—both strategic and tactical are ready for use. Malinovsky then moves to a description of the readiness of Soviet nuclear forces, with special attention given to Europe. (Nikita Sergei'ich can barely pay attention to this. Europe? He wonders to himself. What the hell does this Cuban crisis have to do with Europe? If nuclear war begins in Cuba and spreads to Europe, we are all doomed, he thinks. Besides, he is not interested in how a nuclear war will be fought. He wants to discuss a deal that Kennedy will accept so they can escape from this crisis short of war.) He interrupts the briefing to reiterate an earlier order he had given to Malinovsky: to tell Pliyev that under no circumstances are nuclear weapons to be used in Cuba without a direct order from Moscow—that is, from me, the chairman of the Council of Ministers. He asks Malinovsky pointedly: does Pliyev understand this? Malinovsky replies affirmatively, before resuming his briefing on how the Soviet military is prepared to fight a nuclear war in Europe, and which targets inside the Soviet Union will probably be destroyed by U.S. nuclear forces.

Nikita Sergei'ich is relieved when at last Gromyko arrives bearing the draft letter to Kennedy. Malinovsky's briefing is suspended, and in less than an hour, all are agreed on the content of the letter—which is to say, Nikita Sergei'ich is satisfied with it. The final draft contains some of his hand-written corrections. There is no time for re-typing. Because time is short, the message will be broadcast, rather than sent through the byzantine diplomatic channels that, in both Moscow and Washington, add many hours to the transmission of messages between the two capitols. That evening, the letter is read over Radio Moscow.

During the night, Nikita Sergei'ich is told by Malinovsky that Fidel Castro has given the order to his anti-aircraft batteries to open fire on low-flying U.S. reconnaissance planes, which are suddenly beginning to appear in greater numbers and with greater frequency than before. Moreover, Pliyev requests permission from Moscow to open fire with Soviet anti-aircraft guns and surface-to-air-missiles in the event of a U.S. air attack. Nikita Sergei'ich agrees to the request, in the event of a massive U.S. air attack. He then realizes that he has forgotten about Castro, in his efforts to craft the letters to Kennedy. Nikita Sergei'ich immediately sees his error: if one or more U.S. planes are shot down by the Cubans, Kennedy will assume that the Russians are behind it, that they ordered it or at least approved of it, thus leading Kennedy perhaps to suspect that the war has already begun. Kennedy would probably order the air attack and invasion, after which Nikita Sergei'ich's letters would go into the dustbin of history, assuming anyone is left after Armageddon to write or read such a history. He must write to Castro soon.

Dear Mr. President:

I have already said that our people, our government, and I personally, as chairman of the council of ministers, are concerned solely with having our country develop and occupy a worthy place among all peoples of the world in economic competition, in the development of culture and the arts, and in raising the standard of living of the people. This is the most noble and necessary field for competition, and both the victor and the vanquished will derive only benefit from it, because it means peace and an increase in the means by which man lives and finds enjoyment.

   …

   I think it would be possible to end the controversy quickly and normalize the situation, and then the people could breathe more easily, considering that statesmen charged with responsibility are of sober mind and have an awareness of their responsibility combined with the ability to solve complex questions and not bring things to a military catastrophe.

   I therefore make this proposal: we are willing to remove from Cuba the means which you regard as offensive. We are willing to carry this out and to make this pledge in the United Nations. Your representatives will make a declaration to the effect that the United States, for its part, considering the anxiety and uneasiness of the Soviet state, will remove its analogous means from Turkey. Let us reach agreement as to the period of time needed by you and us to bring this about. And, after that, persons entrusted by the United Nations Security Council could inspect on the spot the fulfillment of the pledges made. Of course, the permission of the governments of Cuba and of Turkey is necessary for the entry into those countries of these representatives and for the inspection

of the fulfillment of the pledge made by each side. Of course it would be best if these representatives enjoyed the confidence of the Security Council, as well as yours and mine—both the United States and the Soviet Union—and also that of Turkey and Cuba. I do not think it would be difficult to select people who would enjoy the trust and respect of all parties concerned.

We, in making this pledge, in order to give satisfaction and hope to the peoples of Cuba and Turkey and to strengthen their confidence in their security, will make a statement within the framework of the Security Council to the effect that the Soviet government gives a solemn promise to respect the inviolability of the borders and sovereignty of Turkey, not to interfere in its internal affairs, not to invade Turkey, not to make available our territory as a bridgehead for such an invasion, and that it would also restrain those who contemplate committing aggression against Turkey, either from the territory of the Soviet Union or from the territory of Turkey's other neighboring states.

The United States government will make a similar statement within the framework of the Security Council regarding Cuba. It will declare that the United States will respect the inviolability of Cuba's borders and its sovereignty, will pledge not to interfere in its internal affairs, not to invade Cuba itself or make its territory available as a bridgehead for such an invasion, and will also restrain those who might contemplate committing aggression against Cuba, either from the territory of the United States or from the territory of Cuba's other neighboring states.

Of course, for this we would have to come to an agreement with you and specify a certain time limit. Let us agree to some period of time, but without unnecessary delay—say within two or three weeks, not longer than a month.

The means situated in Cuba, of which you speak and which disturb you, as you have stated, are in the hands of Soviet officers. Therefore, any accidental use of them to the detriment of the United States is excluded. These means are situated in Cuba at the request of the Cuban government and are only for defensive purposes. Therefore, if there is no invasion of Cuba, or attack on the Soviet Union or any of our other allies, then of course these means are not and will not be a threat to anyone. For they are not for purposes of attack.

If you are agreeable to my proposal, Mr. President, then we would send our representatives to New York, to the United Nations, and would give them comprehensive instructions in order that an agreement may be reached more quickly. If you also select your people and give them the corresponding instructions, then this question can be quickly resolved.

Why would I like to do this? Because the whole world is now apprehensive and expects sensible actions of us. The greatest joy for all

peoples would be the announcement of our agreement and of the eradication of the controversy that has arisen. I attach great importance to this agreement in so far as it could serve as a good beginning and could in particular make it easier to reach agreement on banning nuclear weapons tests. The question of the tests could be solved in a parallel fashion, without connecting one with the other, because these are different issues. However, it is important that agreement be reached on both these issues so as to present humanity with a fine gift, and also to gladden it with the news that agreement has been reached on the cessation of nuclear tests and that consequently the atmosphere will no longer be poisoned. Our position and yours on this issue are very close together.

All of this could possibly serve as a good impetus toward the finding of mutually acceptable agreements on other controversial issues on which you and I have been exchanging views. These issues have so far not been resolved, but they are awaiting urgent solution, which would clear up the international atmosphere. We are prepared for this.

These are my proposals, Mr. President.
Respectfully yours,
N.S. Khrushchev

* * *

#20

Fidel Castro to Nikita S. Khrushchev

October 26, 1962[7]

"however harsh and terrible the solution would be"

Unaware of Khrushchev's latest letters to Kennedy (numbers 18 and 19), Fidel is in constant motion, yet outwardly calm, as he speeds around the Havana area in his Jeep—Havana being ground zero, the grand prize to the American invaders who, Fidel believes, seek to turn it once again into "Sin City," a playground for rich Americans and a haven for U.S.-based mafia criminals. With him are his driver and a Russian-Spanish interpreter. He inspects the trenches being dug across the north side of the island in the areas east and west of Havana. He believes the first wave of U.S. Marines will attempt a landing at one or both points, and then march on Havana. All during the morning of Friday, October 26th, 1962, Fidel can be seen, gesturing from the passenger's side of the front seat of his Jeep, long arms flailing, oddly high-pitched voice shouting orders and encouragement to the Cuban and Russian troops who are preparing for war. It is a familiar sight, by now, to the Cubans, but still strange to behold: a tall barbudo *(a bearded*

revolutionary), with professorial, black, horned-rimmed glasses, dressed in olive battle fatigues showing his rank. Modestly, for a leader with the outsized personality of Fidel, the man the Cubans call their El Maximo Lider *("The Maximum Leader") claims only to be a major. Almost never seen without a cigar, a symbol of Cuba all over the world, he seems to know every Cuban by name, every locale by its nickname.*

He feels the troops are ready. In fact, he believes the Cuban nation is ready for the onslaught he has been expecting ever since the failed Bay of Pigs invasion of April 1961. Every so often, the U.S. low-flying, high-speed reconnaissance planes fly overhead at near-supersonic velocity. At their height and speed it is almost impossible to get a stable visual fix on their location. First, they are seen but not yet heard, silent phantoms against the Caribbean sky. There follows a momentary but excruciatingly loud roar, well after the planes have passed overhead, owing to the differential between the speed of light and of sound. The roar is followed almost instantaneously by the visual disappearance of the planes into the horizon and a long, gradually diminishing roar that fades slowly, as one's sense of hearing returns to normal. Decades later, many Cubans who experienced these over-flights will find it impossible to tell their stories without physically ducking down, as if the planes were about to sever their heads from their bodies. They will recall their conviction that every plane, every time, was probably the first plane to drop the bombs and begin a war that would end with the total destruction of Cuba—bajo el Mar Caribe ("beneath the Caribbean Sea.")

Fidel does not fear these planes, nor do his troops. What he and they feel is anger: the U.S. planes violate Cuban sovereignty at will. By October 26ᵗʰ they all share the conviction that these planes will begin to drop their bombs on Cuba. It is only, they believe, a matter of hours, or perhaps minutes before the massive air attack begins accompanied by an invasion led by U.S. Marines. As he bumps along in his Jeep, Fidel reflects on how the gringos keep finding new ways to violate Cuban sovereignty and to diminish Cuban dignidad *("dignity"). They have occupied the area adjacent to Guantanamo for more than half a century. (Fidel's government refuses to cash the yearly rent check, as a matter of principle.)They facilitate the infiltration of the* gusanos *("worms," i.e., Cuban exiles on the payroll of the CIA) by the hundreds and supply them with explosives with which to terrorize the Cuban population. And now, they assert their right to fly into our airspace whenever they feel like it, the sonic booms breaking windows, terrorizing and angering the population.*

Around noon, feeling that events are racing toward war, Fidel calls the Soviet ambassador, his close friend Aleksander Alekseev, and asks him to come to his command post in south central Havana. Cuban President Osvaldo Dorticos is also present. Fidel complains to Alekseev about what he believes is the overly cautious way the Soviets seem to be approaching the upcoming conflict. Fidel tells Alekseev that he cannot understand why the Soviet troops are sitting on their hands while the Americans overfly the island with impunity. Does Alekseev

know—do the Russians in Moscow know—that the purpose of the gringos' over-
flights is to set up the Cuban and Soviet forces for pinpoint bombing that will,
according to Fidel, begin within the next 24–72 hours. He wants the Soviets
to start shooting the planes out of the air, and he wants the Soviets to know
that he is thinking seriously about ordering his Cuban troops, contrary to Soviet
wishes, to begin firing on the low-flying planes that are within the range of their
antiaircraft guns. Fidel also complains to Alekseev that Cuba is humiliated by
the way the Soviets, at the UN, continue to deny the existence of the nuclear
missiles in Cuba—as if the Soviets and Cubans had done something wrong,
as if they didn't have good and sufficient reasons for wanting to protect Cuba
from the aggressive North American imperialists. Alekseev records all of Fidel's
complaints dutifully, as always, and promises to send them to Moscow as soon
as he returns to his embassy.

All afternoon Fidel moves around the area, encouraging his forces. As his Jeep
carries him from one area of troop concentration to another, Fidel reflects on the
situation in which he and Cuba find themselves. Suddenly, everything becomes
very clear to him: the situation, the strategy of the U.S. aggressor, the response of
his Soviet ally, and his own personal role in the events that are unfolding in and
around Cuba. Some lines of poetry come to him, lines that he memorized as a
schoolboy in eastern Cuba. The lines are by Jose Marti, known to the Cubans as
el Apostal—*the "apostle" of Cuban independence. These lines, known to many*
Cubans, capture the essence of what Fidel believes must be every Cuban's dignified
response to oppression:

> *No me entierren en lo oscuro,*
> *A morir como un traidor;*
> *Yo soy bueno y como bueno,*
> *Morire de cara al sol.*

> *Do not bury me in darkness,*
> *To die like a traitor;*
> *I am good, and as a good man,*
> *I will die facing the sun.*

Marti, Cuba's most famous patriot, was shot dead in May 1895, in the struggle
against Spanish imperialism. Fidel has worshipped Marti ever since he was a
child. On countless occasions, Fidel has felt that he, like Marti, is destined for a
special mission in Cuba's struggle for dignity and independence. Fidel knows doz-
ens of Marti's poems by heart, and he loves reciting them in his speeches.

But Marti is not the only Cuban patriot on his mind. He also sees a parallel
between his own situation and that of another great Cuban patriot of the war
against Spain, Antonio Maceo, the black general who was no poet, but who was a
master of guerrilla war. In March 1878, Maceo rejected overtures from the Span-
ish to settle on a compromise, known as the Zanjon Pact. Maceo, unlike some

other Cuban advocates of independence at that time, wanted nothing to do with compromise. He stood instead for booting the Spaniards off the island once and for all. No deals. No negotiations. Take no prisoners. At a town called Baragua, in the swamps of south central Cuba, Maceo stated his position: he would fight to the death for Cuban dignity and independence. Maceo fought on, until in December 1896, he was shot and killed near Punta Brava, southwest of Havana. Since the triumph of the Cuban Revolution on January 1, 1959, "Baragua" has become synonymous with glorious inflexibility of the committed revolutionaries, who would rather die with dignity than live in what they feel is servitude and degradation.

Fidel breaks into a cold sweat as the historical analogy with Maceo hits home. He, Fidel, is Maceo for the nuclear age, a leader for whom compromise with the imperialists is alien, for whom the objective is the elimination of all imperialist influence and the restoration of dignity and independence to the Cuban people. The Soviets, as he now sees it, keep pushing him toward compromise, they keep telling him not to push the Americans too far, not to provoke them into a war. Jesus Christ in heaven thinks this lapsed product of a Jesuit education, can't the damned Russians see that we don't have that option? The Americans have already decided to crush this revolution. I must find a way to make Khrushchev understand that our choice on this island is not to provoke the Americans or not to provoke them. The Revolution, by its very existence, provokes the gringos. Our choice is to face our fate in a dignified way, or in a cowardly way. The Americans will never compromise because in their arrogance they do not believe it will ever be necessary for them to compromise—not with Cuba, not even with the Soviet Union. This crisis, Fidel thinks, this October crisis, is Baragua *for the nuclear age. And like Antonio Maceo, Fidel will not cave in; he will not surrender to the oppressors; he and his people will go down fighting and take as many of the gringos with them as they can. They will, in Marti's words, "die facing the sun."*

Around 6:00 p.m. he rides in his Jeep to El Chico, *the Soviet command post of Gen. Issa Pliyev, the Soviet field commander, which occupies a former boys reform school southwest of Havana. At El Chico, Fidel is reassured that the Soviet forces on the island are with him in spirit. He is told that all the Soviet forces have now reached combat readiness. Before resuming his inspection of his troops, Fidel makes two requests of Pliyev: to turn on the Soviet radars, so that the Soviets can target and hit the U.S. planes more accurately; and to take off the Cuban uniforms they have been wearing and put on the uniforms of their own country in order to prepare properly for the coming battle, in which many will no doubt perish. Fidel's view is that if a soldier is to perish, he should perish in his country's uniform. Soviets dying for the cause of Cuban dignity and independence ought also, as Fidel sees it, to have the opportunity to "die facing the sun." Pliyev agrees to turn on the radars, but he refuses to order the Russians to dress in battle gear, to Fidel's amazement and disgust.*

Afterward, back again in his Jeep and on the move, Fidel stops on the Male-con, the sea wall and road that fronts the city of Havana for eight kilometers between Old Havana and the near western neighborhood of Vedado. Recognizing his unmistakable figure, the men and boys operating the antiaircraft guns break into a chant: "Fidel, Khru'cho, estano con lo do" (Fidel, Khrushchev, we are with you both"). He orders his driver to stop. Fidel asks his troops if they are ready. They reply that they are ready, but are frustrated at being prevented from trying to shoot down the U.S. planes that have been flying directly over their heads all week. Fidel realizes that the time has come to change this. Inspired by these gunners, Fidel heads straight for his command post, where he issues an order for all Cuban antiaircraft units to begin firing on U.S. planes overflying their positions. He thinks: this will be good for our morale, even if we don't hit anything. We all deserve the right to protect ourselves and to die with dignity as we resist the coming assault.

It is 2:00 a.m. on the morning of Saturday October 27ᵗʰ. At his command post, an exhausted Fidel thinks: I have done all I can here. On this island we are ready to fight and die in a way that will exalt our nation. What else should I do? His thoughts turn to Khrushchev. If he can only find a way to let Khrushchev know what it is like on the island, how willing, even eager, Cubans and Russians are to fight and die for the glorious cause. He decides he will write a letter to Khrushchev to encourage him, to empower him to use his nuclear forces and destroy the United States, in the event of the expected U.S. invasion and occupation of the island. At 3:00 a.m., he arrives at the Soviet embassy and tells Aleksander Alekseev that they should go into the bunker underneath the embassy because the U.S. attack could begin at any moment. A groggy but sympathetic Alekseev agrees, and soon they are set up in the bunker—Fidel dictating, aides translating, writing, reading aloud, with Fidel editing and reediting the letter.

Fidel eventually becomes frustrated. He can't seem to say what is in his mind. After ten drafts, with the sun already rising in the east, Alekseev at last asks Fidel: are you asking Comrade Khrushchev to deliver a nuclear strike on the U.S.? Fidel suddenly stops and becomes silent. Then after some moments of reflection, he resumes: "No," he tells Alekseev, "not quite. I want to tell Khrushchev that an attack is inevitable and an invasion is highly probable. The war will go nuclear, for sure. There is not the slightest doubt about it. I want to say that the choice is yours, Comrade Nikita: you can destroy the enemy, or you can wait for the enemy to destroy you, after he destroys us. But yes, Comrade Alejandro, fundamentally I want to say to Comrade Nikita that he must be prepared to destroy the United States. If, in his judgment, Cuba must also be destroyed in the war, then so be it. Cuba is ready to martyr itself for the cause of global socialism and the destruction of America's imperial empire." Alekseev is shocked, but he dutifully assists Fidel in fine-tuning the final draft of the letter. It is dated "October 26, 1962," even though it is not finished and sent to Moscow until almost 7:00 a.m. on the morning of Saturday the 27ᵗʰ.

At that moment Fidel feels his preparations are complete. He has now written to his patron what may well be the last request of a man and a nation soon to be obliterated. It is a deathbed message, urging Khrushchev to redeem Cuba's approaching destruction by transforming Cubans from victims into martyrs at this nuclear age Baragua. Fidel is quite calm and pleased with the suicide note he and Alekseev have just composed for the six-and-a-half-million citizens of the Socialist Republic of Cuba, and the 43,000 Russian citizens who will die alongside them.

Dear Comrade Khrushchev:

From an analysis of the situation and the reports in our possession, I consider that the aggression is almost imminent within the next 24 to 72 hours.

There are two possible variants: the first and likeliest one is an attack against certain targets with the limited objective of destroying them; the second, less probable although possible, is invasion. I understand that this variant would call for a large number of forces and it is, in addition, the most repulsive form of aggression, which might inhibit them.

You can rest assured that we will firmly and resolutely resist attack, whatever it may be.

The morale of the Cuban people is extremely high and the aggressor will be confronted heroically.

At this time I want to convey to you briefly my personal opinion.

If the second variant is implemented and the imperialists invade Cuba with the goal of occupying it, the danger that that aggressive policy poses for humanity is so great that following that event the Soviet Union must never allow the circumstances in which the imperialists could launch the first nuclear strike against it.

I tell you this because I believe the imperialists' aggressiveness is extremely dangerous and if they actually carry out the brutal act of invading Cuba in violation of international law and morality, that would be the moment to eliminate such danger forever through an act of clear legitimate defense, however harsh and terrible the solution would be, for there is no other.

It has influenced my opinion to see how this aggressive policy is developing, how the imperialists, disregarding world public opinion and ignoring principles of the law, are blockading the seas, violating our airspace and preparing an invasion, while at the same time frustrating every possibility for talks, even though they are aware of the seriousness of the problem.

You have been and continue to be a tireless defender of peace and I realize how bitter these hours must be, when the outcome of your superhuman efforts is so seriously threatened. However, up to the last moment we will maintain the hope that peace will be safeguarded and we are willing to contribute to this as much as we can. But at the same time we are ready to calmly confront a situation which we view as quite real and quite close.

Once more I convey to you the infinite gratitude and recognition of our people to the Soviet people who have been so generous and fraternal with us, as well as our profound gratitude and admiration for you, and wish you success in the huge task and serious responsibilities ahead of you.

Fraternally,

Fidel Castro

* * *

#21

Nikita S. Khrushchev to Fidel Castro

October 28, 1962[8]

"I . . . recommend . . . not to be carried away by sentiment"

An aide comes to tell Nikita Sergei'ich that his defense minister, Rodion Malinovsky, needs to speak to him. It is almost 9:00 p.m. on October 27th, and Nikita Sergei'ich is tired but he knows he must see Malinovsky at once, because he will arrive bearing information about the military operation in Cuba. He also knows that the defense minister never asks to see him urgently unless he has bad news. Nikita Sergei'ich says he will see Malinovsky at once.

Malinovsky's tidings are, as anticipated, about the Cuba crisis, and the news is even worse than Nikita Sergei'ich imagined it might be. Malinovsky arrives, takes a deep breath, and begins. He has just received a report from the Soviet command post in Cuba that an American U-2 spy plane has been shot down over eastern Cuba, and the pilot killed. Malinovsky explains that Gen. Pliyev, the field commander who would normally have fielded any request to take military action, was unavailable, so the second in command, Gen. Stepan Grechko made the decision in Pliyev's absence. It seems, he adds, that the commander of Soviet surface-to-air missiles in Cuba, Col. Georgy Voronkov, had requested guidance when the U-2 entered Cuban territory; Voronkov said he had but two minutes to make a decision. After that, the U-2 would be beyond the range of his missiles. Malinovsky goes on to remind Nikita Sergei'ich that the standing orders from Moscow granted permission to Pliyev to order his forces to shoot down U.S. planes only in the event of a "massive attack." Thus, as Malinovsky acknowledges, this shoot-down represents a violation of those orders. When Nikita Sergei'ich asks Malinovsky for an explanation of why this happened, Malinovsky replies: apparently, the Soviet officers chose to follow the orders Fidel Castro has given to the Cuban anti-aircraft gunners.

At this, Nikita Sergei'ich loses his famous temper and explodes in Malinovsky's very thick and very startled face: "Our people are following Castro's orders? What, have they defected to Cuba and joined the Cuban army?" Malinovsky takes his medicine, like a waiter who serves his customer a bad meal—the chef remaining in the kitchen, unavailable for face-to-face criticism. In fact, Malinovsky feels exactly as Nikita Sergei'ich does, though he says nothing beyond the basic facts he has just reported to his boss. Nikita Sergei'ich sits absolutely still in his desk chair, and is totally silent, as he thinks over what has happened and what needs to be done. Sure, he thinks to himself, normally I would be glad that our forces have shot down another of those annoying U-2s. The Americans think they can violate everybody's airspace anytime they choose. Hah. Not any more. Let the U-2s beware!

But to say the least, this is not a normal situation, with both superpowers poised on the brink of nuclear war. Nikita Sergei'ich becomes convinced at that moment that the situation in Cuba is slipping out of control—out of his control and out of Kennedy's control. If today a Soviet general violated standing orders and shot down an unarmed U.S. spy plane, then perhaps tomorrow the same general, or another general, might violate standing orders and launch a strategic missile at the United States, thus initiating Armageddon.

Nikita Sergei'ich wonders what Kennedy is thinking about the shoot-down—what he thinks it signifies about Moscow's intentions in the crisis. Nikita Sergei'ich fears that he knows what the hawks around Kennedy are telling him. They are saying that Khrushchev has decided to go to war; or Khrushchev is daring you to go to war over the missiles in Cuba; and because the Russians have decided that keeping their missiles in Cuba is important enough to risk war with the U.S., then you, Mr. President, must act first. At a minimum, this means ordering an immediate attack on the Cuban missile sites, followed shortly thereafter by an invasion. As Nikita Sergei'ich imagines Kennedy's aides counseling him to push the button of the U.S.-Soviet global doomsday machine, he wonders whether the young American president has the steely spine required to resist this kind of hawkish advice. Even more terrifying to Nikita Sergei'ich, he can even imagine an aide telling Kennedy, on the heels of this shoot-down, that the time has come for an even more basic decision: a preemptive strike on the Soviet Union. There has been such talk in the U.S. press, and in the Congress, for more than a year.

At this thought Nikita Sergei'ich's palms begin to sweat and his saliva becomes scarce. He thinks: I have never been this terrified in my entire adult life, not even in the two world wars, not even in the darkest days of Stalin's madness. What if? What if? Nikita Sergei'ich decides that this is not a productive line of thought at this critical moment. He realizes that he can suddenly imagine an infinite number of ways a nuclear war might be initiated. Then comes the thought he has been avoiding: what if, as I sit here, the war has already begun?

As Nikita Sergei'ich emerges from the black hole of his reflections on the immi- nence of Armageddon, he notices Malinovsky still standing in front of him, waiting for an order. He gives it: there will be no more independent initiatives. Soviet forces in Cuba are not to shoot at anything without an explicit order from Moscow. He adds, as an aside to Malinovsky, that with everything hanging by a thread, and in anticipation of a positive response to his pair of letters to Kennedy that have already been sent, this is no time to be shooting at American planes, giving Kennedy's hawks an argument for doing what they have wanted to do all along, which is launch a destructive war against Cuba. Malinovsky understands the order, repeats it aloud for confirmation, and leaves to send the message to the Soviet commanders in Cuba.

Now it is almost 10:00 p.m. and Nikita Sergei'ich is exhausted, but also deeply agitated by Malinovsky's news. He is going to need a good night's sleep, which he cannot get if he stays at the Kremlin and sleeps on the couch in his office. So he de- cides that tomorrow, Sunday the 28th, the Presidium will meet at the Novo-Ogaryovo complex, outside Moscow, and that he himself will join his family at his dacha near the complex the following morning. Yes, a change of scenery will do him good. He may need to think quickly tomorrow, depending on Kennedy's response to his letters. He always thinks better in the country than in the city, he believes. He calls an aide and orders him to tell the other Presidium members about the change in venue for the meeting tomorrow, Sunday October 28th, at 10:00 a.m.

As he is about to leave for his apartment in the Lenin Hills, above Moscow, he thinks again about Fidel Castro. It is suddenly clear that Castro has become more than an observer of the crisis, a bit player in the great drama of a superpower con- frontation. In fact, as Nikita Sergei'ich thinks it over, he realizes that Comrade Fidel, his young, impetuous, curiously child-like yet charismatic Caribbean socialist has, in a sense, become *the crisis. He became the crisis today, when his enthusiasm for provoking the Americans into a war became "contagious"—so much so that the usually disciplined Soviet military command broke down and became Fidel's army as much as it is his. These reflections heighten his agitation. He feels he cannot go home until he takes a few minutes to compose some lines he plans to edit tomorrow for a letter to Fidel Castro, who needs to be told in no uncertain terms to cool off and stop provoking the Americans just at the moment when the crisis is being resolved. He calls for a stenographer, and dictates some thoughts containing such phrases as: "friendly advice; you shot down a plane—why? Control yourself at this critical moment in the crisis." And a few others. That's it, he thinks. Now I'm going home and have some tea with lemon and get some sleep. Tomorrow is likely to be at least as difficult as today.*

Nikita Sergei'ich arrives at Novo-Ogaryovo at 10:00 a.m. sharp. The other members of the Presidium are waiting for him, silently, running their fingers through the reports on the Cuba crisis that have been set in front of them. He turns to his foreign policy aide, Oleg Troyanovsky, for a briefing on the Cuba situation. Troyanovsky reports that a letter from Kennedy has arrived overnight, having been broadcast on U.S. radio. He asks Troyanovsky to read the letter aloud, even though everyone at the meeting has a copy of the letter in front of him. This takes about half an hour. Kennedy, it seems, accepts the deal crafted by Khrushchev, except that no mention is made of the swap of missiles in Cuba for missiles in Turkey. Nikita Sergei'ich shrugs at this. It would have been nice to get the missile swap in the deal. But never mind. Overall, it seems they have a deal acceptable to both of them. Nikita Sergei'ich announces that as soon as Troyanovsky's briefing is finished, they will compose a response to Kennedy.

Troyanovsky then reports that a report from Ambassador Anatoly Dobrynin in Washington has been received about a meeting he had the previous evening with Robert Kennedy. The president's brother stressed that time is running out—that they need a positive response from Moscow within twenty-four hours. After that, Robert Kennedy told Dobrynin, there is no guarantee that Kennedy can hold off the hawks any longer. The report from Dobrynin confirms Nikita Sergei'ich's intuition that time is running out and the situation is slipping out of his and Kennedy's control. This is yet another reason, Nikita Sergei'ich thinks to himself, why a positive reply to Kennedy must be drafted this very morning, confirming Nikita Sergei'ich's acceptance of the terms laid out in Kennedy's most recent letter.

But before the dictating and drafting process can begin, Troyanovsky timidly mentions that another message has just come in. (He has received it over the telephone, just now, from the Foreign Ministry.) Nikita Sergei'ich asks him to report on what he has been told. At this point, the normally unflappable aide becomes visibly uncomfortable. After clearing his throat several times, he begins his presentation, guided by his notes. It seems, he says, that Fidel Castro believes an American attack and invasion will occur within 24-72 hours. Under such conditions, Troyanovsky continues, the Soviet Union should, in Comrade Castro's view, be the one to deliver the first nuclear strike—"against the United States, presumably"—adds Troyanovsky.

Nikita Sergei'ich explodes: "This is insane!" He says this at top volume. "Fidel is preparing to die, and the Cubans are preparing to die, and Fidel wants to drag us into the grave with him." He repeats: "This is insane!" The members of the Presidium stare at their briefing folders, unwilling even to make eye contact with anyone. Nikita Sergei'ich turns to Malinovsky and says that he is about to issue new orders for the defense minister to convey immediately to Pliyev in Havana. First, he says, prepare to remove the missiles as soon as possible, before something catastrophic happens. Second, allow no one near the missiles. I repeat: no one! Third, under no circumstances are the warheads to be installed. Fourth, obey no orders to launch a missile unless the order comes from me—from the chairman of the Council of Ministers. Malinovsky repeats his orders aloud to Nikita Sergei'ich's satisfaction, before hurrying to an adjacent office to issue the orders to Pliyev.

Nikita Sergei'ich then asks for his stenographer, Nadezhda Petrovna to read aloud his sketchy notes for a letter to Castro, dictated late the previous night. After making some additions and corrections, Nikita Sergei'ich is satisfied with it, and orders it sent to the Foreign Ministry, to begin making its way through encoding, typing and transmission via telegraph—all on the Moscow end—before going through the entire process in reverse in Havana, whereupon Alekseev will call on Castro and reveal the contents of the letter.

Dear Comrade Fidel Castro:

Our October 27 message to President Kennedy allows for the question to be settled in your favor, to defend Cuba from an invasion and prevent war from breaking out. Kennedy's reply, which you apparently also know, offers assurances that the U.S. will not invade Cuba with its own forces, nor will it permit its allies to carry out an invasion. In this way the president of the United States has positively answered my messages of October 26 and 27, 1962.

We have now finished drafting our reply to the president's message. I am not going to convey it here, for you surely know the text, which is now being broadcast over the radio.

With this motive I would like to recommend to you now, at this moment of change in the crisis, not to be carried away by sentiment and to show firmness. I must say that I understand your feelings of indignation toward the aggressive actions and violations of elementary norms of international law on the part of the United States.

But now, rather than law, what prevails is the senselessness of the militarists in the Pentagon. Now that an agreement is within sight the Pentagon is searching for a pretext to frustrate this agreement. That is why it is organizing the provocative flights. Yesterday you shot down one of these, while earlier you didn't shoot them down when they overflew your territory. The aggressors will take advantage of such a step for their own purposes.

Therefore, I would like to advise you in a friendly manner to show patience, firmness and even more firmness. Naturally, if there's an invasion it will be necessary to repulse it by every means. But we mustn't allow ourselves to be carried away by provocations, because the Pentagon's unbridled militarists, now that the solution to the conflict is in sight and apparently in your favor, creating a guarantee against the invasion of Cuba, are trying to frustrate the agreement and provoke you into actions that could be used against you. I ask you not to give them the pretext for doing that.

On our part, we will do everything possible to stabilize the situation in Cuba, defend Cuba against invasion and assure you the possibilities of building a socialist society.

I send you greetings, extensive to all your leadership group.

N.S., Khrushchev

ACT III

Escape

October 27–31, 1962

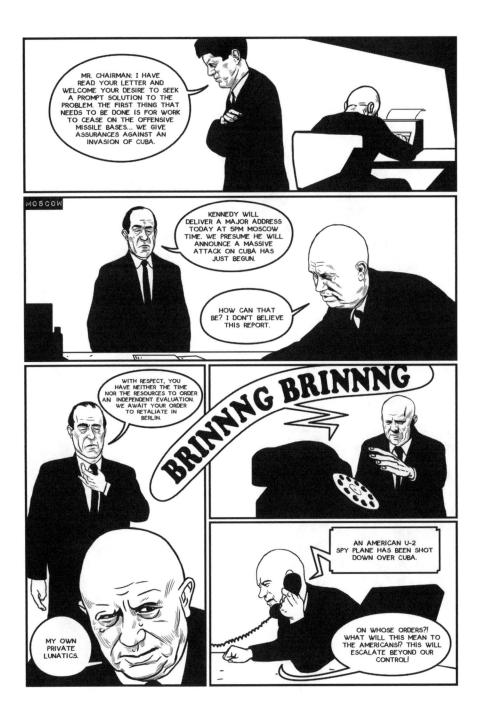

Theatrical Preview

[As Act III begins, Kennedy and Khrushchev stand atop the stairs, on platforms. The spiral staircase is still spinning wildly, from its narrow base to its wide top. Water can be heard roaring. Kennedy and Khrushchev can hardly hold on. They are barely able to avoid being sucked into the vortex. Castro, as before, sits Buddha-like at the base of the stairs, seemingly indifferent to the situation faced by Kennedy and Khrushchev.]

NIKITA SERGEI'ICH: Mr. President, Mr. President: okay, I will pledge publicly to remove the weapons in Cuba you mistakenly refer to as "offensive" if you will pledge not to invade the island with the objective of overthrowing the Cuban government. What do you say to that, Mr. President? Can you hear me?

[Nikita Sergei'ich shouts even louder than before.]

Mr. President, I said …

JACK: Yes, I hear you, loud and clear. You have a deal: you remove the offensive weapons, and we will pledge not to invade Cuba, assuming we can agree on procedures for inspections and safeguards against the reintroduction of the offensive weapons. Can you hear me, Mr. Chairman? It's a deal!

[Suddenly Fidel stands up and stares at the two men at the top of the stairs. He is agitated and angry.]

FIDEL: Comrade Nikita, what in the hell are you talking about? You are going to remove the weapons and leave us vulnerable to the gringos? You don't consult us or even properly inform us of the most basic decisions, and now you propose to strip us of our ultimate security guarantee, the nuclear weapons, for a measly pledge from a gringo who can't be trusted? Comrade Nikita, have you forgotten what happened last year at the Bay of Pigs? Kennedy ordered an invasion of Cuba! And do you remember what Kennedy said just before the invasion? He said, "the U.S. has no intention of invading Cuba?" You have betrayed us, abandoned us!

NIKITA SERGEI'ICH: No, Fidel. No, no, no! You, Kennedy and I have just grabbed our only opportunity to avoid the nuclear abyss. By agreeing with Kennedy, I have saved Cuba from total destruction—well, I mean *we* have saved Cuba from total destruction, assuming, as we do, that you would rather have Cuba survive this crisis than be destroyed in it. Stay cool, Fidel. Don't lose your temper. If you have issues with my deal with Kennedy, then fine, we'll deal with them later. Right now, Comrade Fidel, my young friend, all you have to do is not prevent the removal of the weapons. Oh, and of course, you will have to agree to an onsite inspection scheme, since that is what Kennedy and I have already agreed to. Then you and Cuba are home free, Fidel. Hey, no need to thank us, since we are fraternal brothers in communism, but I think we did pretty well on your behalf.

[At this, Fidel screams and becomes red in the face. He looks to the heavens, King Lear-like, shakes his head back and forth. Fidel then turns directly to the members of the audience and begins speak to them.]

FIDEL: That goddamned Khrushchev actually thinks he saved Cuba. SAVED CUBA?! SAVED CUBA?! What he actually did was invite an American invasion, make sure the world's largest military machine is ready to attack and invade us, and then announce that the only possible deterrent to annihilation by the gringos is now going to be removed, because the lying, brutal American imperialists have "promised" Khrushchev they won't do this year what they did last year and a half-dozen times before that in this century. Is he kidding me? Is he an idiot, or just spineless, or both?

[Fidel is still talking, but now softly and conspiratorially, to the audience.]

We are going to tie Khrushchev and Kennedy up in knots. Ha ha ha! We won't prevent the removal of the weapons. To do that we'd have to kill a lot of Russians, which won't do. We will need them later on. And besides, we don't have any idea how to operate the weapons. But that is it! That is all those two sonsofbitches are getting out of me and out of Cuba. There will be no onsite inspections, and I don't give a shit what Kennedy and Khrushchev have agreed to. No one is going to set foot on this island to inspect anything. Period. End of conversation.

[Fidel now faces Khrushchev, and speaks loudly to him.]

Okay, Comrade Nikita. Take your weapons back home. But your agreement with Kennedy means nothing to us because our demands are not met, or even addressed, in your agreement. We want Guantanamo back; we want the over-flights to cease; we want the exile attacks to cease; we want an end to the pirate attacks; we want an end to the embargo. Oh, and no onsite inspection—by the UN, by the Red Cross, or by anyone else.

NIKITA SERGEI'ICH: No onsite inspections? Wait a minute. Well, okay, for the moment. I am sure the UN people will figure out something. At least, I hope they do.

[The spiral begins to slow down, the noise level of the rushing water decreases, until at last the staircase stops spinning. Now Kennedy and Khrushchev begin to descend the spiral staircase together. When he reaches the bottom, Khrushchev tries to shake Fidel's hand, but Fidel refuses to reciprocate. Kennedy and Castro eye each other warily, before nodding in one another's direction.]

End of Theatrical Preview

* * *

#22

John F. Kennedy to Nikita S. Khrushchev

October 27, 1962[1]

> *"along the lines suggested in your letter"*

Jack has asked his executive committee to reconvene at 10:00 a.m. on Saturday October 27th to consider how he should respond to Khrushchev's long letter of the previous day. Before the meeting, during his morning swim and exercise routine, he has been thinking about what might go wrong: some misunderstanding, misper-ception or misjudgment, either by himself or others. In fact, when he woke up this morning, he had another look at the introduction to a book he ordered all his national security team to read when it appeared earlier this year: Barbara Tuch-man's The Guns of August. *The book shows how the European nations became slaves to their timetables for war preparation, leading to paranoia as to whether they would be able to mobilize in time to counter the threat of country A, country B or country C, which in turn led to the First World War, an epochal tragedy without any overriding purpose or justification for any of the involved countries.*

Millions died, Jack thinks, and for what? For basically nothing, other than some half-cocked slogans about patriotic duty. He thinks: I can't let this crisis get out of control, so that some future historian, if any exist after a nuclear war, will write a book like Tuchman's called The Missiles of October. *The analogy between August 1914 and October 1962 strikes Jack as shockingly close.*

This morning, Jack is especially worried about his military advisers. True, he has had the redoubtable Bob McNamara keeping the generals and admirals in check so far. And his Chairman of the Joint Chiefs, Max Taylor, is smarter and more knowledgeable than any other uniformed military officer he has ever met. Still, he knows how deeply most of his military brass resent the restraint he exercised over the Bay of Pigs invasion, as well as the restraint he is trying to show now over these goddamned missiles in Cuba.

As he gets out of the pool, he remembers that he must tell Jackie to take Caroline and John to their country house in rural Virginia, at least for the time being, far outside the central Washington, DC, area where a nuclear attack would likely be most lethal. As he thinks about them hunkering down out at Glen Ora, he can scarcely believe that today, or tomorrow, or the next day, he may be forced to order the use of U.S. nuclear weapons on Cuba, or perhaps even the Soviet Union. He wonders if Khrushchev feels this absurdity as keenly as he does, and whether the Soviet leader has also reached the conclusion, as Jack has, that nuclear weapons aren't really weapons at all, but instead constitute one big doomsday machine capable of destroying life on earth.

As he enters the meeting with his advisers shortly after 10:00 a.m., he and the others are immediately jolted into an acute awareness of the extreme degree to which they have lost the ability to predict what their Soviet adversary will do next. Someone hands him a piece of paper that contains a news item that will sow chaos, anxiety and fear through the group before the day is over. Everyone stares at Jack, as he reads the news story aloud, just as it appears on the flash bulletin:

BULLETIN
MOSCOW, OCT. 27 (AP)—PREMIER KHRUSHCHEV TOLD PRESIDENT KENNEDY IN A MESSAGE TODAY HE WOULD WITHDRAW OFFENSIVE WEAPONS FROM CUBA IF THE UNITED STATES WITHDREW ITS ROCKETS FROM TURKEY.[2]

Jack is confused. Turkish missiles? He thinks, wait a minute, isn't this different from the offer of yesterday? Didn't yesterday's offer just require a pledge not to invade Cuba in return for Soviet removal of their missiles from Cuba? Didn't it?—he asks his advisers, who confirm that their memories are the same as his. Soon, the entire letter from Khrushchev is received, and it throws the discussions in the White House into something close to pandemonium. On the one hand are Jack's hawks, who put forward such ideas as: there may have been a coup in Moscow and hardliners have replaced Khrushchev; or, if we agree to a trade of NATO missiles in Turkey for Soviet missiles in Cuba, NATO will collapse and the Turks may even fight to keep their weapons. Jack thinks: Jesus Christ, wouldn't that be great? We'd have to attack our allies in Turkey, maybe kill a bunch of them, in order to implement a trade we need to make with our adversary to avoid blowing up the world. On the other hand is a group, led by Jack himself, who believe that a trade, such as Khrushchev is suggesting, will seem fair to most people. To fight a nuclear war over a bunch of obsolete missiles in Turkey is a stupid idea, Jack thinks, though what he actually says is that he doesn't see how the U.S. will have a very good war in Cuba, which may well turn out to be a tragedy of epic proportions, if it becomes known—as it will—that the whole war could have been avoided if the U.S. had just thrown the pile of junk in Turkey into the bargain.

Jack thinks: I like to encourage debate among my advisers, but this is getting ridiculous, as the discussion heats up and rages all day long. Jack steps out of the meeting from time to time to attend to other duties, and relies on his brother Bobby, the attorney general, to report the gist of it to him. Around and around go the advisers. The lack of consensus, or anything close to it, increasingly aggravates him. And as the afternoon wears on, it begins to scare him, after a report arrives that a U-2 spy plane has been shot down over Cuba and the pilot killed. The hawks want to attack immediately by destroying at least the surface-to-air missile (SAM) site in eastern Cuba from which the attack was made. Exhausted and frustrated, some advisers exclaim that the Russians have drawn "first blood," and that it looks as if Khrushchev believes Cuba is worth a war with the United States, and that under these conditions, it makes sense for the U.S. to go in massively, destroying all the missile sites, invading the island, and taking over in Havana. Jack wonders whether his hawkish advisers have any idea what Khrushchev might be forced to do by his own hawks if he were actually to order the attack these advisers are clamoring for this morning.

Jack reaches for a piece of paper on which he has scribbled his notes from a previous briefing by the Joint Chiefs on what would happen, and when, if he decides to give the order to "go for it": bomb the SAM sites—2 hrs; full air strike—17 hrs; invasion—decision day plus 7 days; all forces ashore—decision day plus 18 days; projected American casualties—between 25,000 and 50,000 in the first 2–3 weeks. Jack thinks: this is crazy! Sure, they want to throw out Castro and get someone else in charge in Havana who we can deal with. So do I. But why can I not convince these hotheads that what they are, in all probability, asking me to do is order phase one of Armageddon? No way will the fighting be restricted to Cuba. We are going to have to kill a helluva lot of Russians, as well as Cubans, and Khrushchev can't just sit there and not order retaliation some place—probably Berlin, where the Soviets can kick our ass within hours unless we resort to nuclear weapons. My god! And the bad news keeps on coming: late in the afternoon, he is also informed that another U-2, on an air-sampling mission, has strayed off course over Siberia. Jack has no doubt that Khrushchev's hawks, possibly Khrushchev himself, believe that the U-2 over-flight was only a preliminary step to an attack on Soviet nuclear missiles in Siberia—i.e., World War III, Armageddon, the probable end of human civilization.

By 6:00 p.m. he has had it going round and round with the hawks and doves in his advisory group over how to respond to the two contradictory letters from Khrush-chev. Jack believes that the letter received second, the public announcement, has to be the actual offer. It's public, it's in front of the world, it's operative. That's how Jack sees it. The man in the Kremlin wants or needs a missile trade to close the deal. He puts this to the group. Suddenly Tommy Thompson, Jack's former ambassador to Moscow, who has hardly spoken to this point in the conversation, speaks up. No, Mr. President, Tommy says to Jack. No, I think Khrushchev just needs to say "I saved Cuba," and he can say that with or without the missile trade. So why not just respond to the offer in the first letter. Jack is taken aback. He asks Thompson if that means Khrushchev will actually back down. Tommy Thompson responds by saying that Khrushchev won't pitch it that way; he'll say I have a pledge from President Kennedy that the U.S. will not invade Cuba now, or ever. We got what we wanted from the Americans. I think that will work. Thanks to this exchange with Thompson, Jack thinks he can see a pinpoint of light, finally, at the end of the tunnel of darkness in which they have been operating for nearly two weeks.

Bobby and Ted Sorensen draft a letter consistent with Thompson's argument. Bobby takes it just before 8:00 p.m. to a meeting with Soviet Ambassador Do-brynin. The letter is also revealed in a press release, to insure prompt receipt of its message by Khrushchev. In a meeting at the Justice Department, Bobby explains to Dobrynin that they need an answer the following day. Bobby says this is not an ultimatum, but a statement of fact. His brother can't hold off the hawks any longer than that. After that, war will commence, killing god knows how many Russians, Americans, Cubans and others.

Jack meets privately with his Secretary of State, Dean Rusk, and tells him to prepare a channel to UN Acting Secretary General U Thant that, if activated, would carry this message: U Thant should announce a UN initiative based on the idea of a missile trade, and U Thant should in that event expect a positive response from Jack and his government, as long as the idea is presented as originating with the acting secretary general. It may not be needed, Jack tells Rusk, but if Khrush-chev demands a trade, then he can have his trade via the UN. He tells Rusk to tell no one of this contingency, whether it is activated or not, and Rusk complies.

After more than twelve hours in nearly continuous session, the meeting is ad-journed until 10:00 a.m.the following morning. Jack calls Jackie at Glen Ora and says good night to her and to his children. Jack is acutely aware, as he has never been before, that if things do not go well tomorrow, he may never see them again.

Dear Mr. Chairman:

I have read your letter of October 26 with great care and welcomed the statement of your desire to seek a prompt solution to the problem. The first thing that needs to be done, however, is for work to cease on the offensive missile bases in Cuba and for all weapons systems in Cuba capable of offensive use to be rendered inoperable, under effective United Nations arrangements.

Assuming this is done promptly, I have given my representatives in New York instructions that will permit them to work out this week and—in cooperation with the acting secretary general and your representative—an arrangement for a permanent solution to the Cuba problem along the lines suggested in your letter of October 26. As I read your letter, the key elements of your proposals—which seem generally acceptable as I understand them—are as follows:

1. You would agree to remove these weapons systems from Cuba under appropriate United Nations observation and supervision; and undertake, with suitable safeguards, to halt the further introduction of such weapons systems into Cuba.
2. We, on our part, would agree—upon the establishment of adequate arrangements through the United Nations to ensure the carrying out and continuation of these commitments—(a) to remove promptly the quarantine measures now in effect and (b) to give assurances against an invasion of Cuba and I am confident that other nations of the Western Hemisphere would be prepared to do likewise.

If you will give your representative similar instructions there is no reason why we should not be able to complete these arrangements and announce them to the world within a couple of days...

But the first ingredient, let me emphasize, is the cessation of work on missile sites in Cuba and measures to render such weapons inoperable, under effective international guarantees. The continuation of this threat, or a prolonging of this discussion concerning Cuba by linking these questions to the broader questions of European and world security, would surely lead to an intensification of the Cuban crisis and a grave risk to the peace of the world. For this reason I hope we can quickly agree along the lines outlined in this letter and in your letter of October 26.

John F. Kennedy

* * *

#23

Nikita S. Khrushchev to John F. Kennedy

October 28, 1962[3]

"weapons which you describe as 'offensive'"

Having dealt with Fidel, Nikita Sergei'ich now turns to Kennedy's letter. He is not sure the other members of the Presidium are as keen as he is on the deal proposed by Kennedy. Maybe their attitude, he worries, is "okay, Khrushchev, you got us into this mess, now let's see you get us out of it without having to kowtow to Washington." Nikita Sergei'ich understands this view, because he has the same qualms. He cannot claim to be getting everything he hoped for. He certainly did not dream up the missile deployment plan with the objective of taking them out precipitously, as he is convinced he must do before more incidents occur in or around Cuba that might spark a war that he and Kennedy are trying to avoid. So he feels an uncharacteristic need to let his associates know that while he is proposing a retreat, of sorts, it is an honorable retreat nevertheless.

Toward this end, Nikita Sergei'ich begins a history lecture. He tells the others that there is a time for pressing forward, and a time for strategic retreat. His example is the fledgling Soviet Union in the First World War. In October 1917, the Bolsheviks (including the twenty-three-year-old Nikita Sergei'ich) pressed ahead against the Germans. But in March 1918, Lenin ordered a retreat and codified it in the Brest-Litovsk Treaty, by which the Bolsheviks gained an early exit from the war, but only after granting independence to several countries in northern and central Europe on which they had designs. In 1918, Nikita Sergei'ich tells them, a retreat from their original objective was necessary to save the future of what would become the great superpower, our Soviet Union. Likewise, he says, now we must retreat in order to avoid a nuclear catastrophe—in order to save the human race, including, but not limited to, the Soviet Union. He hopes he is persuasive. But in the end, his mind is made up to agree to the terms in Kennedy's letter, no matter what the others may think. Of course, he would have preferred to get the NATO missiles in Turkey thrown into the bargain. He would have liked that very much. But what the hell, Nikita Sergei'ich reflects, you can't always have everything you want.

In the midst of his historical ruminations, his aide Oleg Troyanovsky is called to the phone in the hallway. When he returns, Troyanovsky reports on a cable from Anatoly Dobrynin describing his most recent meeting with Robert Kennedy. There is, Troyanovsky says, bad news and good news. The bad news is that the Kennedy brothers are desperate to end the crisis as soon as possible because they cannot hold off the Pentagon hotheads much longer. Robert Kennedy told Dobrynin that the Soviets have only until the end of today (Moscow time) to decide. So things are tense and dangerous and time is running out rapidly. As Troyanovsky speaks, Nikita Sergei'ich thinks he notices his aide's hands shaking as he delivers this news to the group. The good news is that the Americans are willing to consider the swap of our missiles in Cuba for NATO missiles in Turkey, but this aspect of the deal must remain confidential or it is null and void. The Turkish missiles, according to Robert Kennedy, will be quietly removed in a few months time. We have the president's word on that, he told Dobrynin. The Presidium, stunned by this authoritative report of the Kennedy brothers' views, asks Troyanovsky to read his notes aloud once more, so that they can more fully absorb the message before considering their options.

At this critical moment, another message is delivered to the meeting that is deeply disturbing: Soviet intelligence is reporting that President Kennedy will be delivering a major address on radio and television at 9:00 a.m., U.S. time, or 5:00 p.m. Moscow time, later that day. The purpose is presumed to be the announcement that a massive attack on Cuba has just begun. Nikita Sergei'ich knows he has neither the time nor the resources to order an independent evaluation of the report about a possible upcoming Kennedy speech. What he does know is that he now has a concrete deadline: he wants to respond positively to Kennedy's letter, and he wants Kennedy and his associates to have his response before Kennedy has to make his speech—if indeed there is to be such a speech. Nikita Sergei'ich is convinced he cannot risk waiting. Once the war starts, he understands, it will likely escalate to monstrous proportions, out of his or anyone's control. So he is determined to treat the news about a Kennedy speech as if it is one hundred percent confirmed. There is a time to get out of this crisis and that time is right now! One look around the huge, polished conference table at Novo-Ogaryovo tells him that the other Presidium members feel the same way.

Nikita Sergei'ich decides he needs to dictate his response to Kennedy immediately. He means to sound conciliatory, even a little bit grateful, but he finds that in dictating it, he is getting angry again at the arrogance of the Americans. Why, he asks Kennedy, are you doing nothing to stop the attacks on Cuba by Cuban exile groups that are obviously receiving their instructions and equipment from Washington? And why, at a moment like this, has an American U-2 spy plane flown over Siberia? Nadezhda Petrovna, his stenographer, takes it all down, as usual. And as usual, most of what Nikita Sergei'ich has said will wind up in the letter, although the staffers at the Foreign Ministry will try to clean it up a little bit before sending it on its way. Also as usual, he is not satisfied with the letter, but there is no time for second thoughts or second guesses. This letter, like the last one he sent to Kennedy, will be read over Radio Moscow at 4:00 p.m., in order to make the deadline imposed by the possibility of a Kennedy speech (at 5:00 p.m. Moscow time).

As the letter to Kennedy is being taken by car to the offices of Radio Moscow, he dictates another letter that brings home to him just how tenuous the situation is. It is to Issa Pliyev, the Soviet field commander in Cuba. There are two parts: first, he tells Pliyev that he and his subordinates were hasty in shooting down the American U-2, because the incident might have derailed our attempts to find a resolution to the crisis. Second, he says he has decided to order the dismantling of the strategic weapons under Pliyev's command, evacuate them from Cuba, and return them to the Soviet Union. After dictating the letter to Pliyev, Nikita Sergei'ich cannot help wondering what sense Pliyev will make of it. Having worked under difficult conditions for months to get the missiles operational and ready for use, Pliyev and his men must now order a complete reversal of the process. Well, he is a good soldier, an experienced commander, Nikita Sergei'ich reassures himself, and he will see to it that the orders are obeyed. I feel better, he thinks, knowing that Pliyev is in charge in Cuba.

It is at that moment, that Nikita Sergei'ich nearly has a panic attack, for he remembers that while the calm, experienced Issa Pliyev is in charge of the 43,000

Russians in Cuba, the excitable, inexperienced, possibly suicidal Fidel Castro leads the more than six million Cubans on the island.

At 4:00 p.m. Nikita Sergei'ich and the Presidium gather around a radio at Novo-Ogaryovo and stare at it, much as they would if they were listening to a Red Army hockey game. They listen to Yuri Levitan, the voice of Radio Moscow, interrupt the regularly scheduled program and read aloud the letter from Nikita Sergei'ich to Kennedy. Nikita Sergei'ich is satisfied with the letter. He didn't get everything he wanted, but he thinks he has done all right, under the circumstances. No, he rephrases it to himself: he and Kennedy have done all right, under the circumstances.

His moment of self-congratulation lasts for only a few seconds after Yuri Levitan has finished reading the response to Kennedy. He cannot get Fidel Castro off his mind. Castro, he thinks, is in some other zone altogether, a zone that Nikita Sergei'ich and Kennedy are not in, that's for sure. He thinks Fidel seems to have gotten the idea that we put the missiles into Cuba to use them—to launch them, to start a war. He seems to think Kennedy wants such a war. And he seems to think, based on his recent letter, that I should want such a war! His negotiating position seems to be: you give me everything we Cubans want or we'll commit national suicide "for the sake of socialism." But such a war will turn Cuba into a radiating ruin. How will that serve the interests of socialism? But I was young once and willing to die for my cause. Maybe with some effort, I will be able to understand him. A way must be found to control Fidel's emotions. In any case, Nikita Sergei'ich thinks, enough is enough for one day. I need to find a way to relax.

He asks Troyanovsky to look at the newspapers and find out what is going on in town tonight. Informed by his aide that a traveling Bulgarian theater troupe is giving its last performance that evening of At the Foot of Vitosh, *Nikita Sergei'ich exclaims, "Let's go see the Bulgarians." And so they do. We are left to wonder whether, while watching the performance by the Bulgarians, Nikita Sergei'ich recalls that it was in Bulgaria, six months ago, when he first had the idea for the Cuban missile deployment and whether, looking back, knowing what he now knows or suspects about Fidel Castro and the Cubans, he would do it again.*

Esteemed Mr. President:

I have received your message of October 27, 1962. I express my satisfaction and gratitude for the sense of proportion and understanding of the responsibility borne by you for the preservation of the peace throughout the world which you have shown. I very well understand your anxiety and the anxiety of the United States people in connection with the fact that the weapons which you describe as "offensive" are, in fact, grim weapons. Both you and I understand what kind of a weapon they are.

In order to complete with greater speed the liquidation of the conflict dangerous to the cause of peace, to give confidence to all people longing for peace, and to calm the American people, who, I am certain, want peace as much as the people of the Soviet Union, the Soviet government, in addition to previously issued instructions on the cessation of further work at building sites for the weapons, has issued a new order on the dismantling of the weapons which you describe as "offensive," and their crating and return to the Soviet Union.

...

The shelling of Havana took place from a piratic ship. It is said that irresponsible émigrés did the shooting. This is possibly the case. However, the question arises: From where did they fire? After all, they, these Cubans, have no territory, they have no private means, and they have no means to wage military action. Thus somebody put the arms needed to shell Havana and carry out their piratic actions in the Caribbean—in Cuban territorial waters—in their hands!

...

In short, Cuba has been under constant threat of aggressive forces which did not conceal their intentions to invade Cuban territory.

...

Mr. President, I want to say clearly again that we could not be indifferent to this. The Soviet government decided to help Cuba with means of defense against aggression—and only with means for purposes of defense. We stationed these means there which you call offensive. We stationed them there in order that no attack should be made against Cuba and that no rash action should be permitted to take place.

Mr. President, I trust your statement, however, on the other hand, there are responsible people who would like to carry out an invasion of Cuba at this time, and in such a way to spark off a war. If we take practical steps and announce the dismantling of the appropriate means from Cuba, then, doing that, we wish to establish at the same time the confidence of the Cuban people that we are with them and are not divesting ourselves of the responsibility of granting help to them.

...

[A] dangerous case occurred on October 28 when your reconnaissance aircraft intruded into the territory of the Soviet Union in the north, in the area of the Chukotka Peninsula, and flew over our territory.

One asks, Mr. President, how should we regard this? Is it a provocation? Your aircraft violates our frontier and at times as anxious as those which we are now experiencing when everything has been placed in a state of combat readiness, for an intruding aircraft can easily be taken for a bomber with nuclear weapons, and this could push us toward a fatal step—all the more so because both the United States government and Pentagon have long been saying that bombers with atomic bombs are constantly on duty in your country.

Therefore, you can imagine what kind of responsibility you assume, especially now, during the anxious times we are experiencing.

…

I would [also] like to ask you, Mr. President, to bear in mind that a violation of Cuban airspace by American aircraft may also have dangerous consequences. If you do not want this, then no pretext should be given for the creation of a dangerous situation.

With respect for you,

N.S. Khrushchev

* * *

#24

John F. Kennedy to Nikita S. Khrushchev

October 28 1962[4]

"Perhaps now, as we step back from danger"

Before breaking up for the evening, Jack and several of his advisers confer informally outside the Cabinet room about what each believes will happen the following day. Everyone is pessimistic, including Jack. Although he does not tell them on this occasion, Jack believes that at this moment, a little before midnight on October 27th, the odds of a war with the Soviet Union are roughly between one out of three and even, with the odds of a conventional conflict escalating to a nuclear war even higher than that. In his ruminations, he finds that he cannot force himself to attach a probability to what happens after a U.S. attack on Soviet missile sites in Cuba. But with the military machines of both superpowers on a hair-trigger alert for possible war, he has little doubt that nuclear weapons will be used, fairly early in the conflict, by one side or the other. After that, the question in his mind is whether the catastrophe will be reversible or not—whether human civilization will stand a chance at survival and regeneration, or whether his failure, and Khrushchev's, will doom mankind to eventual extinction.

The others are also pessimistic. Bob McNamara tells Jack that he is going back to his office to make a list of things that can be done short of going to war in Cuba, if Khrushchev does not respond quickly and positively to the deal proposed in Jack's most recent letter. McNamara tells him that he believes he can come up with at least a dozen ways to buy time and lower the odds that the confrontation over Cuba turns quickly into a nuclear war. McNamara mentions, as an example, laying the missiles in Turkey on their sides, next to their launch platforms, so that Soviet intelligence understands they have nothing to gain from bombing the Turkish missile sites, in response to a U.S. attack on Soviet sites in Cuba. Ted Sorensen is thinking similarly. Before Ted got on a plane for Boston a couple of hours ago, Jack received a note from Sorensen listing several actions that might be undertaken—that would allow the U.S. to stick with the blockade a while longer, giving Khrushchev more time to maneuver out of the box he is in—for example, by letting all Soviet ships bound for Cuba simply sail on through the quarantine line, for the time being, thus lowering the odds of an incident at sea that might escalate into a battle—a battle which might lead quickly to all-out war.

Jack is glad to hear that some of his senior advisers haven't given up trying to find a way out of the crisis without a war. But he also knows that he has other advisers who are itching to attack Cuba. That is the word—"itching"—that keeps coming to him when he thinks, for example, about Air Force Chief Curtis LeMay, who has informed Jack that Monday October 29th is the very last day on which an attack on the Soviet missile bases would probably elicit no response at all from the Soviets in Cuba. After the 29th, according to LeMay, all the missile bases will be operational. Any attack after that may therefore be met with a Soviet nuclear response from the island of Cuba on targets in the southeastern United States. Although Jack detests LeMay's unrelenting hawkishness and his itch to go to war with the Soviet Union, he understands the logic of LeMay's thinking: if there is to be a U.S. attack on the Cuban missile sites, it would be better to order it before the missiles in Cuba can be fired. LeMay's problem, as Jack sees it, is that he is stuck in a way of thinking that served him well in the Second World War, when he commanded the Army Air Corps during the fire-bombings of Germany and Japan, as well as the atomic attacks on Hiroshima and Nagasaki. In the 1940s, the U.S. was not facing a nuclear-armed enemy. Now it is. And that is the problem. If we bomb them now, they just might destroy us in retaliation.

Jack cannot get to sleep because he cannot stop his mind from racing from one version of Armageddon to another, as he imagines what may occur over the next 24-48 hours, if Khrushchev does not accept the terms in his letter of earlier in the evening. He thinks of his daughter Caroline, who will turn five in exactly one month, and who has begun to take an interest in poetry. In fact, Caroline has begun to appear regularly at meetings in the White House specifically to recite a poem she has memorized. Jack liked to memorize poems, too, when he was her age. Lately, Jack has been working with Caroline on his very favorite poem—a poem he memorized years ago, a poem that has meant a great deal to him: through his numerous surgeries and illnesses, and now, in this world-threatening crisis over missiles in Cuba. Jack finally falls asleep reciting to himself the first stanza of the poem, "I Have a Rendezvous With Death," by the American poet Alan Seeger, who was killed on the Western front in 1916, during the First World War:

> *I have a rendezvous with death*
> *At some disputed barricade,*
> *When spring comes back with rustling shade*
> *And apple blossoms fill the air—*
> *I have a rendezvous with death*
> *When spring brings back blue days and fair.*

It is now 9:00 a.m. on the 28ᵗʰ and, following a fitful night's sleep, Jack is dressing for church when he receives a call from his National Security Adviser, McGeorge Bundy, who is phoning him from the White House Mess Hall. Mac Bundy tells Jack an aide has handed him a slip of paper just seconds ago, after he had ripped it from the teletype machine in the White House Situation Room. It is from the CIA's Foreign Broadcast Information Service and, Bundy says, it has news of Khrushchev's response. Jack asks him to read it, which Bundy does, excitedly, and word for word, as follows:

MOSCOW DOMESTIC SERVICE IN RUSSIAN AT 1404GMT ON 28 OCTOBER BROADCAST A MESSAGE FROM KHRUSHCHEV TO PRESIDENT KENNEDY STATING THAT THE USSR HAD DECIDED TO DISMANTLE THE SOVIET MISSILES IN CUBA AND RETURN THEM TO THE SOVIET UNION. 28 Oct 0908A[5]

After a brief moment of disorientation at this unexpected but welcome piece of news, Jack tells Mac Bundy that the previously scheduled meeting of the crisis group should be postponed from 10:00 a.m. to 11:30 a.m. He tells Bundy "I am going to church, and you can tell the others I think they should too, and thank whomever it is they thank for something like this." During the service at the Church of St. Stephen, near the White House, Jack gets his mind organized for the 11:30 a.m. meeting, which will be a different sort of meeting than the one that weighed so heavily on his mind last night.

When he enters the meeting room, his advisers stand and applaud. In the general giddiness and commotion, one of his advisers laughingly says, "Mr. President, now that you are ten feet tall in the eyes of the world, maybe you should try to resolve the India-China border war" (which had begun more or less at the same time as the missile crisis, and which some enterprising—if a bit paranoid—minds feared was part of a global communist plot). Jack responds: "Ten feet tall? Hah, that will last maybe two weeks, if that long, then it will be back to business as usual."

Jack immediately orders the group to settle on a response to Khrushchev. He makes sure that the letter contains a response to Khrushchev's query about the U-2 that was briefly lost over Siberia the day before—that it was unarmed, on an air sampling mission, and so on. He also wants to make sure that the CIA's subversive activity in and around Cuba is to be discontinued, until further notice. He doesn't want to have to field any more inquiries from Khrushchev about why some bridge on the island was blown up or why some building was bombed. He orders those operations "zipped up."

If Jack is tempted to join in the general mood of relief and jubilation, the urge is quickly quashed by a message that just arrived from his Joint Chiefs of Staff. The military brass tells him that, in their view, the offer from Khrushchev is a charade; that the arrangement will give Castro a free hand to cause mayhem in Latin America; that the Soviets will try to hide some of the missiles and warheads in Cuba; and that there should be no relaxation of the military alert (which is currently at the highest level short of the outbreak of war). In short, the Chiefs see no cause for celebration. Rather, LeMay's view is that Khrushchev should be ignored altogether, and that an air attack and invasion should be ordered on the following day, Monday, October 29th.

Thinking about the Joint Chiefs' reaction to Khrushchev's letter is upsetting to Jack for two reasons: first, it shows just how dementedly determined they are to have their war over Cuba; and second, God help us, what if the Chiefs are right? Maybe there will be problems with onsite inspection in Cuba, which is absolutely going to be required if the skeptics are ever to believe that the Russians have actually removed all of their offensive nuclear weapons systems from Cuba. We can't fool around forever with the military alert at Defense Condition 2—with so many of our bombers in the air twenty-four hours a day flying around the perimeter of the Soviet Union, waiting for the order to blow up the Russians and the rest of the world with it. Accidents are bound to happen, and an accident could set off World War III. Thank God for McNamara over in the Pentagon. Who else but Bob, Jack thinks, could keep the likes of Curt LeMay on so tight a leash. No one. Jack thinks to himself: if we get out of this mess somehow, Bob McNamara is my nominee for MVP of the Cuban missile crisis.

Dear Mr. Chairman:

I am replying at once to your broadcast message of October 28 even though the official text has not reached me because of the great importance I attach to moving forward promptly to the settlement of the Cuban crisis. I think that you and I, with our heavy responsibilities for the maintenance of peace, were aware that developments were approaching a point where events could have become unmanageable. So I welcome this message and consider it an important contribution to peace.

The distinguished efforts of Acting Secretary General U Thant have greatly facilitated our tasks. I consider my letter to you of October 27 and your reply of today as firm undertakings on the part of both our governments which should be promptly carried out. I hope that the necessary measures can at once be taken through the United Nations as your message says, so that the United States can in turn remove the quarantine measures now in effect. I have already made arrangements to report all these matters to the Organization of American States, whose members share a deep interest in a genuine peace in the Caribbean area.

You referred in your letter to a violation of your frontier by an American aircraft in the area of the Chukotsk Peninsula. I have learned that this plane, without arms or photographic equipment, was engaged in an air sampling mission in connection with your nuclear tests. Its course was direct from Eielson Air Force Base in Alaska to the North Pole and return. In turning south, the pilot made a serious navigational error which carried him over Soviet territory. He immediately made an emergency call on open radio for navigational assistance and was guided back to his home base by the most direct route. I regret this incident and will see to it that every precaution is taken to prevent recurrence.

...

I agree with you that we must devote urgent attention to the problem of disarmament, as it relates to the whole world and also to critical areas. Perhaps now, as we step back from danger, we can together make real progress in this vital field. I think we should give priority to questions relating to the proliferation of nuclear weapons on earth and in outer space, and to the great effort for a nuclear test ban. But we should also work hard to see if wider measures of disarmament can be agreed and put into operation at an early date. The United States government will be prepared to discuss these questions urgently, and in a constructive spirit, at Geneva or elsewhere.

John F. Kennedy

* * *

#25

Fidel Castro: To Acting Secretary-General of the United Nations, U Thant

October 28, 1962[6]

"The guarantees . . . will be ineffective unless"

It is Sunday morning, October 28th, before 9:00 a.m. Fidel has been prowling the Havana area with the raw energy of a caged lion, making sure that all is in readiness for the air attack and invasion by the gringos. He feels more relaxed while moving, barking out orders, encouraging his forces. They feed off his energy, and vice versa. More than once this hot and sticky morning he has caught himself thinking: well, this could be the last time I will ever see this beach, or that hill, or this friend and comrade. He recalls the briefing he received from a young Foreign Ministry official assigned to study U.S. manuals of nuclear war and describe what would happen in the event of an American nuclear attack on Cuba. The briefer had said simply: "All of us, and all of Cuba, will be destroyed totally." That was all he said. Fidel remembers shaking the young man's hand and thanking him for getting to the heart of the matter. He remembers the spontaneous chant around the briefing room of Viva Cubita! *It was a moment of great poignancy: "Long live little Cuba," a country about to be sunk beneath the surface of the Caribbean by Yankee bombs. Fidel remembers leaving the briefing in a hurry in order to hide the fact that tears were beginning to form at the corners of his eyes—tears that, in the Maximum Leader, might reduce the fighting spirit of his troops. If anything connected to little Cuba is to live after this war, Fidel thought immediately after that briefing, it will be our insistence on our dignity and our courage to pursue it to the last man, woman and child on this island. With that, his nascent sadness was transformed into righteous anger—which he believes is the true and necessary attitude of a revolutionary.*

Fidel arrives back at his Havana command post at 9:00 a.m. and is told that Carlos Franqui urgently needs to speak with him on the phone. Franqui, who fought with Fidel's 26th of July Movement in the struggle against the Batista tyranny, is the editor of Revolucion, *a Havana daily newspaper. Fidel takes the call. He stands totally still, without speaking for what others in the room feel is a very long time, staring straight ahead, telephone receiver in one hand, cigar in the other hand. Suddenly, in one jerky motion, he throws the entire telephone— the receiver and its cradle—against the wall, smashing it to bits, as he screams obscenities, interspersed with Khrushchev's name. He then destroys a mirror with one kick of his military boot. "Sonofabitch, bastard, asshole," he shouts over and over again. Fidel's comrades, having no idea why their commander in chief is act- ing this way, retreat to the part of the room furthest from Fidel's large, gesticulat- ing body. When he finally looks up and sees the terrified looks on the faces of his aides, Fidel pulls himself together and explains quietly what Franqui has told him: the Russians have betrayed the Cubans; Khrushchev has cut a deal with Kennedy; all the nuclear missiles are to be removed in exchange for a pledge from Kennedy not to invade Cuba. Then he shouts again, louder than before: "A pledge, a fuck- ing pledge!" Fidel turns, makes a gesture with the hand that had recently held the now destroyed phone receiver, and indicates to his driver that he wants to hit the road immediately.*

Once in his jeep, Fidel tells his driver to take him to the El Chico *headquarters of Gen. Issa Pliyev, the Soviet field commander. On the short drive to* El Chico, *Fidel tries to piece together what Franqui has told him. The deal, Franqui said, was announced on the CBS radio network, on a broadcast from New York, relayed by the CBS affiliate in Miami, and monitored by the staff at* Revolucion. *There has been no letter from Khrushchev even informing him of the arrangement, much less any consultation. Just a slap across the face with this humiliating and sudden turn of events, in which the whole world will conclude that Cuba has been just a helpless little pawn in the game of chicken being played by the U.S. and USSR.*

Fidel thinks the Russians obviously don't give a damn about Cuba. If they did they wouldn't even consider doing what they apparently have already agreed to do: withdraw the weapons from Cuba that were to guarantee Cuba's security, in exchange for—for what?—a totally useless pledge from Kennedy, who only last year authorized the invasion of Cuba at the Bay of Pigs, and whose forces are now, at this very moment, poised to turn Cuba into a radiating hill of ash. Fidel's overriding thought, as the jeep pulls up to the Soviet command post is: how could I have been so naïve as to believe Khrushchev? That bastard lied to Kennedy about the weapons, and we told him that he would regret it—and now he understands that we were right. But why did we—why did I—believe Khrushchev would tell us the truth, would be honest and forthright with us, with me? That bastard lied to everybody.

Once inside, Pliyev confirms that the missiles are to be dismantled immediately, re-crated and shipped back to the Soviet Union. Fidel asks why Khrushchev is doing this. Pliyev tells Fidel he has no idea, but it is not his job to second-guess Khrushchev. "Yes, of course," Fidel responds, "but did you see this coming, did you suspect Khrushchev was going to cave in like this?" Pliyev tells Fidel he had no inkling whatsoever that this was coming. None. Fidel thanks Pliyev for his time, turns around, and strides out the door and back to his jeep.

So it's really true, Fidel thinks. Khrushchev intends to leave us nothing, or next to nothing. Fidel tells his driver to take a circuitous route back to central Havana. He needs some time to think, to figure out how he should respond to this totally unanticipated circumstance. He thinks: this development creates several big problems for Cuba. Most important, we look like fools—fools to ourselves, fools to our communist comrades elsewhere, fools to the entire world. We are in danger of being perceived as a bunch of naïve Third World idiots who have traded in one master—the Americans—for another exploitative patron—the Soviets. That, as Fidel thinks about it, is the biggest problem facing him and facing Cuba: how to regain self-respect, dignity, independence and sovereignty in the face of this public abandonment by the Russians. Yeah, sure, he thinks, there are other problems, like how will we defend ourselves when the Americans decide to invade—which they are sure to do, once the Russians and their missiles are gone? But we can handle that. We know how to fight. We know how to resist. It is the Cuban way, Fidel thinks. The gringos can beat us, if that is their military objective, but we will fight with dignity. He tells his driver to keep driving along the back roads. He is not finished thinking about how to respond to Khrushchev's betrayal.

Suddenly, Fidel hears some commotion up ahead. He orders his driver to slow down. A group of students who have obviously heard about the Kennedy-Khrushchev deal have gathered in a square and are ripping down posters proclaiming Soviet-Cuban solidarity. Nearby, a Cuban militia unit is chanting something— what is that they are saying, Fidel asks his driver? Then they both hear it loud and clear: "Nikita, mariquita—lo que se da no se quita; pim pam fuera—abajo Caimanera!" ("Nikita you little braggard—what one gives, one gives for keeps; Pim pam out—Yankees out of Guantanamo!") Fidel smiles for the first time this morning. Our people, he thinks, have a genius for figuring out what is what. There, in two lines, they already see that the American and Soviet imperialists see things the same way. We small countries are just here to be exploited and then dropped, as their mood indicates.

It is nearly 11:00 a.m. Fidel tells his driver to take him straight to his command post. He now knows what his moves will be in response to the Kennedy-Khrushchev deal. First, he will draft a short letter to UN Acting Secretary General U Thant, explaining that no matter what Kennedy and Khrushchev have agreed to, Cuba will not honor that agreement unless Cuba's interests are taken into account. He has five points in mind that need to be entered into the discussion. With this letter, Fidel intends to insert Cuba forcibly into the resolution of the crisis, whether Moscow and Washington like it or not. Second, he must write to Khrushchev. He will be honest; he will express his disappointment; but he will not be rude; Fidel is beginning to see how he might be able to turn these recent developments to Cuba's advantage, but he will need the help of the Russians to do so. Cuba will need resources that only the Soviets can provide. Third, he must explain to the Cuban people what has happened and how Cuba will respond: basically, by returning to basic Cuban values, to the fighting spirit of Jose Marti, to Antonio Maceo, to the fearlessness of David confronting Goliath, even to martyrdom if that is what it takes to preserve Cuban dignity.

Fidel has another idea: he must go tonight, perhaps for several nights, to La Colina, *the hilltop campus of the University of Havana, to engage with the students. La Colina is where he first became the political animal he now is, where he first found his voice as a spokesman for Cubans seeking justice and dignity. Yes, he will do this, he thinks. He will rededicate himself to Cuban independence and Cuban values. He will explain to the young people the compatibility of two of the slogans that may be seen on posters all over the island:* "patria o muerte" *and* "socialismo o muerte."

But first Fidel will write to U Thant a letter that demonstrates Cuba's determination to resist pressure from both superpowers. And he will make sure that the letter is made available immediately, all over the world. Fidel thinks: everyone is about to discover that this crisis has a third actor that remains as defiant as ever, as independent as ever—a small country that can resist the big ones.

U Thant
Acting Secretary-General of the United Nations

With reference to the statement made by Mr. John F. Kennedy, President of the United States, in a letter addressed to Mr. Nikita Khrushchev, Chairman of the Council of Ministers of the USSR, to the effect that the United States would agree, after suitable arrangements had been made through the United Nations, to remove the blockade now in effect, and to give guarantees against an invasion of Cuba, and with reference to the decision, announced by Mr. Nikita Khrushchev, to withdraw strategic defense weapons systems from Cuban territory, the Revolutionary Government of Cuba wishes to make the following statement:

The guarantees mentioned by President Kennedy that there will be no aggression against Cuba will be ineffective unless, in addition to the removal of the naval blockade which he promises, the following measures, *inter alia*, are adopted:

1. Cessation of the economic blockade and of all the measures of commercial and economic pressure being carried out by the United States against our country throughout the world.
2. Cessation of all subversive activities, of the dropping and landing of weapons and explosives by air and sea, of the organization of invasions by mercenaries, and of the infiltration of spies and saboteurs—all of which are being carried on from the territory of the United States and certain accomplice countries.
3. Cessation of the piratical attacks being carried out from bases in the United States and Puerto Rico.
4. Cessation of all violations of our air space and territorial waters by United States aircraft and warships.
5. Withdrawal of the naval base of Guantanamo and return of the Cuban territory occupied by the United States.

Accept, Sir, the assurance of my highest consideration.
Major Fidel Castro Ruz
Prime Minister of the Revolutionary Government of Cuba

* * *

#26

Fidel Castro to Nikita S. Khrushchev

October 28, 1962[7]

"violating our airspace . . . day and night"

Fidel has just finished drafting the letter to U Thant. At a meeting of the heads of Cuban radio, television and newspaper outlets, he tells his media people that he wants this short letter to the UN Secretary General to be seen and heard everywhere, immediately. He wants Cuba's perspective, Cuba's courage to resist both superpowers, to inform the discussion of what the crisis is about and on what terms it will be resolved—if it is resolved peacefully, at some point. At a similar meeting of his Foreign Ministry officials, he says he wants all of Cuba's ambassadors to make the distribution of his letter to U Thant their top priority until further notice. Wherever they are posted, Cuban representatives are to approach the host government at the highest level to inform them of Cuba's perspective and Cuba's role in the crisis. He says we must not let the aggressors in Washington and the betrayers in Moscow control the conversation, as if Cuba was just an empty little island, filled with Soviet missiles and little else.

Fidel begins to think about the upcoming visit of U Thant two days from now. This is another opportunity Fidel does not want to miss. He plans to use U Thant's visit to dramatize to the world that Cuba is not a passive victim in this episode, but an active player that matters greatly to the eventual outcome. He thinks: U Thant will be coming here to work out the details of a UN onsite inspection process. That is what he thinks he is coming to Cuba for. But Fidel is absolutely opposed to onsite inspections. To Fidel, they have the same status as U.S. over-flights: they are violations of basic sovereignty, like rape or other kinds of forcible assault, and will not be tolerated. Somehow a way must be found for U Thant to have a successful visit, an important visit to Cuba, but at the same time go back to New York without achieving his objective of onsite inspections, and without the slightest hope of achieving it. This will be tricky, Fidel thinks. He must give it more thought before U Thant arrives. But at a minimum, he already knows that with regard to U Thant's visit, all publicity will be good publicity. Fidel has in mind a certain ambience, an impression he wants to convey: that Cuba and the UN, which have both been stiffed by the superpowers as irrelevant to their superpower game, will in fact be negotiating an end to the crisis about Cuba in Cuba itself. That is the message. He thinks U Thant will find it congenial.

Fidel must write a letter to Krushchev. But before he can organize his thoughts for a letter, he is informed by the Soviet embassy that a letter for him from Khrushchev has just arrived. Minutes later, the letter, quickly translated into Spanish, sits in front of him at his worktable. He feels himself getting angry—very, very angry—all over again, as angry as he was this morning at 9:00 a.m. when Carlos Franqui called to inform him of the Kennedy-Khrushchev deal. As he often does during his speeches, Fidel now begins to address his room full of aides by offering an exegesis of the document in front of him. "Can you believe this?" *he says to no one in particular.* "Khrushchev says he is not going to say anything about his deal with Kennedy because, 'surely, you know the text, which is now being broadcast over the radio.'" *Fidel brings his fist down hard on the table.* "Has the man no shame? No, I guess he doesn't. Not only has he proven himself to be a pathological liar, but he is an ignorant, clueless peasant as well." *Fidel is suddenly and uncharacteristically speechless, as he fumes about Khrushchev's arrogance. Jesus Christ, he thinks, he doesn't consult or inform us about what is going on, and then basically says,* "Oh by the way, you might want to turn on your radio to find out how Kennedy and I have decided between ourselves to deal with this unpleasant Cuban situation." *He looks up at his aides, palms up, shoulders hunched, eyebrows arched, as if to say,* "What in the hell are we going to do with this guy, with these people?" *For the first time since the letter arrived, Fidel's aides permit themselves to smile along with their* comandante en jefe.

"But wait," *Fidel says loudly, as he reads further into the letter,* "listen to this. Khrushchev urges me 'not to be carried away by sentiment.' What the hell is he talking about? Sentiment? We are surrounded by the greatest military force in the world* *which is poised to destroy us; we man our battle stations waiting for Armageddon, and Father Nikita says 'tut tut, now let's be quiet and obedient, like nice children.'"* Fidel is hitting his righteous stride now. Suddenly, it feels very good to express outrage at how he and his country are being treated. *"Is he my father? Is the Cuban Revolution his daughter? Sorry Comrade Nikita, but Cuba is not East Germany, not Poland, not any of the countries of Eastern Europe who adopted socialism at the point of the Soviet bayonet. I'll tell you what those countries are: they are occupied countries, just as Cuba was an occupied country before our Revolution. We in Cuba arrived at socialism on our own, without one peso of help from the Russians and we do not intend to give up any of our independence and sovereignty."*

Fidel realizes that he is not in a good frame of mind to write the letter that needs to be written to Khrushchev. From now on, he wants his communications with Khrushchev to be blunt in their portrayal of Cuban anger and sadness at the Soviet betrayal, but he also wants the criticism of the Soviets to be balanced with gratitude to Khrushchev for having risked so much for Cuba, for putting little Cuba at the center of the world, where it belongs. Fidel also realizes that he is running late for a meeting with the students at the university, to discuss with them the crisis and their own anger at the Soviets. Normally, Fidel's concept of "running late" is highly elastic. He has been known to keep people waiting for days. But he also looks forward to the encounter with the students at his old university, as a way of working out the way he wants to approach the letter to Khrushchev, and the Russians generally, as he tries to find a way out of the mess they have left Cuba in—a way out that preserves Cuban dignity, while also raising the odds that Cuba emerges from the crisis a winner, a force to be reckoned with, not just one more underdeveloped country that goes begging for help from the big powers. He signals his driver, and says, "Let's go to La Colina," the hilltop campus of the University of Havana.

The auditorium is beastly hot, even for Fidel, who is always cold. It is so packed that people can scarcely move. When the door opens and he strides onto the stage, the throng erupts: "Fee-del, Fee-del, Fee-del," as he acknowledges their applause. He quiets them almost immediately, however. He says he has come to discuss a very difficult issue: how to understand what has happened, how Cuba should proceed, now that Kennedy and Khrushchev have apparently made a deal behind the backs of the Cubans. At this, the crowd erupts in angry and threatening shouting: "Kick the Soviets out, Fidel," screams a woman in front. "Put the Russians on trial," yells a young man in the back who has his right fist in the air. "No, Fidel," another hollers, "let us go and take over the missiles and the other weapons. Let Cubans take what is rightfully ours." Fidel can barely suppress a smile. He thinks: these young Cubans remind me of myself ten or fifteen years ago. I would have been the guy in back, he decides. I would be the one leading the students to a missile site, the way I led the 26th of July comrades to the dictator Batista's ammunition depot at Moncada in 1953. I would be the one telling the Russians to put up or shut up and get the hell out of the way.

"I know exactly how you feel," Fidel begins. "Kennedy and Khrushchev have fallen in love—they are having a hot love affair right in the middle of the Cold

War." The students love this; they roar with laughter and approval. They begin chanting Fidel's name again. This time he lets them go on for a while, before raising his left hand to silence them. "And the Russians: they have no cojones, *right? What happened to the Russians'* cojones? *Did they leave them in Russia, for safekeeping? Everything was fine until Kennedy made an ugly face at them, and then they ran for cover." More chanting of "Fee-del, Fee-del." Fidel then puts on a somber, pensive face, and addresses them so quietly that he can barely be heard, in that surprisingly high-pitched, scratchy voice with which everyone in the room is familiar. "Well,* companeros, *the Russians can run for cover if they want to, and they can take their weapons with them—after all, they belong to them, so if they want to take their weapons and go home, then fine. But no one—not even the UN—will ever set foot on this island to inspect the weapon sites. No one! Our commitment to Cuban sovereignty will not permit it. Would Jose Marti have permitted it?" The students shout, "NO!" Fidel says, "Then we will not permit it either." The students shout, "YES!"*

Fidel goes on: "As I said, we all know how it feels to be treated as if we hardly exist, as if we are a bargaining chip for the big powers. We are angry. But young comrades, we have arrived at a critical moment in the history of our Revolution. If we are clever, courageous and relentless in pursuit of Cuba's interests, we have an opportunity never before experienced by a country like ours—small, without big weapons of our own, underdeveloped, with a history of colonialism and imperialism. Listen to me: we will never take orders from the Soviet Union; but we should take their resources if they offer it to us in fraternal solidarity. We will never march to the Soviet drumbeat, but we should learn from their expertise, if it is offered to us in friendship and brotherhood. Let's give the Soviets a chance to learn from their mistakes. Let's educate them as to what Cuba and Cubans stand for—especially how totally different we are from the comrades they are used to dealing with in Eastern Europe. Let's give Khrushchev a chance to start over with Cuba. Patria o muerte! Venceremos!" *("Homeland or death! We will win!")*

With the students shouting ecstatically, "Fee-del, Fee-del, Fee-del," Fidel leaves the stage and in a moment, he is gone. He can hear the students, still chanting, as he heads for his jeep. He thinks: now I am ready to write that letter to Khrushchev.

Dear Comrade Khrushchev:

I have just received your letter.

The position of our government concerning your communication to us is embodied in the statement formulated today, whose text you surely know.

I wish to clear up something concerning the antiaircraft measures we adopted. You say: "Yesterday you shot down one of these [planes], while earlier you didn't shoot them down when they overflew your territory."

Earlier isolated violations were committed without a determined military purpose or without a real danger stemming from those flights.

This time that wasn't the case. There was the danger of a surprise attack on certain military installations. We decided not to sit back and wait for a surprise attack, with our detection radar turned off, when the potentially aggressive planes flying with impunity over the targets could destroy them totally. We didn't think we should allow that after all the efforts and expenses incurred and, in addition, because it would weaken us greatly, militarily and morally. For that reason, on October 24 the Cuban forces mobilized 50 antiaircraft batteries, our entire reserve then, to provide support to the Soviet forces' positions. If we sought to avoid the risks of a surprise attack, it was necessary for Cuban artillerymen to have orders to shoot. The Soviet command can furnish you with additional reports of what happened to the plane that was shot down.

Earlier airspace violations were carried out de facto and furtively. Yesterday the American government tried to make official the privilege of violating our airspace at any hour of the day and night. We cannot accept that, and it would be tantamount to giving up a sovereign prerogative. However, we agree that we must avoid an incident at this precise moment that could seriously harm the negotiations, so we will instruct the Cuban batteries not to open fire, but only for as long as the negotiations last and without revoking the declaration published yesterday about the decision to defend our airspace. It should also be taken into account that under the current tense conditions incidents can take place accidentally.

I also wish to inform you that we are in principle opposed to an inspection of our territory.

I appreciate extraordinarily the efforts you have made to keep the peace and we are absolutely in agreement with the need for struggling for that goal. If this is accomplished in a just, solid and definitive manner, it will be an inestimable service to humanity.

Fraternally,

Fidel Castro

* * *

#27

Nikita S. Khrushchev to Fidel Castro

October 30, 1962[8]

"the overall situation had to be considered."

Nikita Sergei'ich has just learned of Fidel Castro's five points, listed in his letter to U Thant. His reaction is, Fidel can't count. He really has six points. He forgot to include the point about how opposed he is to onsite inspection by the UN (or anyone!) to verify that we have removed our missiles and destroyed the launching pads. Nikita Sergei'ich feels his blood begin to boil when he thinks about the huge obstacle Fidel has thrown onto the road Kennedy and Nikita Sergei'ich have been traveling together for the past forty-eight hours. They had almost pulled a peaceful victory from the nuclear bonfire of defeat—they had agreed in principle to an equitable deal—and now this Cuban crazy man thinks he has the right to veto all we have accomplished. Sometimes I wonder, Nikita Sergei'ich thinks, whether Fidel is disappointed that the war did not occur, that Cuba still exists. His five (really six) points just raise the odds, yet again, that the warmongers around Kennedy will find a way to have their war, dragging both Kennedy and me into it.

Nikita Sergei'ich feels he must write to Fidel and try to get him to face the facts of life as the leader of a nation. He must learn to act responsibly, on the basis of the overall situation faced by his nation and the world as a whole. Nikita Sergei'ich begins to make mental notes for the letter. He begins with Fidel's mistakes: he ordered a U-2 plane shot down, which nearly caused the outbreak of war. That was ridiculous, the result of a lack of patience. I must teach him patience. Later, after this crisis is behind us, he and I will get together and I will counsel him to have patience. Then there was the bizarre request that I authorize a nuclear attack on the U.S. and destroy it. Whoa! That was not just impatience. That was lunacy! He and I will definitely have to talk about the facts of life in a world filled with nuclear weapons. I will show him the numbers. He is smart. He will begin to see how crazy it would have been for us, especially with our inferior nuclear force, to attack the U.S.

And now, Fidel has asserted that he has veto power over any deal Kennedy and I work out. I know, I know, Alekseev, our man in Havana, keeps telling me not to lecture Fidel, not to engage in polemics with Fidel, not to repeat over and over again that he is wrong in this or he was mistaken to have said or done that. But is it polemical, Nikita Sergei'ich wonders to himself, to tell someone who has crazy ideas that his ideas are crazy? Sometimes, I wonder what we have gotten into in Cuba. I wonder if all Cubans are like Fidel. Do all Cubans prefer a beautiful death to continued life, as we pursue our dream of a socialist world?

Nikita Sergei'ich knows what he must do. He must send Anastas Mikoyan to Cuba as soon as possible. But it will be complicated. Anastas Ivan'ich's wife, Ashken, is near death. He may be reluctant to go to Cuba, fearing that he may never see her alive again. That is understandable. But Mikoyan is also a revolutionary who knows his duty. Nikita Sergei'ich calls a Presidium meeting to discuss sending Mikoyan to Cuba. When he puts the question to his longtime ally and friend, Mikoyan sits silent, staring into space, unable to answer yes or no. The others at the meeting become very uncomfortable, unable to watch Mikoyan on the verge of tears, not wanting to go to Cuba, yet knowing that Nikita Sergei'ich is right: he is the man to do the job that must be done. He is the man to talk Fidel Castro, one of the world's famous talkers, out of his temper tantrums and his obstructionism.

Maybe, thinks Nikita Sergei'ich, Mikoyan is like this because, like Fidel, he is from the south—well, from Armenia, anyway, and in the Soviet Union that qualifies as "the south." Nikita Sergei'ich smiles to himself as he imagines the old man wearing out the young firebrand in Havana. Besides, Anastas Ivan'ich is the only Presidium member who has ever been to Cuba. He is the only one who knows the territory—and who knows all the important Cubans.

Finally, Nikita Sergei'ich cannot stand the oppressive silence any longer. Without waiting for Mikoyan to say yes or no, he tells him, "Go Anastas Ivan'ich; go to Cuba and work with Fidel on all these problems. Only you can do this. I will take care of everything here, with Ashken. Everything! She would want you to do your duty. You know she would." At last, Mikoyan, still unable to speak, nods yes. He will do it. Finally, he says haltingly that he will go to Cuba and not leave the island until his job is done—that is, until Fidel agrees to climb down from his position, his five (or six) points, his obstructing, and his wild ideas. Nikita Sergei'ich thinks: this man is a true revolutionary. As the meeting ends, the Presidium members begin to leave the room, when Nikita Sergei'ich grabs Mikoyan by the shoulders and stares straight into his eyes and nods his approval. Like Mikoyan, Nikita Sergei'ich discovers that he cannot speak at the moment. But his eyes say to Mikoyan: thank you, my old friend, for accepting this incredibly difficult mission, under these conditions.

At last, Nikita Sergei'ich sits down to compose his thoughts so he can send a "fatherly" letter to Fidel. He will tell him, he thinks, that Cuba's difficulties are only temporary, only part of the transition of this crisis from a military phase to a diplomatic phase. He will also tell Fidel something about leadership, about why leaders need to get out in front of their people and lead them in ways they may not like at the moment, but which are nevertheless necessary. Another thing: Fidel has said he was not consulted, that he was left out of our calculations to end the crisis with Kennedy. This is total rubbish. Of course, Nikita Sergei'ich thinks, I won't put it that way. But as a matter of fact our calculations were based almost entirely on our objective of saving Cuba, or preserving Cuba, so that it can take its place in the family of socialist nations. Nikita Sergei'ich thinks Fidel will like this: that we Soviets had the salvation of Cuba uppermost in our minds. And finally, Nikita Sergei'ich thinks, I had better remind him yet again, as Alekseev has reminded him numerous times, that his request that we launch a nuclear strike at the U.S. was—how shall I phrase it?—was, incorrect, was wrong, was basically crazy. Yes, Nikita Sergei'ich thinks, that should do it.

While he is waiting for his stenographer, Nadezhda Petrovna, to take his dictation, he looks down at his desk to find yet another report about how the Chinese are accusing him of "adventurism" for putting the missiles into Cuba, and "capitulationism" for agreeing to pull the missiles out of Cuba and for not insisting that the Americans abide by Fidel's Five Points. Screw the Chinese, Nikita Sergei'ich thinks. If they keep this up, I will fix them by selling our best MiG fighter jets to their nemesis, India. Mao is as old as I am but he is crazier than Fidel. He says a nuclear war with the U.S. imperialists is inevitable. He says the Chinese have lots of surplus people—he actually said that—and a hundred million dead, more or less, is a price he would gladly pay to destroy the U.S.

Just then Nadezhda Petrovna comes through the door, and he begins his "fatherly" letter to his adopted "son," Fidel Castro.

Dear Comrade Fidel Castro:

We have received your letter of October 28 and the reports on the talks that you as well as President Dorticos have had with our ambassador.

We understand your situation and take into account the difficulties you now have during the first transitional stage after the liquidation of maximum tension that arose due to the threat of attack on the part of the U.S. imperialists, which you expected would occur at any moment.

We understand that certain difficulties have been created for you as a result of our having promised the U.S. government to withdraw the missile bases from Cuba, since they are viewed as offensive weapons, in exchange for the U.S. commitment to abandon plans for an invasion of Cuba by U.S. troops or those of its allies in the western hemisphere, and lift the so-called "quarantine," that is, bring the blockade of Cuba to an end. This led to the liquidation of conflict in the Caribbean zone which, as you well realize, was characterized by the clash of two superpowers and the possibility of it being transformed into a thermonuclear world war using missiles.

As we learned from our ambassador, some Cubans have the opinion that the Cuban people want a declaration of another nature rather than the withdrawal of the missiles. It's possible that this kind of feeling exists among the people. But we, political and government figures, are leaders of a people who don't know everything and can't readily comprehend all that we leaders must deal with. Therefore, we should march at the head of the people and then the people will follow us and respect us.

Had we, yielding to the sentiments prevailing among the people, allowed ourselves to be carried away by certain passionate sectors of the population and refused to come to a reasonable agreement with the U.S. government, then a war could have broken out, in the course of which millions of people would have died and the survivors would have pinned the blame on the leaders for not having taken all the necessary measures to prevent the war of annihilation.

Preventing the war and an attack on Cuba depended not just on the measures adopted by our governments but also on an estimate of the actions of the enemy forces deployed near you. Accordingly, the overall situation had to be considered.

In addition, there are opinions that we, as they say, failed to engage in consultations concerning these questions before adopting the decision known to you.

For this reason we believe that we consulted with you, dear Comrade Fidel Castro, receiving the cables, each one more alarming than the previous one, and finally your cable of October 27 [October 26 in Cuba], saying you were nearly certain that an attack on Cuba would be launched. You believed it was merely a question of time, that the attack would take place within the next 24 to 72 hours. Upon receiving this alarming cable from you and aware of your courage, we viewed it as a very well founded alarm.

Wasn't this consultation on your part with us? I have viewed this cable as a signal of extreme alarm. Under the conditions created, also bearing in mind the information that the unabated warmongering group of U.S. militarists wanted to take advantage of the situation that had been created and launch an attack on Cuba. If we had continued our consultations, we would have wasted time and this attack would have been carried out.

We came to the conclusion that our strategic missiles in Cuba became an ominous force for the imperialists: they were frightened and because of their fear that our rockets could be launched, they could have dared to liquidate them by bombing them or launching an invasion of Cuba. And it must be said that they could have knocked them all out. Therefore, I repeat, your alarm was absolutely well-founded.

In your cable of October 27 you proposed that we be the first to launch a nuclear strike against the territory of the enemy. You, of course, realize where that would have led. Rather than a simple strike, it would have been the start of a thermonuclear war.

Dear Comrade Fidel Castro, I consider this proposal of yours incorrect, although I understand your motivation.

We have lived through the most serious moment when a thermonuclear world war could have broken out. Obviously, in that case, the United States would have sustained huge losses, but the Soviet Union and the whole socialist camp would have also suffered greatly. As far as Cuba is concerned, it would be difficult to say even in general terms what this would have meant for them. In the first place, Cuba would have been burned in the fire of war. There is no doubt that the Cuban people would have fought courageously or that they would have died heroically. But we are not struggling against imperialism in order to die, but to take advantage of all our possibilities, to lose less in the struggle and win more to overcome and achieve the victory of communism.

...

Naturally, in defending Cuba as well as the other socialist countries, we can't rely on a U.S. government veto. We have adopted and will continue to adopt in the future all the measures necessary to strengthen our defense and build up our forces, so that we can strike back if needed. At present, as a result of our weapons supplies, Cuba is stronger than ever. Even after the dismantling of the missile installations you will have powerful weapons to throw back the enemy, on land, in the air and on the sea, in the approaches to the island...

...

We feel that the aggressor came out the loser. He made preparations to attack Cuba but we stopped him and forced him to recognize before world public opinion that he won't do it at the current stage. We view this as a great victory...

I wish you success, Comrade Fidel Castro. You will no doubt have success. There will still be machinations against you, but together with you, we will adopt all the measures necessary to paralyze them and continue to the strengthening and development of the Cuban Revolution.

N.S. Khrushchev

* * *

#28

Fidel Castro to Nikita S. Khrushchev

October 31, 1962[9]

"we knew . . . we would have been annihilated."

Fidel is spending about half of Monday October 29th preparing for the visit on the following day of acting UN Secretary General U Thant. He meets with Jorge Enrique Mendoza, who has the second most famous voice on the island of Cuba, after Fidel. Mendoza was the voice of Radio Rebelde (Rebel Radio) *during the Revolution against Batista, and he continues in that role now, even though he has many added administrative responsibilities, overseeing all the Cuban media. Many who know Mendoza believe that he consciously tries to imitate the voice of Fidel, just as he has many of the* comandante en jefe's *mannerisms—such as putting a finger in the air and over his head, to emphasize a point, and waving his hands furiously together then apart, as if each hand is at war with the other.*

Fidel tells Mendoza to work up several programs on the U Thant visit: the secretary general will meet with Fidel and other Cuban officials; he will be briefed on the missile disassembly and re-crating by the Russian field commander; Fidel will report to the nation on radio and television on November 1st, the day after U Thant's departure, on what has happened between Cuba and the UN leader. Fidel has one caveat: Mendoza is to be absolutely straightforward about the Cuban position on UN inspection of Soviet missile sites in Cuba—we Cubans are not slippery and deceitful, like the Russians. There will be no inspections, Fidel says. Cuba will stand up for its rights and its dignity and its sovereignty. Mendoza takes it all down. Fidel then sends him on his way, before having a similar conversation with Carlos Franqui, editor of the Cuban daily newspaper, Revolucion. *Mendoza and Franqui pass one another in the room outside Fidel's office. They are rivals for Fidel's attention and they eye each other warily.*

Fidel thinks they must get the tone just right: Cuba welcomes U Thant; Cuba is honored that he has, in this moment of peril, come to Cuba to negotiate with the Cubans; but there will be no on-site inspections on this island. U Thant is from Burma, Fidel muses, he knows all about the heavy hand of British and Japanese imperialism, about the problems small countries have trying to be taken seriously by the great powers. So he will understand why Cuba is adamant about the inspections issue. And if U Thant is clever and creative, as people say he is, then he will find a way to claim that the visit was a success even though he will not get us to agree to inspections on Cuban territory. His musing about the U Thant visit at an end, Fidel tells his driver he wants to go to the Soviet embassy.

In less than ten minutes his jeep pulls into the driveway and is met by both Cuban and Soviet security officers. The ambassador, Aleksander Alekseev, is waiting for him at the entrance to the embassy. Fidel hollers his customary, "Que pasa, Alejandro?" ("How are things, Alexander?") Alekseev responds to his friend in kind, with a phrase for which he is becoming famous in Havana: "Fidel, las cosas van de mal en peor!" ("Fidel, things are going from bad to worse!") Once inside, sipping strong coffee, Fidel discovers what is now troubling Alekseev. "Fidel," he says, "you know how much I am in love with your Revolution, with your whole glorious project here on this isle of freedom. And you also know that I am here to serve as a go-between for you and Nikita Sergei'ich—that is mainly how I spend my time, trying to make sure the two of you understand each other. Yes, there is a language barrier, but that is not the main problem. The main problem is—Fidel, please sit down, won't you?" Fidel has been pacing back and forth, as he listens to the man the Cubans know simply as Alejandro, or occasionally, "Don Alejandro," Russia's greatest friend of the Revolution. "Okay, sure," Fidel responds. "What's up?"

Alekseev finally gets to the point: "I want you and Nikita Sergei'ich to declare a moratorium on writing to each other, now that the crisis has reached a somewhat less intense phase. Every time you two write to each other, the misunderstandings increase, you both get angry and the accusations fly. As you are well aware, Nikita Sergei'ich thinks you are hotheaded, immature, and, well, I really believe he thinks you are occasionally suicidal. But he is also stubborn—like you—and he is confident that if he continues to lecture you about how to behave as a leader, then in the end you will be, well, you will be a good Russian!"

Before Alejandro's line about becoming a "good Russian," Fidel was just about to tell his friend that he had more important things to do than be lectured by the Russians—any Russian, but especially Khrushchev (channeled by Alekseev), who at the moment is his least favorite Russian. But Fidel smiles at the image of himself as a Russian: short, with blond hair, a thick neck, and standing like a vertical corpse on top of Lenin's tomb, as thousands of other short, blond, thick-necked soldiers go goose-stepping by. "Look, Alejandro," Fidel says, "I know what you mean. I know that Comrade Nikita and I are on different wavelengths, I know that he and I …"

"YOU AND NIKITA SERGEI'ICH ARE TOO MUCH LIKE EACH OTHER!" Alekseev blurts out. "I'm sorry for the outburst, but neither of you will ever cease on your own until you convince your antagonist of the correctness of your views. But this means your argument with Nikita Sergei'ich will go on forever. And unfortunately for me, the argument—in both directions—goes through me. And although I am a Russian and I serve my Russian masters in Moscow, you know, Fidel, that I am more Cuban than Russian—except for your baseball, which makes no sense to me, and your cigars, which do not give me as much pleasure as my cigarettes—with these two exceptions, I am a Cuban. This is why I am counseling you to back off, let Nikita Sergei'ich do the same, and revisit your differences on some future face-to-face encounter, perhaps in the Soviet Union, once this crisis has passed."

Fidel is sympathetic to Alekseev's point. In corresponding with Khrushchev, he has felt as if he is knocking his head against a brick wall. "All right, Alejandro," Fidel responds, "I will agree to your moratorium, on one condition: that the moratorium will go into effect after *I try one more time to clarify Cuba's position to him. In his letter, which you have seen—which just arrived and is dated today, the 30ᵗʰ, he is patronizing and condescending—don't you agree?" Fidel notes that Alekseev nods his agreement. Fidel continues: "Why can he not grasp the strategy of little peoples, like us Cubans? Why can he not see that unlike the Soviet Union, we can only rely on our supreme commitment to the Revolution and its integrity— our willingness to die for our cause. That is really all we have, when compared to the USSR and the U.S.*

"Alejandro," Fidel says in a suddenly barely audible and conspiratorial tone of voice, "let me refine my argument a little bit and then you tell me whether I should try one last time to convey my argument to Comrade Nikita. Okay? Here goes: we Cubans are not crazy, not suicidal. We do not seek to destroy ourselves. But we are small, relatively powerless in ordinary military terms, and we therefore have to rely on our moral missiles, our missiles of courage, our willingness to risk everything for what we believe in." As Fidel's voice continues to increase in volume, Alekseev understands that he has no choice in the matter: Fidel will now practice his argument on him; and he will then send another letter to Khrushchev, which will aggravate the situation even further, necessitating still more intercession by Alekseev, if Khrushchev insists on replying. Thus resigned, Alekseev bites his lip, forces a smile and says, "Fidel, I give you permission to go ahead."

"Look, Alejandro," Fidel says, "this is what I want to say. We Cubans had two options, once it became clear that Kennedy was dead set on destroying our Revolution. We saw it coming right after Girón *[the Bay of Pigs]. So did Comrade*

Nikita. Okay. Now we could choose option one: which is to wait and cringe and
count the days until the Americans invade and occupy our country, as they have
so many times in the past. Sure, we would fight, and resist and take as many of
the gringo bastards with us as possible. But the ultimate outcome is assured. We
can resist them but we cannot vanquish them. They know this, and that is why we
cannot deter them from attacking us. They do not fear us.

"But comrade Nikita's offer of nuclear missiles gave us a second option: we
could face the danger directly and provoke a crisis in which the Soviet Union's
security interests were at risk every bit as much as ours—I am talking about a
nuclear crisis, a crisis in which the world might disappear in the flames of Arma-
geddon. Our hope was—are you listening, Alejandro?— that Washington and
Moscow are not suicidal, and that they come to their senses and call off their
nuclear war before it starts. It is risky, of course. The world might have been
destroyed by American and Soviet nuclear bombs. But that is the option we pre-
ferred—to risk everything, on the chance that Kennedy and his people would be
too scared to threaten us anymore, because in threatening to destroy us, he would
also be threatening to destroy the Soviet Union. But that would have put the U.S.
at risk of being attacked by Soviet nuclear missiles. That was more or less how we
approached the crisis. And I would emphasize: this was the thinking of the entire
leadership and of the Cuban people.

"Now, why are we angry with Comrade Nikita and his associates? We are
angry at the moment with the Soviet Union because of the way we are being
treated—as an afterthought, as not having interests of our own, as a country
that just does not really matter—this is the way the gringos have treated us for a
hundred years. This is imperialism and, Comrade Nikita is an imperialist when
he treats us this way, as he has done by refusing to consult with us about how we
would prefer to see the crisis end—by refusing to include our demands in any deal
he makes with Kennedy.

"What do you think, Alejandro? Will Comrade Nikita understand and accept
this?"

"I see," Alekseev says, feigning a pensive face. "You want to tell Nikita
Sergei'ich that, in your view, he is an insane imperialist, and you want him to
write back and say, 'thank you for pointing this out to me—I never really thought
about it this way before.'" Both men smile at this. Alekseev understands that Fi-
del is not really asking him whether he should write such a letter to Khrushchev;
Fidel is instead declaring his intent to send such a letter to Khrushchev. Fidel
will continue to express his anger and his frustration, just as Nikita Sergei'ich
has expressed his anger and frustration to Fidel. Fidel will imply that Khrushchev
is mentally sluggish, patronizing and condescending. Fidel will be eloquent and
elegant, as always, but also as always, Nikita Sergei'ich will not accept a word of
it. But Alekseev feels that Nikita Sergei'ich is sufficiently keen on bringing Cuba
into the Soviet bloc for the long haul that if Fidel avoids extreme language and
concludes with an expression of gratitude for Soviet assistance, a moratorium on

the war of letters between Moscow and Havana is possible. Alekseev believes he has
already convinced Nikita Sergei'ich that Fidel must be dealt with in person, not
in letters. Alekseev says, finally, still smiling, "Fidel, if Nikita Sergei'ich had any
hair, he would tear it out after reading the argument you have just articulated to
me. Just make sure you thank him at the end of the letter."

They both laugh and embrace. Fidel then heads out the door, climbs into his
jeep, and tells his driver to head back to his command post. First he will make
some notes about the letter he wants to write to Khrushchev, which he plans to
draft in two days' time, after U Thant has gone back to New York. He plans to
write the letter right after U Thant's departure on the 31ˢᵗ. He knows it will be
a difficult letter—as difficult, in its way, as his letter of October 26ᵗʰ, urging
Khrushchev to launch a nuclear attack on the U.S. if the Americans invade Cuba.
How, Fidel wonders, can I say what needs to be said without seeming to be crazy,
and without seeming ungrateful for all Khrushchev has done for us? How do I
say "thank you" to a friend we really need to keep, but whom we also think has
betrayed our country?

Dear Comrade Khrushchev:

I received your letter of October 30. You understand that we were
indeed consulted before you adopted the decision to withdraw the
strategic missiles. You base yourself on the alarming news that you say
reached you from Cuba and, finally, my cable of October 27. I don't
know what news you received. I can only respond for the message that I
sent you the evening of October 26, which reached you the 27th.

What we did in the face of events, Comrade Khrushchev, was to prepare ourselves and get ready to fight. In Cuba there was only one kind
of alarm, that of battle stations.

When in our opinion the imperialist attack became imminent I
deemed it appropriate to so advise you and alert both the Soviet government and command—since there were Soviet forces committed to fight at
our side to defend the Republic of Cuba from foreign aggression—about
the possibility of an attack which we could not prevent but could resist.

I told you that the morale of our people was very high and that the
aggression would be heroically resisted. At the end of the message I reiterated to you that we awaited the events calmly.

Danger couldn't impress us, for danger has been hanging over our country for a long time now and in a certain way we have grown used to it.

The Soviet troops which have been at our side know how admirable
the stand of our people was throughout this crisis and the profound
brotherhood that was created among the troops from both peoples during the decisive hours. Countless eyes of Cuban and Soviet men who
were willing to die with supreme dignity shed tears upon learning about

the surprising, sudden and practically unconditional decision to withdraw the weapons.

Perhaps you don't know the degree to which the Cuban people were ready to do their duty toward the nation and humanity.

I realized when I wrote them that the words contained in my letter could be misinterpreted by you and that was what happened, perhaps because you didn't read them carefully, perhaps because of the translation, perhaps because I meant to say so much in too few lines. However, I didn't hesitate to do it. Do you believe, Comrade Khrushchev, that we were selfishly thinking of ourselves, of our generous people willing to sacrifice themselves, and not at all in an unconscious manner but fully assured of the risk they ran?

No, Comrade Khrushchev. Few times in history, and it could even be said that never before, because no people had ever faced such a tremendous danger, was a people so willing to fight and die with such a universal sense of duty.

We knew, and do not presume that we ignored it, that we would have been annihilated, as you insinuate in your letter, in the event of nuclear war. However, that didn't prompt us to ask you to withdraw the missiles, that didn't prompt us to ask you to yield. Do you believe we wanted that war? But how could we prevent it if the invasion took place? The fact is that this event was possible, that imperialism was obstructing every solution and that its demands were, from our point of view, impossible for the USSR and Cuba to accept.

And if war had broken out, what could we do with the insane people who unleashed the war? You yourself have said that under current conditions such a war would inevitably have escalated quickly into a nuclear war.

I understand that once aggression is unleashed, one shouldn't concede to the aggressor the privilege of deciding, moreover, when to use nuclear weapons. The destructive power of this weaponry is so great and the speed of its delivery so great that the aggressor would have a considerable initial advantage.

And I did not suggest to you, Comrade Khrushchev, that the USSR should be the aggressor, because that would be more than incorrect, it would be immoral and contemptible on my part. But from the instant the imperialists attack Cuba and while there are Soviet armed forces stationed in Cuba to help in our defense in case of an attack from abroad, the imperialists would by this act become aggressors against Cuba and against the USSR, and we would respond with a strike that would annihilate them.

Everyone has his own opinions and I maintain mine about the dangerousness of the aggressive circles in the Pentagon and their preference for a preventive strike. I did not suggest, Comrade Khrushchev, that in the midst of this crisis the Soviet Union should attack, which is what your letter seems to say; rather, that following an imperialist attack, the USSR should act without vacillation and should never make the mistake of allowing circumstances to develop in which the enemy makes the first nuclear strike against the USSR. And in this sense, Comrade Khrushchev, I maintain my point of view, because I understand it to be a true and just evaluation of a specific situation. You may be able to convince me that I am wrong, but you can't tell me that I am wrong without convincing me.

I know that this is a delicate issue that can only be broached in circumstances such as these and in a very personal message.

You may wonder what right I have to broach this topic. I do so without worrying about how thorny it is, following the dictates of my conscience as a revolutionary duty and inspired by the most unselfish sentiments of admiration and affection for the USSR, for what she represents for the future of humanity and by the concern that she should never again be the victim of the perfidy and betrayal of aggressors …

We will struggle against adverse circumstances, we will overcome the current difficulties and we will come out ahead, and nothing can destroy the ties of friendship and the eternal gratitude we feel toward the USSR.

Fraternally,
Fidel Castro

ACT IV

Squeeze

October 30, 1962–November 20, 1962

Theatrical Preview

[Kennedy and Khrushchev are deep in conversation as they circle the bottom of the spiral staircase, at the base of which Fidel sits in his modified Buddha pose. Their conversation is indistinct, but certain words can be heard repetitively. They speak in unison, as if they were chanting. They do not appear to be particularly agitated, but are instead merely intense, as they work through the program of what needs to happen to fully end the Cuban crisis.]

    NIKITA SERGEI'ICH AND JACK: Blah blah blah overflights; blah blah blah onsite inspection; blah blah blah dismantle the quarantine; blah, blah, blah offensive weapons; blah, blah, blah defensive weapons.

[All of a sudden, Castro stands up and begins speaking loudly and distinctly, gesticulating furiously with his hands and arms.]

    FIDEL: Excuse me, fellas, but I guess you didn't hear what I said: *there will be no onsite inspections on the island of Cuba by anyone who is not a Cuban!* We will endorse no violations of our sovereignty. We will allow the removal of the missiles by the Soviets, but nothing beyond that. We will resist all such attempts to compromise our sovereignty and destroy our dignity. Anyone coming to this island to "inspect" anything had better come well armed, because we will shoot to kill. Did you hear me this time, O leaders of the superpowers? No inspections!

    JACK: [To Khrushchev.] Hey wait a minute, Mr. Chairman, you and I agreed to onsite inspection—we have got to have inspection rights or our deal won't wash domestically. After all, you lied to me for many months about putting the missiles into Cuba; now we must have a way of verifying that you are doing what you said you would do—which is remove the missiles from Cuba.

NIKITA SERGEI'ICH: I know, I know, but we haven't been able to get Fidel to agree to it yet. He's being stubborn again. Give us some time to work on him, will you? Meantime, please stop the over-flights—they really piss off Fidel and the Cubans. Oh, and you may as well dismantle the quarantine while you are at it. Trust me, Mr. President, we'll get Fidel to come around. By taking down the quarantine immediately, you will facilitate our efforts to talk some sense into him.

JACK: No way can we do that, Mr. Chairman. We have to see hard evidence that the withdrawal is complete before we can take down the quarantine.

[Both Jack and Nikita Sergei'ich now re-ascend the spiral staircase, as their argument heats up. By the time they are halfway to the top they begin shouting at one another.]

NIKITA SERGEI'ICH: But, Mr. President, I have already told you that Fidel hasn't agreed to the conditions yet. He will, he will. But he needs time. Fidel is difficult.

JACK: [Raising his voice.] That is your problem, not ours. I must warn you, Mr. Chairman, that I don't know how long I can constrain the hawks in my administration, in the Congress and the general population. Until you actually carry out what you have agreed to, we will remain at our very high state of war-readiness.

[The argument appears to be getting out of hand, with both men edging ever closer to the precipice. As they get nearer to the precipice, the staircase begins to spin, as before, and the noise of the maelstrom becomes progressively louder, also as before.]

JACK: By the way, Mr. Chairman, you are going to have to withdraw your IL-28 nuclear-capable bombers from Cuba as well, along with some other systems we regard as offensive.

NIKITA SERGEI'ICH: [Appearing stunned.] What? Wait a minute, we only agreed to withdraw the missiles. You said they are "offensive"—you are wrong, but never mind—so we agreed to withdraw them.

JACK: Sorry, Mr. Chairman, but you agreed in your letter to me of October 27th to remove, and I quote, "the weapons you [meaning we, the Americans] regard as offensive." Those are *your* words. And those IL-28 bombers can reach deeply into the American heartland—in an offensive mode. So they are going to have to come out. It is non-negotiable. You already agreed to it, as I have just demonstrated.

NIKITA SERGEI'ICH: Mr. President, why are you complicating things like this? Why are you squeezing me—just to see how much you can get away with?

JACK: Look, Mr. Chairman, I am getting squeezed harder than you can imagine by my hawks. Day and night, they badger me, urging me to bomb Cuba to smithereens, throw you Russians off the island for good, and eliminate the Castro regime for good. They tell me this is a golden opportunity, that they have had enough "political talk," as they put it. Now they say it is time to turn the military loose on Cuba. The pressure is very, very intense. Just talking about it is nerve-wracking.

NIKITA SERGEI'ICH: Okay, Mr. President, I am sorry to hear about your problem with the American hawks. And yes, I did say that we would remove the weapons you say are offensive. I admit it. Okay, I will send our best negotiator, Anastas Ivan'ich Mikoyan, to Havana and instruct him to bring Fidel around to the deal you and I have agreed to. [Turning away from Kennedy, and stares off into the distance.] Anastas Ivan'ich, good luck on your mission. [Turns back to Kennedy.] Poor man. What a mission.

[The stage is dark and silent for ten seconds.]

FIDEL: Comrade Nikita: sorry, but I did not agree to any of this. Cuba chooses to preserve its sovereignty and dignity, rather than accept slavery at the hands of either or both of the superpowers. Therefore, Comrade Nikita, we will soon begin shooting down the low-level U.S. reconnaissance planes. Get used to it: you are dealing with proud Cubans, not with passive, subservient East Germans or Poles.

NIKITA SERGEI'ICH: Oh my God! That's it. I have had it with Fidel. He still wants to die beautifully, apparently, rather than preserve his country under socialism. [Turns toward Kennedy.] Okay, Mr. President, we will withdraw the IL-28 bombers, no matter what Fidel says. The hell with Fidel. Consider it done, in less than thirty days.

JACK: That is what I want to hear, Mr. Chairman. For our part, we will dismantle the naval quarantine of Cuba; and we will cease the low-level over-flights that Castro objects to, at least for now. And by the way, Mr. Chairman, since we still need daily reassurance—well, our hawks need it more than I do—since we still have to inspect the island in some fashion, what would you say if we limited the high-level U-2 flights to one a day, if you will instruct the crews of your surface-to-air missile sites in Cuba to ignore us and hold their fire?

NIKITA SERGEI'ICH: Yes, of course, Mr. President. You have a deal. At last this crisis is over. Just imagine, you and I, after all we have been through together, have six more years to try to end this dangerous Cold War and eliminate nuclear weapons from the face of the earth.

JACK: [laughing.] Only if I get reelected two years from now. And you know, I have made one helluva lot of enemies in the past couple of years because—this may interest you, Mr. Chairman—because, frankly I have not authorized an air attack and an invasion of Cuba. In fact, I have some crazies in Washington who are even angry with me because I didn't authorize a pre-emptive attack on the Soviet Union.

NIKITA SERGEI'ICH: [Stands silent, following Kennedy's comment, staring at Kennedy, shaking his head back and forth.] I know what you mean. The vultures are circling in Moscow as well. But I know who they are. They don't dare oppose me. And I will make sure that I stay healthy—important at my age, 68—so that you and I can build on having successfully faced down our hawks and saved the human race. And that is just what we did, Mr. President. We saved the human race. Now we must eliminate the Cold War conditions and the weapons that brought about the crisis.

[Khrushchev then begins to descend the spiral staircase, which has now stopped spinning. The roar of the maelstrom has ceased as well.]

NIKITA SERGEI'ICH: [Turns to Kennedy, with outstretched hand.] Come, my friend. We have work to do. [Kennedy shakes his outstretched hand. They descent the stairs together, carefully avoiding Castro, who ignores them as they pass by.]

End of Theatrical Preview

* * *

#29

Nikita S. Khrushchev to John F. Kennedy

October 30, 1962[1]

> *"people have felt . . . the flames of thermonuclear war"*

It is Tuesday in the Kremlin, forty-eight hours after the miraculous Sunday on which Nikita Sergei'ich received the message from Kennedy that the crisis over the missiles in Cuba was over. "Well," as Nikita Sergei'ich reflects alone in his office, "that is what I allowed myself to believe on Sunday: that all would be well now that Kennedy and I have made a deal. He pledges not to invade Cuba; I pledge to remove the missiles. Done! Beautiful!"

But what a difference a couple of days makes. Nikita Sergei'ich now sees that his optimism on Sunday was possible only because, for a moment, he managed to forget about Fidel Castro—hotheaded, high-strung, hypersensitive, moody Fidel Castro. Nikita Sergei'ich now feels he has merely exchanged one terrible fear for another: his fear of an insane nuclear war between the Soviets and the Americans has been replaced by the fear that his possibly crazy protégé, Fidel Castro, may ruin everything Nikita Sergei'ich and Kennedy have accomplished. Fidel might still reverse this October miracle. Everything was going fine, he muses, until Fidel told the world (also on Sunday, three hours after the crisis was apparently resolved) that Kennedy and I had, in effect, concocted a superpower deal that excluded Cuba in the give and take leading to the deal—that together we had screwed over Cuba, making Cuba the victim of a superpower plot.

It is unbelievable, Nikita Sergei'ich thinks, that Fidel demands that the Americans give Cuba back Guantanamo, for example, or there will be no deal, and that he will see to it that no deal is possible by preventing onsite inspection on the island of Cuba. Sure, we support this idea, Nikita Sergei'ich admits, but does Fidel really believe the Americans will give him back Guantanamo as part of the deal to end this crisis? If he does, he is out of his mind.

Nikita Sergei'ich's fear and gloom is relieved only when he remembers that his incomparable negotiator and a great Soviet friend of Cuba, Anastas Mikoyan, will be in Cuba in a couple of days to straighten out their young ally and his colleagues. He thinks—he hopes—that Anastas Ivan'ich will make Fidel understand how we— we Soviets, we mature great friends of the young and impetuous Cubans—saved Cuba from annihilation. And that's exactly what we did, he thinks, as he pounds both fists down on his desk at the same time, a gesture for which he is famous all over the world. We saved Fidel's ass and now he is angry because he says we didn't get his permission!

As Nikita Sergei'ich thinks about all the loose ends still hanging over all three countries, he realizes that Kennedy and the Americans may hold the key to dealing successfully with Fidel Castro. He thinks: the damned Americans are going to have to give me something to work with, something to trade, something to offer Fidel in exchange for getting him to agree to some sort of onsite inspection procedure. Kennedy says this is an absolute, non-negotiable demand that must be met before he will stand down his forces and declare an end to the crisis. All right, fine, Nikita Sergei'ich thinks, but Kennedy must help me persuade Fidel by unilaterally removing the blockade. Then it will be obvious, he reasons, even to Fidel that Kennedy is serious about his pledge not to invade Cuba. That might do it. So he decides to write to Kennedy and tell him how much such a gesture would be worth at this moment.

Before calling for his stenographer, however, he is handed the latest summary from his intelligence services, and what he finds in the report gives his decision to write to Kennedy added urgency. The Americans, according to the report, are moving more troops—a lot more troops—into the Caribbean region. Soviet intelligence believes these concentrations of fighting men will be used in any U.S. follow-up to an air attack on the island, should Kennedy order an invasion. In addition, Nikita Sergei'ich discovers that the Americans have not even begun to reduce their war-readiness. In fact, one eyewitness report says that U.S. strategic nuclear missiles at one base stand obscured by the mist of oxygen clouds, presumably "in *preparation for their final fueling and launch." Reading the word "launch" gives him the chills. Nikita Sergei'ich calls his young KGB chief, Vladimir Semichastny, and asks him to confirm what he has just read. His chief spy, alas, does confirm it. It suddenly occurs to Nikita Sergei'ich that unless he and Kennedy find a way to deal successfully with the obstinate Fidel Castro, the crisis could still blow up in their faces. This is what Kennedy needs to understand: that removing the blockade is essential to reaching a resolution. Kennedy must stop squeezing us as a way of squeezing Cuba, or the Khrushchev-Kennedy deal could be remembered as just a missed opportunity, a prelude to Armageddon.*

As he calls for his stenographer, Nadezhda Petrovna, he imagines Kennedy sitting in his White House office as a fundamentally changed man in at least one respect: he knows, and the American people know for the first time, that they are vulnerable to our power. We may not have as many missiles or warheads as the Americans, but we have enough to really scare them and make them negotiate with us as equals. Yes, America, he thinks, even you have to acknowledge from now on that there is another superpower in the world, your equal, whom you must treat with respect, even though it is not an American tradition to treat adversaries with respect. Nikita Sergei'ich finds this thought comforting, though it must coexist in his mind with the constant anxiety he feels regarding what he and Kennedy will do about Fidel Castro if he refuses to agree to the terms of their deal to end the crisis. For Nikita Sergei'ich knows that however much they may try to squeeze Fidel, the Cubans will counter-squeeze to the best of their ability. This scares Nikita Sergei'ich, not just because he knows that Fidel is impossible to predict or control, but also because he suspects Kennedy has no clue about how zealously, creatively, and recklessly Fidel can assert his independence.

As Nadezhda Petrovna prepares to take dictation, Nikita Sergei'ich smiles inwardly, as he imagines a private meeting, sometime in the distant future, when he can tell Kennedy some of the details of what it is really like to deal with Fidel.

Dear Mr. President:

First of all, I would like to express a wish that you already now remove the quarantine without waiting for the procedure for the inspection of ships on which an agreement has been reached to be put into effect. It would be very reasonable on your part. You yourself realize that the quarantine will in fact accomplish nothing since those ships that are now heading for Cuba naturally, after we have agreed on the removal of our missiles from Cuba, do not carry any offensive weapons, but, as I have already stated it publicly and informed you confidentially, any weapons at all. Immediate lift of the quarantine would be a good gesture.
    ...

We, the Soviet people and the peoples of Asian and European countries saw war. War often rolled through our territory. America participated in the two wars but it suffered very small losses in those wars. While huge profits were accumulated as a result of the wars. Of course, it was monopolists who benefitted but workers, working people got something out of it, too. War did not touch the soil of the United States. The American people did not experience destruction, suffering, they only received notifications about deaths of their kin. Now during this crisis, war was knocking at the gates of America.

These, in effect, are my considerations after the crisis situation. I want to tell you that in this crisis, as our saying goes, there is no evil without good. Evil has brought some good. The good is that now people have felt more tangibly the breathing of the burning flames of thermonuclear war and have a more clear realization of the threat looming over them if the arms race is not stopped. And I would say that what has just happened will serve especially good the American people.

...

Having eliminated this crisis we gave each other mutual satisfaction...To our mutual satisfaction we maybe even sacrificed self-esteem. Apparently, there will be such scribblers who will engage in hair-splitting over our agreement, will be digging as to who made greater concessions to whom. As for me, I would say that we both made a concession to reason and found a reasonable solution which enabled us to ensure peace for all including those who will be trying to dig up something.

Sincerely,
N.S. Khrushchev

* * *

#30

John F. Kennedy to Nikita S. Khrushchev

November 3, 1962[2]

"the quarantine can be of assistance to Mr. Mikoyan"

This morning, Jack is pacing back and forth on the veranda outside the White House. He has begun to realize that the Cuban affair has entered a phase that one of his aides has begun calling "the November crisis." As usual, the devil is in the details, he thinks, and the damned details involved in trying to end this crisis are driving him batty. He yearns for the relative simplicity and peace of mind of five days ago, when he and Khrushchev reached their agreement, and before he heard, a few hours later around noon on Sunday, October 28ᵗʰ, that Castro and the Cubans would not permit onsite inspection of the missile sites by anyone—not even neutral or friendly third parties. It has been apparent to Jack since that moment that the Soviets and the Cubans are at loggerheads, with the Soviets on the same side of the onsite inspection issue as the U.S., while the Cubans—stubborn, filled up with themselves, and basically irresponsible—are flashing an index finger at both Washington and Moscow. At times like this, Jack wishes (or almost wishes) he and Khrushchev could talk on the phone or, better yet, meet face-to-face and talk about how to deal with Castro, the fly in the ointment of what is otherwise a better than expected conclusion to one helluva dangerous couple of weeks. Maybe someday, he thinks, but not anytime soon.

It is apparent to Jack from Khrushchev's letter of October 30ᵗʰ that he thinks Jack is just being stubborn and greedy in not agreeing to dismantle the quarantine until onsite inspection take place in Cuba and the removal of the offensive weapons systems is positively confirmed. Jack tells his brother Bobby, who is pacing along side him, that the operative part of Khrushchev's letter might be summarized as, "C'mon, Kennedy, just tell your Navy to leave the Caribbean, and then I will be able to talk some sense into Castro and get him to agree to onsite inspections. Stop being stubborn, and give me a goddamned break, will ya?" Bobby's response is, "Doesn't Khrushchev read the damn newspapers? Does he think Keating and his Republican pals in Congress are kidding when they say that the Kennedy administration won't get a plugged nickel for national defense unless and until we can prove that all the missiles and related stuff has been removed from Cuba?"

"Yeah," Jack tells Bobby, "I guess Khrushchev must think this is all some kind of game and that we are bluffing about the necessity of onsite inspection." Bobby's reference to New York Republican Senator Kenneth Keating reminds Jack of how much he detests this particular senator. Keating has already said publicly that the Russians are not actually removing the missiles, but rather are hiding them in the caves of northern Cuba. With the congressional election in three days, this kind of talk is inflammatory, in addition to being ridiculous. Jack tells Bobby, "Khrushchev must think that I can just ignore the fact that Keating has strong ties to the military establishment and to the Cuban exile community—two groups with a lot of political clout that don't exactly embrace what we have done in dealing with Cuba over the past couple of years."

Bobby then reminds his brother that Anastas Mikoyan has just landed in Cuba. Castro, he says, has made things tough for Mikoyan, by failing to respond positively to U Thant's [October 30–31] mission to Cuba. The UN secretary general proposed several schemes for inspection and the Cubans rejected all of them. Jack says, "Yeah, I know. I feel like my head is caught between an irresistible force and an immovable object: the Republicans and our administration hawks are pushing, pushing, pushing to get onto the island with their fine tooth combs so they can look for Soviet weapons, on the one hand; and, on the other hand, Khrushchev seems totally unwilling to put the hard squeeze on Castro and get him to allow inspectors of some sort onto the island. Maybe Mikoyan can talk some sense into the Cubans. He was clever enough to survive Stalin. Maybe he'll be clever enough to persuade Castro."

Bobby, arms folded, nods and says, "Maybe. But there is no way in hell we can take down the quarantine before inspectors verify the removal of the weapons systems. What if," Bobby adds, "we tried to give Khrushchev a little help by. . . ."

Jack interrupts because he instinctively knows what Bobby is thinking. "Right, that's right, Bobby," he says, "we've got to find a way to help Khrushchev put the squeeze on Castro. We can't do much more than we're doing without actually going to war in Cuba, which for chrissake is what we are trying to avoid. Besides, Castro reacts to everything we do as if it's designed to remove him from power—as if that's all we think about up here." Jack and Bobby smile slyly at each other, briefly, as each recalls the dozens or maybe hundreds of schemes they have heard proposed by various individuals and groups, inside and outside the government, designed to get rid of the Castro regime. Jack continues, "What if we let Khrushchev know, maybe not so subtly, that this is exactly what we are doing, that he and we are on the same team with regard to bringing the Cubans to heel on the inspections issue, and that if Castro can't be brought around, then we may head right back into the gun barrel of nuclear war."

He says, "I need to respond to Khrushchev's letter of a few days ago—where he asks that we take down the quarantine. What if I just tell him straightaway that—how should we put this—that the quarantine line might be used by Mikoyan as leverage to, uh, help me out Ted." [Jack calls on his all-purpose aide and wordsmith, Theodore Sorensen, who has now joined the Kennedy brothers' peripatetic conversation, to complete his thought.]

"Mr. President," Sorensen replies, "why don't we tell Khrushchev that we prefer to leave the quarantine line intact, in part to help Mr. Mikoyan in his negotiations with the Cubans. Unless, Mr. President, you think this is too blatant an approach, too clear that we and the Russians are ganging up on Castro."

Jack replies: "No, not at all. That's perfect. Let's respond just to that part of the letter and hold off responding to Khrushchev's flowery, philosophical stuff for another occasion. Get it drafted and I'll sign off on it."

Jack, with his taste for irony, cannot fail to note the weirdness of what is happening. He, the president of the United States, is about to send a letter to the Soviet Chairman informing him that he prefers to maintain the quarantine—which looks a lot like a blockade, which is an act of war, so some say—in part as a favor to the Soviet vice-premier, just arrived in Cuba, in his efforts to get a stubborn Soviet ally to knuckle under and accept a violation of its sovereignty by international weapons inspectors. Bobby cannot suppress a laugh. Sorensen smiles as well, on his way out the door to go and write the letter. Jack says to Bobby, "I sure as hell hope Keating doesn't discover that you and I are working part-time for the Soviet government."

Dear Mr. Chairman:

I wish to thank you for your letter of October 30. I am commenting now only on a problem raised in your letter that relates to the Cuban affair.

With respect to the quarantine on shipments to Cuba, I am hopeful that arrangements can be worked out quickly by the United Nations which would permit its removal. We were happy to agree to your suggestion that the International Committee of the Red Cross undertake responsibility for inspection. You are, of course, aware that Premier Castro has announced his opposition to measures of verification on the territory of Cuba. If he maintains this position this would raise very serious problems. So far as incoming shipments are concerned, I understand that efforts are being made to have the International Red Cross carry out the necessary measures at sea and I hope that these will be successful. In the meantime, perhaps the existence of the quarantine can be of assistance to Mr. Mikoyan in his negotiations with Premier Castro. I should also like to point out that in an effort to facilitate matters, I instructed our delegation in New York to inform your representative there, Mr. Kuznetsov, that for the next few days any Soviet ships in the quarantine area would be passed without inspection…

I am hopeful we can dispose of this pressing matter so that we can go on in a better atmosphere to the broader questions. We both must make our best efforts to this end.

Sincerely,

John F. Kennedy

* * *

#31

Nikita S. Khrushchev to John F. Kennedy

November 4 1962[3]

"Why start now . . . complicating the situation?"

Nikita Sergei'ich has a good laugh when he reads Kennedy's comment that he has decided to leave the blockade line intact to provide assistance to Anastas Ivan'ich in his negotiations with Castro. He appreciates Kennedy's sense of humor and irony, two characteristics in which Nikita Sergei'ich believes he is also not lacking. Unfortunately, the refusal to dismantle the quarantine is unlikely to be helpful to Anastas Ivan'ich in Cuba. Nevertheless, the point is made and understood by Nikita Sergei'ich: he and Kennedy are in the same boat and if they are not careful, Fidel Castro can still sink it.

His secretary informs him that his Foreign Minister Andrei Gromyko has asked to see him about an urgent matter related to Cuba. He asks that Gromyko be let in. Andrei Andrei'ich is not his favorite adviser. But, Gromyko—obsequious, and often mysterious, even a little weird in his presence—is nevertheless efficient and is proving to be a dogged representative of Soviet interests around the world. Nikita Sergei'ich has heard via one of Gromyko's aides that the

Americans refer to Andrei Andrei'ich as "Old Stone Face," which makes Nikita Sergei'ich laugh out loud whenever he thinks about what it must be like to face the enigmatical foreign minister as an adversary. Nikita Sergei'ich is thankful that he will never have a problem often complained about by the Americans— Andrei Andrei'ich's tendency to speak for an hour or more, without interruption, with sequential translation, as his interlocutors drift off into a twilight zone of semi-consciousness. On the contrary, Nikita Sergei'ich can sometimes barely get him to speak at all. He is the living embodiment of a principle he is said to teach at the Soviet Foreign Ministry's School of International Relations: "one error of commission is more dangerous than a thousand errors of omission." It occurs to Nikita Sergei'ich at this moment, as it has many times before, that if he were a student at a school run on Andre Andrei'ich's principle, he would probably be expelled on his first day.

Andrei Andrei'ich looks glum as he walks through the doorway, but then, Nikita Sergei'ich thinks, he always looks glum, so maybe the news isn't as bad as his face indicates it might be. But this time the news really is cause for gloom. Andrei Andrei'ich has brought with him Anastas Ivan'ich's report of his discussions in New York with the U.S. delegation negotiating an end to the Cuban crisis with the Soviet representatives. The foreign minister delivers the news orally, after handing Nikita Sergei'ich a copy of the written report. Two aspects of the report send Nikita Sergei'ich spiraling into anger at Kennedy and the Americans. In the first place, the report says the Americans treated Anastas Ivan'ich as an enemy. They seem to have gone out of their way to insult him, during and immediately after the conversations in New York. "Goddamned arrogant Americans," Nikita Sergei'ich bursts out.

"Exactly my feeling, Nikita Sergei'ich. Exactly."

"Yes, well, of course, it would be," Nikita Sergei'ich replies, leaving it to his obsequious foreign minister to interpret this remark as he wishes.

But a second part of the report is truly disturbing. Not once, but twice, the American representatives tried to force him to accept a list of new American demands that were presented as non-negotiable. Not only has Kennedy refused to dismantle the quarantine. Now he and his henchmen in New York have indicated that in addition to demanding the removal of the strategic missiles and their associated equipment, they are now saying that the IL-28 light bombers and a half-dozen other weapons systems must be removed. They are now labeling these weapons as "offensive," and therefore subject to the terms of the Khrushchev-Kennedy deal. Nikita Sergei'ich repeats the terms of the deal to Andrei Andrei'ich, who stares at him with his usual irritating, blank look of supplication. "But the deal," he says, "is clear: we Soviets remove the missiles; the Americans pledge not to invade Cuba. Isn't that it, Andrei Andrei'ich?"

"Not exactly, if I may say so. In your letter to Kennedy, I believe you said that 'we agree to remove the weapons you regard as offensive,' or words to that effect." Silence now descends on both men.

"Are you saying," Nikita Sergei'ich asks rhetorically, "that I walked into a trap of my own making? Is that what you are saying?"

"No, no, no, Nikita Sergei'ich. I would say that Kennedy, in the arrogant, pushy way of the Americans, is seeking to exploit a verbal distinction to his own advantage."

Nikita Sergei'ich mulls this over. He has little interest in the verbal game—who is allowed to call which weapons "offensive," and so on. The point of importance is that if the Americans are serious about adding the IL-28 bombers to the list of "offensive" weapons that have to be removed, Anastas Ivan'ich's task in Cuba has just been made even more difficult than it already was. We will have to—God help us!—actually consult with the Cubans about this, or at least pretend to consult with the Cubans, regarding the American demand that we remove the IL-28s. Of course, Fidel will have a fit, and of course Anastas Ivan'ich will have to deal with him.

Nikita Sergei'ich notices, as he emerges from his reflection, that Andrei Andrei'ich is once again staring at him in silence. Nikita Sergei'ich continues his reflection aloud. "You know, those IL-28s aren't worth a damn, anyway. We were only going to use them for scrap metal, before we shipped them to Cuba. But I thought Kennedy and I had established a new kind of relationship on the basis of having gone through the Cuban crisis together—resolving it together. I guess I have deceived myself. Anyway, who cares? I am like the man who hands his empty wallet to a thief, who does not yet know there is nothing of value in it." For now, however, I think I had better send Kennedy a letter explaining how we feel about the addition of the IL-28s to the list of offensive weapons—why it is ridiculous and so on."

"That is exactly what I would do, Nikita Sergei'ich," Gromyko says in his deep droning bass voice. "Exactly."

Nikita Sergei'ich, irritated by both Kennedy's demand and Gromyko's demeanor, does not respond to his foreign minister. He merely waves toward the door and tells Gromyko to send in Nadezhda Petrovna, as he is ready to dictate a letter.

Dear Mr. President:

I have just received information from Mr. V. Kuznetsov, our representative at the negotiations in New York for liquidation of the tense situation around Cuba, that Mr. Stevenson handed him a list of weapons which your side calls offensive. I have studied the list and, I must confess, the approach of the American side to this matter has seriously worried me. In such a move, I will say frankly, I see a wish to complicate the situation, because it is impossible indeed to place into the category of "offensive" such types of weapons which have always been referred to as defensive weapons even by a man uneducated militarily—by a common soldier, not to say of an officer.

...

I think you will understand me correctly. For you and I have to deal not only with elimination of the remnants of the present tension—there lies ahead for you and me a great, serious talk on other questions. Why then start now complicating the situation by minor things? Maybe there exist some considerations, but they are beyond our comprehension. As for us, we view the introduction of additional demands as a wish to bring our relations back again into a heated state in which they were but several days ago.
Sincerely,
N.S. Khrushchev

* * *

#32

John F. Kennedy to Nikita S. Khrushchev

November 6, 1962[4]

> *"withdrawal of the missiles and bombers is essential."*

"It looks as if our friend Khrushchev doesn't get it yet with regard to the IL-28 bombers," Jack says to his brother Bobby and several other aides gathered in the Oval Office. "He claims in this letter dated November 4ᵗʰ that we have just gratuitously added the bombers to the list—as if we hadn't given fair warning to the Soviets that we regard the bombers as offensive weapons, given that they can carry nuclear bombs and are basically useless for defense of the island. What do you make of it, Bobby?"

"Two things," Bobby responds. "Number one, Khrushchev doesn't have a leg to stand on. The issue of the IL-28s is not new. They are alluded to in the September 4ᵗʰ statement you issued about how we would respond if offensive weapons were found to be in Cuba. And since November 1ˢᵗ or thereabouts our low-level recon flights have been overflying both the missile sites and the IL-28 airfields to monitor progress on dismantling of both weapons systems. They know this. No, it is too late to turn back on the bomber issue. We had that big discussion in a meeting a couple of days ago and we agreed—you agreed—that the bombers have to come out. Period. So I think Khrushchev is just grasping at straws here, trying to save face."

Jack thinks about what Bobby has said. Bobby usually sees things more or less the way Jack does, except Bobby sees things in sharper relief, mostly in blacks and whites, whereas Jack, at least in his own mind, tends to see more gray areas. "Bobby, I agree with you," Jack says, "but we have to be careful not to push Khrushchev into a corner. He needs to be able to save face. After all, he is in a helluva tough situation at the moment, trying to bring Castro into line, and maybe looking over his shoulder at his own hardliners, who think he chickened out when he struck the deal with us to end the crisis."

"Right," Bobby responds, "but I just don't think giving him the bombers back is the way to help Khrushchev save face. Now, that brings me to my second point. We put a lot of things on that laundry list that the Stevenson group handed Mikoyan and Kuznetsov in New York the other day—a lot of hardware, in addition to the missiles and bombers. Why can't you say to Khrushchev: 'sorry, the bombers have to come out. But if we can agree on that much, then we would be willing to consider dropping some of the other items on the list, like the patrol boats, ground-to-air missiles, and so on.'"

Jack asks the others in the room what they think of Bobby's idea. After all of them nod their approval, Jack says, feigning seriousness, "What are you, a bunch of 'yes-men' in the Kennedys' politburo?" This cracks everybody up except Ted Sorensen who, while not lacking a sense of humor, even now does not, after working with the Kennedys for ten years, know whether certain of their remarks are uttered in jest or in earnest. Sorensen is especially mystified by Jack's frequent references to Ivy League culture, Irish history and culture, women in general, and sex in particular. Jack says, "Ted, what do you think? You're our favorite Russian in this politburo." (Sorensen's family, on his mother's side, had migrated to the U.S. in the late nineteenth century from Russia.)

Somewhat sheepishly, the naturally shy and reserved Nebraskan, Sorensen, says without smiling, "da," which sends everyone in the room into hysterical laughter, including Jack and Bobby.

"Okay, then, Ted," Jack says, "why don't you go ahead and pull a draft together." As Jack thinks about what to do, he knows he must make sure Sorensen finds room in there to say that we have not forgotten the issue of onsite inspection—of both the missile sites and bomber airfields. In fact, this is a much more serious issue, potentially, than the IL-28s. Khrushchev probably doesn't give a damn whether he leaves those useless old bombers in Cuba or not. So he'll probably find a way to let Castro know that they are coming out. But the issue of onsite inspections is one he can't solve without Castro's agreement. He doesn't think Khrushchev wants to get into a shooting match with the Cubans over this or any other issue. But he has got to put a harder squeeze on Castro on the inspections issue, along with squeezing the bombers out of Cuba at the same time.

As the meeting breaks up, Jack says, "Ted, make damn sure Khrushchev knows how we feel about the inspections issue. The Republicans and other hawks are going to eat us for lunch if we can't provide proof that the offensive weapons systems are coming out of Cuba."

Dear Mr. Chairman:

I am surprised that in your letter, which I received yesterday, you suggest that in giving your representative in New York a list of the weapons we consider offensive there was any desire on our part to complicate the situation. Our intention was just the opposite: to stick to a well-known list, and not to introduce any new factors. But there is really only one major item on the list, beyond the missiles and their equipment, and that is the light bombers and their equipment. This item is indeed of great importance to us.

...

Your letter says—and I agree—that we should not complicate the situation with minor things. But I assure you that this matter of the IL-28s is not a minor matter for us at all. It is true, of course, that these bombers are not the most modern of weapons, but they are distinctly capable of offensive use against the United States and other Western Hemispheric countries, and I am sure your own military men would inform you that the continued existence of such bombers in Cuba would require substantial measures of military defense by the United States. Thus, in simple logic these are weapons capable of offensive use. But there is more in it than that, Mr. Chairman. These bombers could carry nuclear weapons for long distances, and they are clearly not needed, any more than missiles, for purely defensive purposes on the island of Cuba. Thus in the present context their continued presence would sustain the grave tension that has been created, and their removal, in my view, is necessary to a good start on ending the recent crisis.

...

These recent events have given a profound shock to relations between our two countries. It may be said, as Mr. Kuznetsov said the other day to Mr. McCloy, that the Soviet Union was under no obligation to inform us of any activities it was carrying on in a third country. I cannot accept this view; not only did this action threaten the whole safety of this hemisphere, but it was, in a broader sense, an attempt to change the worldwide *status quo*. Secret action of this kind seems to me both hazardous and unjustified. But however one may judge that argument, what actually happened in this case was not simply that the action of your side was secret. Your government repeatedly gave us assurances of what it was *not* doing; these assurances were announced as coming from the highest levels, and they proved inaccurate.

...

In the aftermath of this shock, to which we replied with a measured but necessary response, I believe it is vital that we should reestablish some degree of confidence in communication between the two of us. If the leaders of the two great nuclear powers cannot judge with some accuracy the intentions of each other, we shall find ourselves in a period of gravely increasing danger—not only for our two countries but for the whole world.

...

I should emphasize to you directly, Mr. Chairman, that in this respect there is another problem immediately ahead of us which could become very serious indeed, and that is the problem of continuing verification in Cuba. Your representatives have spoken as if this were entirely a problem for the Castro regime to settle, but the continuing verification of the absence of offensive weapons in Cuba is an essential safeguard for the United States and the other countries of this hemisphere, and is an explicit condition for the undertakings which we in our turn have agreed to. The need for this verification is, I regret to say, convincingly demonstrated by what happened in Cuba in the months of September and October.

...

In the immediate situation, however, I repeat that it is the withdrawal of the missiles and bombers, with their supporting equipment, under adequate verification, and with a proper system for continued safeguards in the future, that is essential. This is the first necessary step away from the crisis to open the door through which we move to restore confidence and give attention to other problems which ought to be resolved in the interest of peace.

Sincerely,
John F. Kennedy

* * *

#33

Nikita S. Khrushchev to John F. Kennedy

November 11, 1962[5]

"we will remove the IL-28 planes . . . not now but later."

Nikita Sergei'ich has called a meeting of the Presidium for 10:00 a.m. on November 10th. The goddamned Cuban crisis refuses to go away, he muses, as he gets his thoughts together in preparation for the meeting. In fact, it seems to be on the verge of spiraling out of control yet again. It is just ridiculous, Nikita Sergei'ich thinks: I am getting squeezed by both Kennedy and Fidel. It's as if a long towel is wrapped around my head. Kennedy has one end and Fidel has the other end. The only thing they ever want to communicate to one another is a threat, which they have begun to convey to each other by twisting the towel ever tighter around my head—from both directions. "Make Castro do this and this and this [twist, twist]. Make Kennedy do that and that and that [twist, twist]." No wonder I have this terrible headache, he thinks, as he rubs his temples in an effort to relieve the tension.

Nikita Sergei'ich's "woe is me" reverie is suddenly interrupted as the door opens and the other Presidium members file in. Nikita Sergei'ich watches them and thinks that they look like gray ghosts—lifeless, stiff and mechanical. Obviously, it's up to me, as always, to deal with all these difficult problems. I will ask for their views, of course but they won't have any views to speak of, as usual. The bastards are just waiting for me to screw up this Cuban crisis, so they can begin anew at what they do best: conspire and scheme to make trouble for those to whom they must answer—in this case, me. Kennedy at least has his brother, who though he often acts like a thug, according to our ambassador in Washington, is at least loyal and efficient. Who do I have to rely on? Just look at these guys. Not one of them has ever said anything worth remembering.

After nodding in the direction of the other Presidium members, Nikita Sergei'ich tells them he wants to review the cables sent to Moscow by Alekseev Mikoyan from Cuba over the past week, before moving on to a consideration of how to respond to Kennedy's demand for the removal of the IL-28 bombers from Cuba. After the review, he says, he will offer some thoughts on a letter to Kennedy for them to consider.

First, he begins: here is a cable from our ambassador, Alekseev. Now, we know that Alekseev loves Cuba and Cubans. So what are we to make of his comment that the Cubans, including Fidel, have treated him "like a leper" since they found out about the way Kennedy and I resolved the crisis? This is galling. These ungrateful children, these clueless Cubans—they can't have things exactly as they wish, so they are going to go off into their corner and pout and not speak when spoken to. Nikita Sergei'ich feels himself getting angry. At some point, if the Cubans don't grow up and act like adults, he tells the others, we may have to consider just packing up all our people and stuff on the island and bringing them home. Not yet. Mikoyan may still pull a few rabbits out of his hat. He usually does. But if he can't, then we may need to be prepared to wash our hands of our Caribbean communist friends. With friends like these, we don't need any enemies.

Next, he says, here is another cable from Alekseev—this one is not in your folder, because Anastas Ivan'ich instructed Alekseev to send it to me personally, for reasons that will be obvious. I am not going to read it aloud. But when I read it, I was heartbroken. Alekseev describes bringing the news to Anastas Ivan'ich of Ashken Lazarevna's death; of going with him to the Cuban guest house where he was staying; of being told to leave him alone for one hour, so he could meditate by a pond beside the guest house (called El Laguito, apparently, a "Little Lake" with flamingos wading through the water—just imagine!); and finally, of Anastas Ivan'ich slowly emerging from his meditation, gray with grief, telling Alekseev to put his son Sergo on a plane to Moscow immediately. Sergo will represent him at his wife's funeral, he told Alekseev. Anastas Ivan'ich said he would stay and do his duty to his country and to revolutionary principles. I gave him his choice. I told him he could leave Cuba at any time to return for the funeral. This was his choice.

At that moment, Nikita Sergei'ich is almost overcome with guilt. He recalls his promise to his friend that he would attend Ashken Lazarevna's funeral, a promise he has broken, because he can't stand funerals. He lied when he told his friend that he would go. Well, he thinks, as he pulls himself together, that is not the biggest lie I have ever told, that's for sure. Then he almost bursts out laughing when he thinks: like recently, when I lied to Kennedy about the missiles in Cuba. The melancholy mood has passed, and he feels himself once more "filling up with vinegar," as they say in the rural areas.

"So much for the atmosphere," Nikita Sergei'ich says. "I feel sorry, as I am sure you do, that Alekseev has been treated terribly by the Cubans, and that Anastas Ivan'ich has to carry on under such difficult personal circumstances, made much more difficult by what I want to discuss next—which is the possibility, emerging from his cables from the island, that the members of the Cuban leadership are all crazy! Have you read these cables?" (He looks up to see the Presidium members fumbling with their papers, a sure indication that they have not read the cables.) No? Well, listen to this, listen to what Anastas Ivan'ich is saying about his conversations. This is from five days ago, at a meeting with Fidel and the others at the "Little Lake" place with the flamingoes where he is staying. Nikita Sergei'ich reads from the cable, as follows:

A.I. MIKOYAN. When we complete the evacuation of the missiles, many issues will be seen in a different light. While we have not withdrawn them, we must maintain a different line. For that, 5-6 days are necessary. It is necessary to hold the line; otherwise they will accuse us of treachery. After we complete the evacuation, we will be able to adamantly oppose overflights, the quarantine, verification by the Red Cross, violations of airspace. …

It is necessary to get the UN on our side … We mustn't underestimate the value of diplomatic means of struggle. They are very important in periods when there is no war. It is important to know how to use the diplomatic arts, displaying at the same time both firmness and flexibility.

Now, in response, Nikita Sergei'ich interposes, "Here is what Che Guevara said to him":

E. GUEVARA. In this, in my opinion, lies the crux of the recent events. Even in the context of all our respect for the Soviet Union, we believe that the decisions made by the Soviet Union were a mistake. I am not saying this for discussion's sake, but so that you, Comrade Mikoyan, would be conversant with this point of view.

I think that the Soviet policy had two weak sides. You didn't understand the significance of the psychological factor for Cuban conditions. This thought was expressed in an original way by Fidel Castro: "The USA wanted to destroy us physically, but the Soviet Union with Khrushchev's letter destroyed us legally."

"Anastas Ivan'ich responds to him correctly," says Nikita Sergei'ich, "but Guevara refuses to bend":

A.I. MIKOYAN. But we thought you would be satisfied by our act. We did everything so that Cuba would not be destroyed. We see your readiness to die beautifully, but we believe that it isn't worth dying beautifully.

E. GUEVARA. To a certain extent you are right. You offended our feelings by not consulting us. But the main danger is in the second weak side of Soviet policy. The thing is, you as if recognized the right of the USA to violate international law. This greatly damages your policy. This fact really worries us. It may cause difficulties for maintaining the unity of the socialist countries. It seems to us that there already are cracks in the unity of the socialist camp.

A.I. MIKOYAN. That issue worries us too. We are doing a lot to strengthen our unity, and with you, comrades, we will always be with you despite all the difficulties.

E. GUEVARA. To the last day?

A.I. MIKOYAN. Yes, let our enemies die. We must live and live. Live like communists. We are convinced of our victory. A maneuver is not the same as a defeat.[6]

Nikita Sergei'ich explodes: "'To the last day?' You see? The Cubans seem to be disappointed that they didn't die a beautiful death a couple of weeks ago. 'To the last day?' What we did was prevent a 'last day.' We didn't expect thanks for saving Cuba. But we didn't expect insolence either—insolence and suicidal thoughts.
"Well, okay," he goes on, "you might think that while Che is a little bit off the wall, surely Fidel, their Maximum Leader, has got a better hold on reality. If you think that, then think again. Listen to what he told Anastas Ivan'ich four days ago in a meeting at Fidel's apartment:

Then suddenly Fidel, in a calm tone, made the following unexpected statement:
"A unilateral inspection would have a monstrous effect on the morale of our people. We have made large concessions. The American imperialists freely carry out aerial photography, and we do not prevent them from doing so because of a request by the Soviet government. We need to search for some other formula. I want to say to Comrade

Mikoyan, and what I am telling you reflects the decision of our entire people: We will not agree to an inspection. We do not want to compromise the Soviet troops and risk peace throughout the world. If our position puts peace throughout the world at risk, then we would think it more correct to consider the Soviet side free of its obligations and we will resist by ourselves. Come what may. We have the right to defend our dignity ourselves."

"Then Anastas Ivan'ich says this:

I was not worried about his refusal to allow the inspections at the ports. I was shocked by the final part of his statement. Everyone was quiet for several minutes. I thought: how do I proceed with this matter? I decided not to comment on this shocking statement.[7]

"My comrades," says Nikita Sergei'ich, "do you see what Fidel is saying here? He is saying: 'Okay, if you Soviets are too cowardly to go to the brink of nuclear Armageddon to preserve the integrity of the Cuban Revolution, or even over the brink, very well then, that is fine with us. Better than fine, actually. Why don't you just take all of your missiles and your planes and boats and troops and go straight back to the USSR or straight to hell or wherever you may want to take your weapons that you lack the courage to use.' 'Come what may?' 'Come what may?' You see? This is what we are up against: we have a small ally that has lost its mind. Time will tell whether this is just temporary insanity, and our relationship with Fidel's revolution can thrive, as Fidel and his comrades learn from their mistakes and grow into mature leaders.

"Come what may." Nikita Sergei'ich pauses over this phrase again, saying it out loud to his associates. Since October 28th he has believed that if Fidel had possessed nuclear weapons under his control in the crisis, he would have initiated a war in which the whole world would have been destroyed in nuclear fire. He understands why Fidel may have felt that way in the depths of the crisis—or at least he thinks he is beginning to understand. He thought he had no options. He thought the Americans were determined to destroy his country. Okay, fine, thinks Nikita Sergei'ich. But now? Now Fidel wants to antagonize and push the Americans to the brink again, "Come what may?" Nikita Sergei'ich concludes by asking his colleagues whether or not these cables show lunacy among the Cubans. All nod agreement in unison, as usual.

Nikita Sergei'ich has been reading and reflecting and exhorting his colleagues nonstop for nearly an hour and a half. He is about to turn to the principal business of the day—the response to Kennedy about the IL-28s—but as he shuffles the papers in front of him, he looks up and catches the eye of Leonid Brezhnev. Nikita Sergei'ich has a sudden premonition, which connects to his reflections about whether Fidel and his colleagues are crazy, and it gives him the chills. He does not entirely trust Leonid Illych, who is obviously ambitious and a schemer of the old school. What he sees in Brezhnev's eyes is an accusation that goes as follows: "Yes, Nikita Sergei'ich, Fidel may well be crazy. But whose idea was it to put our nuclear forces and top echelons of our fighting machine at this crazy man's disposal? It was yours, and yours alone, Nikita Sergei'ich. Maybe you are just as crazy as Fidel. Maybe neither of you are fit to rule a progressive bastion of Marxisim-Leninism." Nikita Sergei'ich looks away, but he will never forget the implied accusation in Brezhnev's stare.

"Comrades," Nikita Sergei'ich says, "Anastas Ivan'ich believes we should give Fidel and our Cuban friends one more chance. He thinks we should consult with them intensively on the issue of whether the IL-28s are to be removed or not. I agree with Anastas Ivan'ich, partly to see if he can bring Fidel and the others along. Maybe Fidel and the others will learn some valuable lessons from Anastas Ivan'ich as they discuss the IL-28 issue. But we have also just received some contradictory information from Kennedy—actually from both Kennedys—about the U.S. position on the bombers. Just the day before yesterday, Robert Kennedy told a representative in our embassy in Washington that the following two options would be acceptable to Kennedy, and would result in dismantling the quarantine and ceasing the overlights of Cuban territory: we should pledge to withdraw the IL-28s; or—this is the interesting part—we should pledge that only Soviet pilots would fly the IL-28s, and that we would not train the Cubans to do so. But then later on the same day—the 9th, I believe—Robert Kennedy told our representative that only the first option is on the table. It seems the Americans are confused about what to do.

"In light of Anastas Ivan'ich's willingness to persevere with Fidel, and in light of the possibility that we can dicker with the Americans to keep the bombers in Cuba for a while, I propose that we instruct Anastas Ivan'ich to discuss the IL-28s in great detail, trying to get the Cubans to see the wisdom of their removal (rather than to risk re-starting the deep crisis all over again), on the one hand; and, on the other hand, that I respond to Kennedy's letter dated November 6th by hedging our bets. I propose to offer a 'gentlemen's agreement,' that we intend to withdraw the bombers at some point, when it is convenient for us to do so. In return, the Americans should dismantle their blockade and stop their over-flights of the island. At the same time, we should instruct our negotiators in New York that our fallback position on the IL-28s is to remove them, because the Americans believe they are 'offensive.' But they should also be instructed not to fall back to this concession unless they are directed by us to do so. They should simply say that we agree to have only Soviets pilot the planes, or words to this effect—over and over again, like a broken record, in the manner of our best negotiators."

Nikita Sergei'ich is finished at last, fully two hours into his performance before the Presidium. He asks if all approve of consulting with the Cubans at greater length and pledging a Soviet pilots-only policy for the IL-28s. All nod their approval. As the Presidium members file out, Nikita Sergei'ich asks his secretary for some aspirin. After he takes the aspirin, he asks for his stenographer, and he begins to dictate the letter to Kennedy.

Dear Mr. President:

Now the elections in your country, Mr. President, are over. You made a statement that you were very pleased with the result of these elections. They, the elections, indeed were in your favor. This success does not upset us either—though that is of course your internal affair. You managed to pin your political rival, Mr. Nixon, to the mat. This did not draw tears from our eyes either.

...

Now about the matter that, as you state, worries you today about the IL-28 planes which you call an offensive weapon. We have already given you our clarification on this point and I think you cannot but agree with us. However, if you do not agree—and this is your right—ask your intelligence [agency] after all and let it give you an answer based not on guesswork but on facts. If it really knows anything it must tell you the truth and namely that it is long since the IL-28s have been taken out of production and out of use in our armed forces. And if some planes remain now—and a certain number of them have been brought by us to Cuba—that was done as a result of your action last year when you increased the budget and called up reservists. We on our part had to take measures in response at that time, having postponed taking those planes out of use as well.

Had there been no such action on your part we would not have IL-28s in existence because they would have been used for scrap. Such is this "formidable offensive" weapon...

Nevertheless we regard your concern with understanding though on our part we share the desire of the government of Cuba to possess defensive weapons which would permit the defense of the territorial integrity of its country.

Therefore if you met this with understanding and if we agreed with you on solving other questions in implementing the mutually assumed obligations then the question of the IL-28 bombers would be solved without difficulties.

...

We will not insist on permanently keeping these planes in Cuba. We have our difficulties on this question. Therefore we give a gentleman's word that we will remove the IL-28 planes with all the personnel and equipment related to those planes, though not now but later. We would like to do that sometime later when we determine that the conditions are ripe to remove them. We will advise you of that.

Sincerely,

N.S. Khrushchev

* * *
#34

John F. Kennedy to Nikita S. Khrushchev

November 12, 1962[8]

" the U.S. will immediately lift the quarantine"

Jack's advisers are droning on about the IL-28s and he is getting impatient. In fact, he is getting a headache from listening to the hawks in his Executive Committee— the damned hawks, both military and civilian. One of them will periodically pound the table and demand that Jack do this or that in order to salvage our country's honor, or some such thing. General Maxwell Taylor, who is a close friend of Jack's, seems unusually quarrelsome today. He is explaining why the quarantine must be tightened to prevent petroleum from getting to Cuba—this is part of what he calls the "squeeze-em-out" strategy. So far so good, Max, Jack muses. But then Max says that since the Soviets probably will not comply even if the quarantine is tightened, we must be ready to bomb all the IL-28 airfields the Soviets have built on the island. He calls that the "shoot-em-out" strategy, which he says he personally favors right now, along with the rest of the Joint Chiefs. Here we go again, Jack thinks. What will it take to make these hawks realize that this is the nuclear age and we've gotta be goddamned careful we don't start something that escalates to Armageddon?

After a short absence from the meeting to attend to other presidential business, Jack comes in on a more promising conversation being orchestrated, more or less according to plan, by his brother Bobby. The negotiating team is down from New York, and they are saying that a package deal should be offered to the Russians: they pledge to remove their IL-28s; we agree to lift the quarantine. Their only caveat is that the Soviets should remove the bombers first, then we can dismantle the quarantine. Otherwise, they claim, it will look as if we are caving into pressure from the Soviets. Jesus Christ, Jack thinks, who gives a damn who goes first, as long as we believe the other side will follow through? After all, Khrushchev had to take it on faith that we will remove the missiles from Turkey next year—which we will—but he took my word on that. And I took his word that the Soviets would keep the secret—which they have, so far.

As often happens, everything rides on the way we read the Soviets, Jack realizes. Suddenly he interrupts the debate and turns to his expert on the Soviet Union and Khrushchev, Tommy Thompson. "Tommy," Jack says, "what do you think?"

Thompson, a reserved, relatively low-ranking member of the committee, responds, "Mr. President, I think Khrushchev wants to get out of this mess—to end the crisis as soon as possible. I think one of the reasons is that Castro is giving Mikoyan fits down in Cuba. I also think that he is concerned, as we are, that something might happen, some dangerous mistake or accident, and with both militaries on high alert, it could lead to war. So I would say he will welcome the package deal recommended by our New York group: they remove the bombers; then we remove the quarantine."

"All right, then, let's try that. We can always squeeze 'em harder later on, if it comes to that."

After the meeting, Jack meets with Bobby and Ted Sorensen in the oval office. Sorensen has already drafted a brief message to Khrushchev consistent with Jack's decision of a few minutes ago. As he is looking over the draft, Jack laughs and says, "You know, Bobby, we've got to get you under control—not entirely under control, of course, but I don't want you telling Dobrynin that they can keep the IL-28s if they put Russian pilots in them—not this time, anyway. This time, Bobby, we're going to constrain you a little bit with this message, which looks fine, and which I'd like you to deliver personally to Dobrynin at the Soviet embassy. So that's the main message. Now, if you want to scare the shit out the Russians by telling them that time is running out, go ahead and tell him that, too. Because, damn it, time is running out—again!"

Bobby, who is pacing around the room with his arms folded in front of him, as usual, gets a pouty look on his face, as if to say to his big brother, you can take this message and shove it! But he can't sustain the pout, and he bursts into laughter as Jack hands him the message. After Bobby closes the door behind him, Jack says to Sorensen, "Ted, he'll have poor Dobrynin pinned to the mat in less than five minutes, telling him about what the hawks want to do in Cuba. Unfortunately, he will just be stating the facts. I hope Dobrynin realizes it. Time is getting short."

Chairman Khrushchev and the president agree in principle that the IL-28 aircraft shall be withdrawn within a specified period of time. Following this agreement the U.S. will immediately lift the quarantine, without waiting for the aircraft pullout. The U.S. side would, of course, prefer that the agreed time period for withdrawing the IL-28 aircraft were made public. However, if the Soviet side has any objections to making it public, the president will not insist. Chairman Khrushchev's word would be quite sufficient. As for the period of time, it would be good if the aircraft were withdrawn within, say, 30 days.

* * *

#35

Nikita S. Khrushchev to John F. Kennedy

November 13, 1962[9]

"the threat of the dreadful catastrophe"

"Damn," Nikita Sergei'ich says to no one in particular, when he reads the message from Dobrynin containing Kennedy's latest message on the IL-28 issue. "This is

not helpful. Kennedy obviously wants us to pledge publicly to remove the IL-28s according to some schedule or other, before *he gives the order to take down the quarantine, stop the over-flights and end the crisis. Why is he extending the crisis? Why is Kennedy making things so difficult? It is possible, he wonders, that Kennedy's hawks are circling, smelling blood, wanting to go into Cuba for the kill? They probably think they can still do it. They still have all their troops and hardware encircling Cuba. So we have to be careful."*

What makes this so complicated, Nikita Sergei'ich thinks, is that I have already told Anastas Ivan'ich that we want to consult the Cubans every step of the way with regard to the removal of the IL-28s. To be more precise, we want Anastas Ivan'ich to convince the Cubans to endorse the removal of the bombers. We have no idea how long it will take Anastas Ivan'ich to convince the Cubans—if they are capable of being convinced—that the IL-28s will have to go. So I guess that we are not actually consulting with them after all. This is more like informing them, but in slow motion. It is not a matter of "if," but "when." Our negotiating team in New York knows this; Anastas Ivan'ich knows this. If I only knew how long Kennedy's fuse is—how long we can delay the withdrawal of the IL-28s without risk of reentering a deep crisis. But I don't.

Nikita Sergei'ich decides he needs to do three things in his reply to Kennedy. First, he will send a trial balloon: he will say that the IL-28s can be removed in, say, two to three months. He will see if Kennedy can accept this "gentleman's agreement"—take his word on the withdrawal, the way he took Kennedy's word about the eventual withdrawal of the missiles in Turkey. Second, he will return to the issue of the over-flights. Surely Kennedy will find it easier to stop the over-flights than to abandon the quarantine. If he would just stop those invasions of Cuban airspace, he thinks, then Anastas Ivan'ich would really have something valuable to trade with the Cubans. Third, he will congratulate Kennedy again on the recent success of his party in the November 6th congressional elections, and that this must mean that he is in a sufficiently strong position to go ahead and make a concession on the IL-28s.

Nikita Sergei'ich finds himself at this moment angry toward both Kennedy and Fidel. His Cuban protégé is temperamental and erratic. Even the great Anastas Ivan'ich may not be able to calm him down and bring him around to the Soviet position. But Kennedy is aggravating him as well. Why doesn't Kennedy see how humiliating the over-flights of the island are to the Cubans, how these random violations of their sovereignty are really threats, or perceived as threats? The Americans are flying over the island and the Cubans can't do a damn thing about it. It makes Fidel and all Cubans feel helpless, even panicky. I know all about this, Nikita Sergei'ich thinks, as he remembers August 1960, when the Soviets shot down a U-2 spy plane near Sverdlovsk. They had been trying to shoot one down for years, but had only recently succeeded in building a missile that could attack the U-2s up at 75,000 feet, from which they take their photographs. Nikita Sergei'ich remembers well his anger at being told about the U-2 over-flights, and his frustration at not being able to do anything about it for many years. For Fidel, the situation is even *worse, he thinks. The U-2 is only a spy plane. But the planes swooping in over Cuba at very low altitude every day might be carrying bombs. The next flight might be the beginning of the American attack. That is what all the Cubans must be thinking. No wonder Fidel is angry and on edge. Still, the main objective must be to get the hell out of this crisis. And the last major hurdle seems to be agreement on the IL-28s. If only Kennedy would cut me some slack by stopping the over-flights and/or ending the quarantine, we could get out of this mess no worse for the wear, and not have to keep ramming the Americans' demands down the throats of the Cubans.*

As he authorizes the message about to go out to Kennedy, he feels instinctively that it will not work—that Kennedy will not bend in his direction, that Castro will not yield to Anastas Ivan'ich's tactics in Cuba, and that twenty-four or forty-eight hours from now, he will once again be disappointed and angered by Kennedy and mad as hell at Fidel all over again. But it's worth a try, he thinks, to stall for a little more time before we agree publicly to Kennedy's demand that we pull the bombers out.

Dear Mr. President

I have read with great satisfaction the reply of the president of the United States and I agree with the considerations expressed by the president.

...

The question of the withdrawal of the IL-28s within the mentioned 30 days does not constitute any complication. Yet this period will probably not be sufficient...It can be done in 2-3 months...

You understand that when we say that it is necessary to announce now the withdrawal of the IL-28s at the time when your planes are flying over Cuba it creates for us no small difficulties. I have no doubt that you will understand—and the Cuban government understands this—that such actions constitute violation of sovereignty of the Cuban state. Therefore it would be a reasonable step to create in this respect conditions for the normalization of the situation, which would in a great degree make it easier to meet your wish of expediting the withdrawal of the IL-28s from Cuba.

...

I will allow myself to express some other considerations and I believe you will not take offense and not consider that I intrude too much into the sphere of internal affairs. Voting in the elections to the Senate, House of Representatives and in gubernatorial elections which just took place has resulted in the defeat of your former rival who was clearly preparing again for the next presidential elections. It is significant that as a result of the elections precisely those candidates were defeated who, if I may use such an expression, were making the most frenzied bellicose speeches.

This indicates that the American people have already begun to feel that if the arms race continues further, if a reasonable solution is not found and an understanding is not achieved between our countries then our peoples will feel still more strongly the threat of the dreadful catastrophe of a thermonuclear war.

N.S. Khrushchev

* * *

#36

Fidel Castro to Acting Secretary-General of the United Nations, U Thant

November 15, 1962[10]

"We are sounding the necessary alarm"

Things are not going well between Mikoyan and Fidel. It is obvious to Fidel what is going on: by pretending to "consult" with us, he concludes, Mikoyan does nothing but lecture us about the importance of being patient, being obedient (though he does not use this term, "obedient," that is exactly what he is preaching), and being careful not to anger the Americans. He says this is a pivotal moment in the crisis, and that we must not allow our emotions to carry us away. Actually, Fidel thinks, this is about as much "consultation" as the Russians provided when they threw in the towel and surrendered to the Americans on October 28th. Then, we heard about it on a radio broadcast from Miami. Now, we get Mikoyan, who goes on and on nonstop like a radio with no "off" button, and whose mission is obviously to get us to surrender to him, to allow the gringos to over-fly our island and blockade our country until—until when? Until they feel that they have extracted everything they can get out of Khrushchev. Then the Russians will go home, leaving Cuba wide open for the Americans to attack and invade us.

Yesterday, November 14th, Fidel refused to meet with Mikoyan, claiming illness. Tonight, he has been invited to an 8:00 p.m. dinner with Mikoyan at the Soviet embassy, where he is sure he will be treated to yet another four-hour monologue by Mikoyan on Cuba's duty as a small revolutionary country led by the big guys, by the USSR—always, they make this point, that we Cubans are now to be "led by the USSR." Bullshit! How can those spineless, careless bastards ever lead us? They have totally forgotten what it is like to be a revolutionary, if they ever knew. Now the Soviet mode of operation, Fidel thinks, is be cautious; don't rock the boat; don't offend the big bad Americans; and be sure that smaller socialist countries like Cuba understand that their orders come from Moscow. Fidel just cannot keep the word "bullshit" from entering his mind. He feels he is drowning in a sea of Russian bullshit, and he is not happy about it.

Fidel has scheduled a meeting with his aides just before he goes to the Soviet embassy for dinner this evening. But on an impulse, at about 4:00 p.m., still

obsessing about the arrogance and cluelessness of the Russians, he orders his driver
to take him to an anti-aircraft battery in west Havana, near the Hotel Comodoro,
between Fifth Avenue and the beach. Fidel feels the need to touch the reality, the
physical danger, as faced by his anti-aircraft crews. They have been ordered to
hold their fire at the low-flying U.S. planes, until further notice. Fidel feels ter-
rible about this—his order to hold fire, which was really just a relay of the orders
he received from Khrushchev and the Russians. If he were in the shoes of the men
in his anti-aircraft crews, Fidel tells his driver on the way to the Comodoro, he
would feel as if the Maximo Lider had put handcuffs on his own troops, preventing
them from doing what they should be doing, which is protecting Cuban life and
property, and preserving Cuban pride and integrity. Fidel almost tells the driver
to turn back, feeling that he cannot face his own men under these circumstances.
After all, what will he say if a U.S. jet flies over them while he is talking to them?
What then? Will he stand helpless, humiliated, along with his men?

But the turn-back option is immediately foreclosed, as the driver pulls up beside
the anti-aircraft guns, and the men recognize Fidel. They shout "Fee-del, Fee-del,"
as always. But this time, Fidel does not feel as if he is worthy of their loyalty and
admiration. They talk—Fidel and his men. After a half hour of discussion with his
frustrated men, Fidel takes a turn lining up an anti-aircraft gun as if he were going
to shoot at a plane. Just as he is getting out of the gunner's seat, Fidel is startled
when a U.S. jet flying at a few hundred feet above the ground, from west to east,
is suddenly directly overhead. He instinctively ducks his head, as do the other men.
A second or two later, the sonic boom almost bursts Fidel's eardrums. As the plane
disappears over the central city on the eastern horizon, there is total silence around
the anti-aircraft gun. Fidel stares at the eastern horizon. Unused to an eerily silent
Fidel, the men look at each other and then down at their feet, hoping that Fidel
breaks the silence soon. Instead, he gestures toward his driver to bring the jeep over
and pick him up. Then he orders him to head straight to Fidel's headquarters in
central Havana. For one of the few times in his life, Fidel Castro is too angry to talk.

Fidel enters his main office approximately a half hour before the others arrive. He
goes immediately to his desk, grabs a pen, and begins to write a letter to UN Act-
ing Secretary General U Thant. It is Cuba's turn, he thinks as he smiles, to squeeze
the big guys, to make them squirm, to make it obvious that they are dealing with
Cubans, not with some former U.S. colony and future Soviet colony. The letter goes
through several drafts, all in Fidel's own handwriting, even though his secretarial
assistant is in another part of the office complex. He wants to do this himself. It
enforces discipline, he thinks, and prevents him from getting expansive and turning
his idea into a long letter. This one will be short and it will be shocking. He finishes
it at 6:00 p.m. or thereabouts, just as his two comrades walk through the door.

This meeting is between Fidel, his brother Raul, the defense minister, and Celia
Sanchez, the founder of the 26th of July Movement in Manzanillo province, and
a trusted adviser to Fidel on all matters, though she has no official designation in
the government. It is widely believed on the island of Cuba that Raul and Celia

are the only two people in the world Fidel absolutely trusts, whose loyalty can be counted on and who—this is what really distinguishes them—will fearlessly oppose Fidel when they think he is wrong, though they will only do this when they are alone with him. Rumors fly on the island about what these meetings are like. Many believe they throw things at each other and scream and yell at each other. Why not? It is the Cuban way. As Raul and Celia enter, all the others know that they must leave. They form a phalanx around the headquarters, almost (but not quite) out of earshot of Fidel, Raul and Celia. They will remain in their positions, and will await their orders once the meeting is over.

Celia asks Fidel whether he is going to the dinner at el bunker, *("the bunker"), which is what the Cubans call the Soviet embassy. Fidel says he has decided to go, because it will provide an opportunity to put the fear of god into the damned Russians.*

Celia and Raul glance at each other. Right on cue, Celia says to Raul something that is a standing joke between them—"Aqui viene el problema" *("Here comes trouble"). Many Cubans around Havana have picked up the phrase and as they say,* "aqui viene el problema," *they tug on their chins, as if pulling a beard—another of many coded references to Fidel. She and Raul chuckle briefly. Then Celia asks Fidel how he intends to scare the Russians. Before Fidel can answer, the ever-cautious Raul, no longer smiling, asks his brother why he thinks this is a good idea.* "I have told you," *he says,* "that we need these people and that offending them is not the way to cultivate them."

As often happens, Raul's caution sends Fidel through the roof and into an angry tirade. He tells Raul that the Cubans have had it up to here (he gestures at his throat) with caution, with obedience, with listening to Mikoyan lecture them like children. Raul tries repeatedly to interrupt, but Fidel ignores him. He then relates, at top volume and high velocity his experience at the anti-aircraft battery over by the Comodoro, and his determination not to tolerate this anymore. He tells them he was embarrassed to confront his own men. He says he wants to earn their respect, not just assume it. He tells them that he does not believe his full hearing capacity has yet returned, as if to remind him of the humiliation of the overflights—something the men at the anti-aircraft site must contend with more than two dozen times every day. "It's a goddamned wonder," *Fidel says,* "that those guys haven't already joined the counterrevolutionaries." *By the time he finally takes a breath, Fidel is shouting and as he shouts, his voice is reduced, as always, to a labored, thin squeak, like the sound emitted by a pressure cooker on the stove that is about to explode. It is always surprising to Celia, after all these years, that Fidel, tall and muscular, has a squeaky, crackling voice, while Raul, short and skinny, has a deep, authoritative baritone.*

Celia interrupts the Castro brothers by returning to Fidel's stated desire to shock the Soviets this evening. "What," *she asks,* "does he have in mind?"

"Celia," *Fidel says,* "I have just written to U Thant, telling him that we Cubans will no longer tolerate violations of our sovereignty and our dignity by sitting on* *our hands as the gringos fly over our country setting us up for an attack and an invasion. My letter says that in the future, those over-flying our country will risk being destroyed. In other words, we are going to try, to the best of our ability, to begin to squeeze the gringos and the Russians, the way they have both been squeezing us—or trying to squeeze us. "Here," Fidel says, "go ahead and read it."*

Celia reads it without comment, and hands it to Raul, who also reads it in silence. Raul is visibly upset. Raul is the old-line communista in the family. It goes way back to 1953, when Raul went to Czechoslovakia to attend a conference of communist youth, and was befriended by a young Soviet KGB officer named Nikolai Leonev, who spoke very good Spanish, and who was heading to Mexico to open up a KGB station run out of the Soviet embassy in Mexico City. He and Raul traveled by ship from Europe to Latin America, and by the time Raul arrived back in Cuba—at least in Fidel's telling of this family saga—Raul was as much a Russian as a Cuban. Though he is upset, all Raul says is, "Are you sure this is a good idea? After all, Mikoyan is trying to help us, you know. He will be shocked by this, if you send it without consulting him."

Fidel almost blurts out "Without consulting him?—you mean the way they have consulted us?" But he thinks better of it and remains silent. Fidel knew this would be Raul's response. It doesn't bother him. Raul is like this, he thinks. He loves the Soviets and he is very cautious. I do not love the Soviets, and I am—so he says to me all the time, the way our mother said it—"salvaje" ("a wild barbarian")! He is more interested in Celia's reaction. She is unpredictable. And her perspective is not constrained by a family history of big brother-little brother dynamics.

Celia says she thinks both Castro brothers are right. Looking at Fidel, she says, "The letter should be sent to U Thant. Cuba's dignity is at stake, and so is the possibility in the future of Cuba taking a leading role in the revolutionary movement." Then, turning to Raul, she says, "By sending the letter, Cuba stands a chance of putting the Soviets right where we want them. Don't forget," she says to both Fidel and Raul, "the Soviets need us at least as much as we need them. That's why the Soviets have sent Mikoyan to the island—to try to calm us down, to try to convince us that they love us, even though we are 'unruly children.' Frankly," she says, "I think this letter will scare them. It will get their attention. If a war doesn't break out and destroy us, the imperialists in Moscow will know forevermore whom they are dealing with when the time comes for Cuba and Russia to kiss and make up. They will be prepared to pay mightily for our allegiance. They will know we mean business—that we are not kidding. Support for Cuba does not mean control of Cuba."

Raul adds, "If a war doesn't destroy us. But I see your point, Celia. We have to be prepared to risk everything, to get something. That is how it is with small countries like ours when we are playing with the big boys. Okay, comrade brother, put the squeeze on them."

Fidel reaches up and tugs the brim of his military cap, as he smiles at both of them. He calls for an aide and hands the letter to him, instructing him to type it

up exactly as it is, and to cable it immediately to U Thant in New York, via the
new Cuban UN Ambassador, Carlos Lechuga.

"*Time to go,*" *he says.* "*Time to show the Russians who they are dealing*
with." *After they are outside, Celia and Raul head east toward Old Havana,*
while Fidel's driver heads for el bunker, about five minutes' drive in the opposite
direction.

Your Excellency:

...

I should like to refer solely to the following matter: we have given you—
and we have also given it publicly and repeatedly—our refusal to allow
unilateral inspection by any body, national or international, on Cuban
territory. In doing so we have exercised the inalienable right of every sovereign nation to solve all problems within its own territory in accordance
with the will of its government and its people.

...

The Soviet government, carrying out its promise to Mr. Kennedy,
has withdrawn its strategic missiles, an action which was verified by the
United States on the high seas.

...

What have we obtained in exchange? The violations have increased
in number; every day the incursions of war planes over our territory
become more alarming; military aircraft harass our air bases, make low-
level flights over our military defenses and photograph not only the
strategic missile installations but in fact our entire territory, foot by foot
and inch by inch.

...

Today again through this communication we are sending you as
secretary-general of the United Nations, we wish to give warning that to
the extent of the firepower of our anti-aircraft weapons, any war plane
which violates the sovereignty of Cuba, by invading our air space, can
only do so at the risk of being destroyed.

...

We are sounding the necessary alarm for the defense of world peace,
we are defending the right of the small countries to be considered on a
footing of equality, we are telling all the peoples of the earth that before
the imperialist enemy there can be no weakening. The path of calm
and stern vigilance, strong in the security of a response commensurate
with the magnitude of the aggression, is the only way to the salvation of
peace.

Our right to live is something that cannot be discussed by anyone.

But if our right to live is made conditional upon an obligation to fall
to our knees, we reply once again that we will not accept it.

We believe in the right to defend the liberty, the sovereignty and the dignity of this country, and we shall continue to exercise that right to the last man, woman or child capable of holding a weapon in this territory.

May I reiterate to you the expression of my highest consideration.

Fidel Castro

Prime Minister of the Revolutionary Government

* * *

#37

John F. Kennedy to Nikita S. Khrushchev

November 15, 1962[11]

"the trouble here may be in Cuba."

"Dammit, Mac," Jack says to his National Security Adviser McGeorge Bundy, "Khrushchev is stalling. I have told him repeatedly that the IL-28s have got to come out, and come out soon, or we will be heading back into another Cuban crisis. This stalling tactic really aggravates me. Hell, we know Khrushchev can turn the screw on Castro if he wants to. I mean: what can Castro do other than bitch about it? Nothing much, as far as I can see."

Bundy responds by telling Jack that all present available evidence suggests that Khrushchev is just as unhappy about the situation as Jack is. As we know, he adds, negotiating with a stubborn little ally can be as tough as a negotiation can be.

"Yeah, I know," Jack responds. "The goddamned Israelis have been driving me crazy. The sonsofbitches won't listen to reason over that damned nuclear facility at Dimona. I told Ben Gurion at least a dozen times that we were dead serious about non-proliferation of nuclear weapons, that we opposed their acquisition of nukes, that we would guarantee their security, that nuclear weapons wouldn't enhance their security in any case. And what did Ben Gurion say: basically he told me to go to hell. What are we going to do, bomb them? No. Cut off the foreign aid? No. They know that and we know that. We know how powerful their lobby is in this country. The net result is that we get into a shouting match with an ally who just will not cooperate. So Mac, you're saying that's basically what's going on right now between Khrushchev and Castro? You think Khrushchev is me and Castro is Ben Gurion?"

Bundy responds that this comparison is just what he had in mind and that, to him, the comparison is instructive. Jack then asks what Bundy derives from the comparison.

He responds by telling Jack: you need to write a letter to Khrushchev that lets him know that you believe he has failed in his commitment to resolving the crisis: there is still no onsite inspection; the IL-28 bombers are still in Cuba; and there

have been no assurances issued against their reintroduction, or against the reintroduction of the missiles. You need to let him know you haven't forgotten that
he has not followed through. But I think you also need to remind him that this
is a standoff between Moscow and Washington, and that Castro and the Cuban
government should be second-order concerns for both him and you. You should
remind him that we have our own means of influencing Castro, but our means are
more or less limited to bombing suspected weapons sites and invading the island.

"But Mac," Jack responds, "I don't want to invade Cuba. Sure, we may have
to, but that is only a last resort."

"Yes, of course, Mr. President," Bundy continues. "But what would you say to
reminding Khrushchev that he has less violent means of influencing Castro. He
can simply order his people to pack up their merchandise, put it back in the boxes
it came in, and ship it back to the Soviet Union. Has it occurred to you, Mr.
President, that with every passing day, Khrushchev has less and less enthusiasm for
leaving nuclear-capable weapons systems in a Cuba run by the erratic Castro regime? How do you think Khrushchev feels about this latest Castro broadside—the
one from earlier today that was relayed to us by our UN mission in New York—in
which Castro threatens to start shooting down our planes if we over-fly the island?
I am betting Khrushchev is mortified. This might actually be a good time to write
to the Soviet chairman and tell him in so many words: it's your move, or it will be
our move, and if we have to move, it won't be pretty. Castro is out of control, and
we are losing patience. That is why we prefer to give you, Khrushchev the option
of making the next move. If it involves ignoring Castro, then so be it."

Bobby breaks into the conversation by telling his brother and Bundy and Ted
Sorensen, "There is another reason why a letter like the one Mac is suggesting is
called for now. [New York Senator Kenneth] Keating is shooting off his mouth
again. It's ridiculous. Every day, we hear from Keating, 'I said there would be missiles in Cuba, blah, blah, blah, and I was right; and now I am telling you that they
are still there and that we should blah, blah, blah bomb and invade, etc.' I had
someone catalogue his recent speeches and other comments on Cuba. Yesterday's
statement by Keating was his twenty-fourth on this issue in the past two months.
Sure, he's a nut case, but he's also a nut case who has received leaked classified
information, and he's a nut case who wants to run for president in 1964. Just the
other day he said if he is proven to be wrong in any particulars about weapons in
Cuba, he will eat his hat."

Jack interrupts: "He said that? I'd love to give that sonofabitch a steady diet of
fried fedora," he says, as laughter breaks out in the group. "I sent [CIA Director
John] McCone to see Keating last month to shake him down, to challenge him to
reveal where he was getting his information. But he stonewalled McCone. Apparently they got into a shouting match and McCone said, 'Okay, don't tell us where
you're getting your information. Just tell us where your sources think the weapons
are and we'll be happy to over-fly that site and give you the results.' Keating
wouldn't bite on that. McCone called him unpatriotic—which he is—and even

that didn't have any impact on him. The only way to shut him up and lower the political temperature on the Cuba issue is to get Khrushchev to start moving on the IL-28s. I agree with both of you."

"Ted, work up a draft letter for me to look over that covers the points we've been discussing."

"Of course, Mr. President," Sorensen replies. "I just wonder whether you might want to include a comment about how much you and Mrs. Kennedy enjoyed last night's performance of the Bolshoi Ballet. As you know, Khrushchev is very proud of Soviet cultural achievements."

"No way," Bobby breaks in. "He will have already gotten his report on the ballet from his ambassador who hosted you, who will say that you and Jackie loved it. We don't want Khrushchev distracted. We want him feeling the pressure that we are feeling—feeling squeezed the way we are feeling squeezed—and that this can't go on. I say you just send a letter that says, between the lines, 'get off your ass and get that shit out of Cuba because time is running out.' He needs to understand that we're dealing with some crazies here who have a lot of clout, and Khrushchev holds the key to shutting them up and reducing the danger."

"Bobby," Jack says, "we've got to find a way to bring you out of your shell so that you are able to really say what's on your mind, instead of keeping everything bottled up inside you." Jack laughs as he looks straight at Ted, who understands this Kennedy dog and pony show perfectly. Without another word being said, Sorensen disappears through the doorway to go and write exactly the letter he has just been instructed to write.

Dear Mr. Chairman

I am glad to learn of your assurance of agreement that the IL-28s should be withdrawn. All that remains is to reach understanding on the timing.

...

I cannot agree with your statement that you have fulfilled your commitments and that we have not fulfilled ours. Let us recall what, in fact, has occurred. You have removed a certain number of missiles from Cuba—not under United Nations supervision—but you did cooperate in arrangements which enabled us to be reasonably sure that forty-two missiles were in fact taken out of Cuba. There has been no United Nations verification that other missiles were not left behind and, in fact, there have been many reports of them being concealed in caves and elsewhere, and we have no way of satisfying those who are concerned about these reports. The IL-28s are still in Cuba and are of deep concern to the people of our entire hemisphere. Thus, three major parts of the undertakings on your side—the removal of the IL-28s, the arrangements for verification, and the safeguards against [re-]introduction—have not yet been carried out.

We suppose that part of the trouble here may be in Cuba. The secretary general of the United Nations was not allowed to make arrangements for the experts he took with him to Cuba to verify removal of the offensive weapons; The Cuban government did not agree to International Red Cross inspection at ports; they have refused the secretary general's suggestion that the Latin American ambassadors in Havana undertake this verification; they have rejected a further suggestion of the secretary general concerning the use of various non-aligned chiefs of mission in Havana for this purpose. It is difficult for me to understand why the Cubans are so resistant to the series of reasonable proposals that have been made to them by U Thant unless, for reasons of their own, they are determined to see the crisis prolonged and worsened. We both have means of influencing the Cuban government and I do not believe that we can allow that government to frustrate the clear understandings our two countries have reached in the interests of peace.

In these circumstances we have so far been patient and careful, as we have been, indeed, at every stage. As you know from your own reports, we have always applied the quarantine with care and with regard for the position of others, and in recent days we have relied on oral assurances of the masters of your ships and other ships. Moreover I myself held back orders for more forceful action right to the limit of possibility during the week of October 27 and 28. But we cannot make progress from here—or avoid a return of danger to this situation—if your side should now fall into the mistake of claiming that it has met all of its commitments, and refusing to help with the real business of carrying out our purpose of untying the Cuban knot.

What, in these circumstances, should be done? We are entitled to insist on removal of the IL-28s and on safeguards against reintroduction of offensive weapons before we lift the quarantine or give assurances of any sort. But we are interested in making rapid progress, step-by-step, and that is why we have proposed an arrangement more favorable from your standpoint: that as soon as you give the order for the removal of the IL-28s and their men and equipment, to be completed within thirty days (and I am glad you say the length of time is not the real problem) we will announce the lifting of the quarantine. That is more than we agreed to on October twenty-seventh and twenty-eighth, but we wish to end this crisis promptly.

...

In the absence of any arrangements under the United Nations or otherwise for international verification or safeguards, we have of course been obliged to rely on our own resources for surveillance of the situation in Cuba, although this course is unsatisfactory. Just today we learned of new threats by Castro against this necessary surveillance. I should make it very clear that if there is any interference with this surveillance, we shall have to take the necessary action in reply, and it is for just this reason that it is so urgent to obtain better safeguards.

...

But the first step is to get the bombers started out, and the quarantine lifted—for both are sources of tension...

John F. Kennedy

* * *

#38

Nikita S. Khrushchev to John F. Kennedy

November 19, 1962[12]

"Now . . . we speak of . . . eliminating the remnants of the crisis"

November 16, 1962. *Nikita Sergei'ich is angrily pacing back and forth in front of his associates in the Presidium. In his left hand he is holding a copy of Kennedy's letter dated the day before, November 15th, which shows that Kennedy is unwilling or unable to bend on the issue of the IL-28 withdrawal. "He says he won't dismantle the blockade until after I announce a timetable for taking out the IL-28s. After!" As he says this he holds up his left hand for emphasis.*

In his right hand, Nikita Sergei'ich is holding a copy of Fidel's letter, also dated November 15th, to U Thant, informing the UN secretary general that the Cubans are about to open fire on all low-flying U.S. reconnaissance planes in an effort to shoot them down. He blurts out, "He's going to shoot them down! He is going to torpedo everything and we are once more going to be on the brink of war with the Americans."

Attached to Fidel's letter is a cable from Anastas Ivan'ich Mikoyan. Nikita Sergei'ich continues: "Anastas Ivan'ich says that Fidel basically just threw this letter at him at dinner last night. He didn't consult with Anastas Ivan'ich or even properly inform him of what he was doing. Fidel basically threw a tantrum in the form of this damn letter to U Thant. Oh, and of course he says he still opposes the withdrawal of the IL-28s. Anastas Ivan'ich says he is saddened by this turn of events. These Cubans are good people, he says, but they are high strung, sentimental and ignorant of the facts of life in a world of nuclear weapons.

"Well, comrades, I for one am not saddened, I am angry—angry at these ungrateful, spiteful, childish Cubans. Think about it—think about what they have done. First, they refuse onsite inspection, even after they know that Kennedy and I have agreed to it. Then Fidel refuses all of U Thant's ideas for onsite inspection. All of them! Then they refuse to deal with Anastas Ivan'ich for days on end, and when Fidel does see him at last he just tells him that they are going to try to shoot down the American planes, 'come what may.' That's it," Nikita Sergei'ich says

as he continues his peripatetic monologue, pacing back and forth, back and forth, and as the heads of the Presidium members swivel through an arc of about ninety degrees, so as not to offend their agitated chief by appearing to be uninterested in his loud, boisterous ruminations. "I've had it with the Cubans," he continues. "I am going to write to Kennedy today and tell him that the IL-28s will be out in less than thirty days from now, that he can absolutely count on it, so he can dismantle the quarantine and stop the over-flights of the island, and we can end this crisis. That's what I want to tell him. What do the rest of you think about my plan?"

At first, the Presidium members, as usual, stare down at their papers, and pretend to rearrange them in their folders. Also as usual, when the shuffling is completed, silence rules. Occasionally, someone will look up, as if to ask, is it over yet? Can we go yet? Are you done with us yet, Nikita Sergei'ich? "I'll take that as a show of unanimous support," Nikita Sergei'ich says, and he calls for his stenographer, Nadezhda Petrovna. The letter is dictated quickly. Nikita Sergei'ich's mind is clear, his purpose is simply to inform Kennedy that he is willing to do what Kennedy demands, the Cubans be damned. As an afterthought, he cannot resist a couple of remarks that reflect his ongoing frustration with Kennedy's relentless pressure on him to remove the IL-28s. On the second run through he inserts a sarcastic comment about Kennedy's reference to some American hawks claiming that the Russians are hiding the nuclear missiles in Cuban caves. And for what seems like the twentieth time, he tells Kennedy that the Americans could help end this crisis sooner rather than later if they would simply cease and desist from the over-flights.

Nikita Sergei'ich asks for a show of hands to authorize the sending of the letter to Kennedy. To his utter amazement no one raises his hand. No one. Taken aback, and impatient as always, Nikita Sergei'ich says, "Well?" At this point the previously unthinkable happens. His foreign minister, Andrei Andrei'ich Gromyko, timidly raises his hand just slightly above the conference table, then, his hand shaking visibly, a little higher, just high enough for Nikita Sergei'ich to see it. "Well, Andre Andrei'ich, so you agree," Nikita Sergei'ich says. "What about the rest of you?"

Suddenly Andrei Andrei'ich, sounding even more than ever like one of those professional actors who are also announcers for Radio Moscow, asks if he might express an opinion about the letter. Nikita Sergei'ich nods in his direction, indicating he can go ahead. "Nikita Sergei'ich," he begins droning in his basso profundo of a voice, "I agree with the text of the letter. We cannot allow the Cubans to twist us around in this manner. As you say eloquently in your letter, it is too dangerous. But I wonder if it might make sense to give Anastas Ivan'ich one more try with Fidel—one more chance to show Fidel why the crisis must be brought to an end now, and in the manner indicated in your letter. My suggestion is this: that we have your letter ready to send to Kennedy, but that we delay sending it for a few days—until Anastas Ivan'ich has a chance to educate our Cuban friends as to what must be done. If Fidel proves to be impervious to reason, or if Kennedy suddenly demands an immediate answer, then you can send it at that time."

Nikita Sergei'ich thinks about this for a moment. Certainly, he muses, it would be better if Fidel would publicly endorse the decision to withdraw the IL-28s. He abruptly says, "good. That's what we'll do. Until Anastas Ivan'ich gives up on Fidel, or Kennedy demands an immediate answer, I'll just keep the letter on my desk, and send it when it seems appropriate." As he says this, he looks around the room. He thinks Andrei Andrei'ich looks even more self-satisfied than he usually does, like one of those Easter Island heads, only with a smirk on his face. He also wonders, yet again, whether that is a barely visible sneer of satisfaction on Brezhnev's face—a sneer which seems to indicate that Leonid Ilyich is far from inconsolably sad in the face Nikita Sergei'ich's continuing Cuban difficulties.

November 19, 1962. *Nikita Sergei'ich is told by his foreign policy aide, Oleg Troyanovsky, that there are several new developments in the Cuban crisis. First, Oleg Alexandr'ich says that Kennedy is scheduled to give a major statement and press conference at 4:00 p.m. Washington time the following day regarding the Cuban crisis. Reports coming out of the Soviet embassy in Washington and from the negotiating team in New York carry the following message: Kennedy wants to know which of two statements he should deliver tomorrow: one indicating that the crisis has deepened over the IL-28 issue and that Washington is preparing to take stronger action in the Caribbean; or one informing the public that Moscow has agreed to withdraw the IL-28s, and that Kennedy is ordering the dismantling of the quarantine, which signals the end of the crisis.*

"There are also two other developments," Oleg Alexandr'ich continues. "First, we have heard authoritatively that if you agree to Kennedy's demand for the withdrawal of the IL-28s, then Kennedy will agree that all subsequent inspection can be done at sea, and via high-altitude, U-2 reconnaissance—that in effect he will drop the demand for onsite inspection of the sites in Cuba, and he will suspend the low-level flights that so offend the Cubans. And second, our intelligence services are picking up some ominous indications in the Caribbean that Kennedy may be on the verge of ordering an attack on Cuba—pending, of course, your response to his propositions. That is where things stand, Nikita Sergei'ich."

"That's it," he responds immediately. "It is time to send my letter to Kennedy. Just change the date from November 16 to November 19 and send it. We can't wait for Fidel to see the light. Have a copy of my letter sent to Anastas Ivan'ich as well. The man is a saint. But, as the saying goes, Oleg Alexandr'ich, "You cannot get water from a rock," a comment that draws a smile from Troyanovsky. Oleg Alexandr'ich had earlier taught the expression to Nikita Sergei'ich, having learned it from the Americans while growing up in Washington DC, where his father was the Soviet Union's first ambassador to the U.S.

"Exactly," Oleg Alexandr'ich responds, "whether the rock is in Washington or in Havana." Nikita Sergei'ich smiles at this, in anticipation of ending the Cuban crisis once and for all.

Dear Mr. President

I have studied attentively your considerations which were forwarded through our ambassador in Washington on the evening of November 15. I wish first of all to express satisfaction with regard to your statement that the United States is also interested in untying the Cuban knot...I fully share also the thought expressed by you about the necessity to act with caution, to take into consideration the position of others. Now when we speak of eliminating the remnants of the crisis this is as important as at any of its past stages.

…

Furthermore, your planes continue to fly over the Cuban territory. It does not normalize the situation but aggravates it. And all this is taking place at a time when we have removed the missiles from Cuba, have given you the possibility to ascertain through appropriate observation and when we declare our intention to remove the IL-28 planes from Cuba.

…

As for the rumors alleging that the missiles may have been left in Cuba somewhere in the caves, one can say that we do not live in the caveman age to attach great significance to the rumors of this sort.

In conclusion I wish to stress that much time has already passed since an agreement was reached between us and it is not in the interests of our countries, not in the interests of peace to delay the fulfillment of the agreement that has been reached and the final settlement of the Cuban crisis. Such is our conviction.

N.S. Khrushchev

* * *

#39

John F. Kennedy to Nikita S. Khrushchev via the Soviet ambassador in Washington

November 20, 1962[13]

"the president . . . has ordered a lower state of alert"

It is 2:00 p.m. and Jack is alone in the White House living quarters, preparing for his 4:00 p.m. press conference. He is going over all the reports, sample questions prepared by members of his staff, possible answers and warnings regarding possible "odd" questions from specific journalists. Earlier this morning, he received

Khrushchev's November 19th letter via Georgy Bolshakov of the Soviet embassy. Jack felt that when he read the letter, he took his first deep breath since October 28th, when a previous letter from Khrushchev arrived, and he had prematurely assumed the crisis was over.

White House wordsmith Ted Sorensen has drafted his introductory statement on the Cuban crisis with which the press conference will begin. Jack already knows the opening paragraph by heart, having refined it a half-dozen times since this morning:

I have been informed by Chairman Khrushchev that all of the IL-28 bombers now in Cuba will be withdrawn in thirty days. He also agrees that these planes can be observed and counted as they leave. Inasmuch as this goes a long way towards reducing the danger which faced this hemisphere four weeks ago, I have this afternoon instructed the secretary of defense to lift our naval quarantine.[14]

What a relief it is, Jack thinks, to be able to read these words and explain to the nation that the Cuban crisis is coming to an end. There are still unsatisfying loose ends regarding the lack of onsite inspection. But as the saying goes in Washington, this is "good enough for government work." Good enough, indeed.

At 2:30 p.m., Ted Sorensen arrives for some last minute tweaking of his preparatory materials. Sorensen reminds him for the hundredth time not to tell too many jokes, not to poke fun of too many of the questions asked by the journalists, and to limit the number of his puns and double entendres to a minimum. Jack tells Sorensen he will try, but that Ted must understand that it is often the lesser of two evils to poke fun at a questioner rather than to simply say that he or she has asked a goddamned stupid and irrelevant question. Sorensen merely looks as his boss helplessly. And to be honest, Sorensen thinks, I really enjoy his jokes. In fact, as he has thought about it on numerous occasions, most of the really funny jokes he knows he first heard from Jack, with one exception: an old Nebraska joke about a specialty poultry worker—a pheasant plucker, actually—who has a few drinks and begins to tell the woman he has just met about his work, and as he does so he transposes a few consonants from "pheasant" to "plucker," and vice versa. Then for one horrifying moment, Sorensen thinks: what if he tells that one at the press conference? But before he can say anything more, Jack tells him to tell Tommy Thompson to deliver a message to Khrushchev via Ambassador Dobrynin: that in addition to everything else he will discuss at the press conference, he is also lowering the level of U.S. war-readiness.

Sorensen makes a quick exit, having been given his assignment. Jack tightens up his tie, grabs his folder of "cheat-sheets," and heads downstairs to a car waiting to take him to the State Department auditorium for the press conference.

[An hour before his press conference, President Kennedy directed Llewellyn Thompson to communicate to the Soviet ambassador the following message for Nikita Khrushchev]

In addition to what the president intends to announce at the press conference, he has also ordered a lowered state of alert for the U.S. armed forces, that had been introduced in the beginning of the Cuban events. Simultaneously, those air squadrons that had been called to active duty during the Cuban crisis have been ordered back to reserve.

As Sorensen foresaw, Jack is given plenty of material to have fun with at the press conference, in spite of the fact that most of the discussion concerns the closest call to Armageddon in recorded history. Toward the middle of the press conference, Jack has the following exchange with a solicitous journalist from Florida:

JOURNALIST: Mr. President, the people of Florida are hoping that you and your family will again spend Christmas with them. Can you tell us what your present plans are, sir?

JACK: My father and mother are going to Florida in December, and my wife and children hope to go there for Christmas, and if my situation permits, I will go for Christmas. If the question is the result of some stories that the tourist business in Florida is off because of our difficulties, I hope it will not be too dangerous in Florida this year. [Laughter][15]

Back in the White House after the press conference, Ted Sorensen feels compelled to tell his boss that the complaints had already started coming in from the chambers of commerce all over Florida. "Mr. President," Sorensen says, "I don't think they got your joke."
"Of course they didn't," Jack laughs, "because all that heat and humidity down there rots the brain. It can't be helped. That's why I don't want to spend too much time down there. Oh, and Ted: happy post-Cuban crisis!"
After Sorensen leaves the Oval Office, Jack walks to a window, leans over and places his palms down on the table immediately in front of the window. He has discovered that this often helps him manage his severe back pain. As he looks out the window, slightly bent over, occasionally massaging his lower back and suddenly overcome with fatigue, he asks his secretary, Evelyn Lincoln, what day of the week it is. After learning that it is Tuesday, he pulls a Harvard football schedule out of his pocket and is ecstatic to learn that this coming Saturday is "The Game"—the Harvard-Yale game, played this year at Harvard Stadium in Allston, MA, across the river from Harvard Yard. Going to the Harvard-Yale game, he decides, will be excellent therapy for both his back and his spirits, something both frivolous yet fully engaging to a Harvard man like Jack.

POSTSCRIPT

Hope

December 10, 1962–October 15, 2010

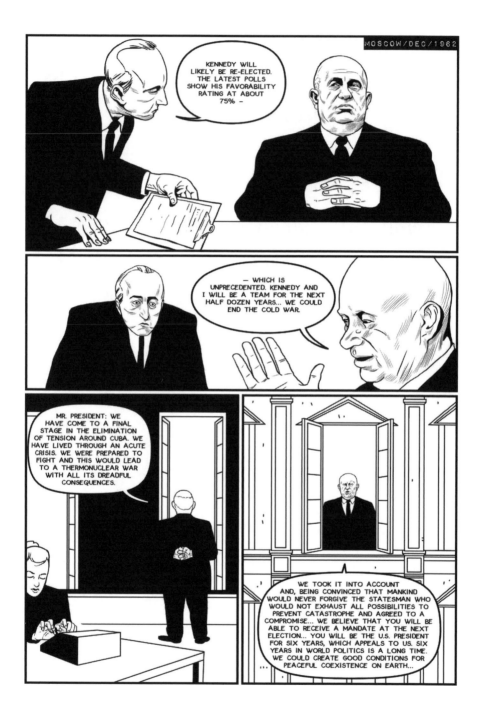

...TO BE CONTINUED AT ARMAGEDDONLETTERS.COM

Theatrical Preview

[The spotlight is on Khrushchev. He is sitting in a chair, weeping, with his face in his hands. After a few seconds, he turns to the audience.]

NIKITA SERGEI'ICH: It's all over. Kennedy has been murdered. We thought we had six years to work together on peace and disarmament. But we only had one year. We made a good start—with the Limited Test Ban Treaty and the Hotline—but it was only a start. It is impossible to start all over again with his successor. Johnson was not in the trench with me during the Cuban crisis. He doesn't know what Kennedy and Fidel and I know. He never will. With Kennedy, everything was possible. Now . . . [He begins weeping again *[Suddenly Khrushchev looks out at the audience.]*

You think I exaggerate? Do you? You think I'm just a sentimental Russian, given to emotional outbursts? Is that what you think? Well, think again, my friends. Listen to what Kennedy said last June:

[The spotlight shifts to Jack Kennedy *standing at a podium. He shuffles some papers, then begins]*

It is with great pride that I participate in this ceremony at the American University,
    . . .
    I have chosen this time and place to discuss a topic on which ignorance too often abounds and the truth is too rarely perceived—yet it is the most important topic on earth: world peace . . .
    . . .

219

I speak of peace because of the new face of war. Total war makes no sense in an age where great powers can maintain large and relatively invulnerable nuclear forces and refuse to surrender without resort to those forces. It makes no sense in an age where a single nuclear weapon contains almost ten times the explosive force delivered by all the allied air forces in the Second World War. It makes no sense in an age when the deadly poisons produced by a nuclear exchange would be carried by wind and water and soil and seed to the far corners of the globe and to the generations unborn.

...

First: Let us examine our attitude toward peace itself. Too many of us think it is impossible. Too many think it is unreal. But that is a dangerous, defeatist belief. It leads to the conclusion that war is inevitable—that mankind is doomed . . .

We need not accept this view. Our problems are manmade—therefore they can be solved by man. ...

...

Second: Let us reexamine our attitude towards the Soviet Union. . . . No government or social system is so evil that its people must be considered as lacking in virtue. . . . Among the many traits the peoples of our two countries have in common, none is stronger than our mutual abhorrence of war. Almost unique among the major world powers, we have never been at war with each other. And no nation in the history of battle ever suffered more than the Soviet Union in the Second World War. At least 20 million lost their lives. Countless millions of homes and families were burned or sacked. A third of the nation's territory, including two-thirds of its industrial base, was turned into a wasteland—a loss equivalent to the destruction of this country east of Chicago.

...

While we proceed to safeguard our national interests, let us also safeguard human interests. . . . The United States, as the world knows, will never start a war. This generation of Americans has already had enough—more than enough—of war and hate and oppression. We shall be prepared if others wish it. We shall be alert to try to stop it. But we shall also do our part to build a world of peace where the weak are safe and the strong are just. We are not helpless before that task or hopeless of its success. Confident and unafraid, we must labor on—not toward a strategy of annihilation but towards a strategy of peace.[1]

[The spotlight then returns to Khrushchev sitting in a chair. The rest of the stage is dark. Khrushchev looks out at the audience, shaking his head back and forth.]

NIKITA SERGEI'ICH: Our sources believe Kennedy was killed by a right-wing conspiracy that could not tolerate his failure to attack and invade Cuba, and his failure to start a war with us. The Kennedy family has been in touch with us and they said the same thing. If it is true, it is lunacy. Kennedy was killed for his failure to blow up Cuba and then to blow up the world? These are failures? What kind of sick minds think this way? Nina Petrovna and I must be the first in line tomorrow at the U.S. embassy. We must sign the book of mourning before the others.

[The stage goes dark for a few seconds. The spotlight then shines on Khrushchev as he is sitting in the dock of a courtroom. A disembodied voice then gives the brief against Khrushchev, who is being removed from power.]

[*Voice-over*]:

On this fourteenth day of October 1964, Nikita Sergei'ich Khrushchev, these are the conclusions of your former colleagues on the Presidium with regard to your foolish Cuban adventure:

- The Cuban crisis was too dangerous—a product of your own risky adventurism. It was not a victory, as you have claimed, but the worst defeat suffered by our country since World War II.
- You foolishly tried to go around the Party apparatus. If you had consulted with us in the proper fashion, you would have been prevented from making such a costly mistake, and our country would have avoided humiliation.
- You caved into your fantasies when you brought the young, dangerous and arrogant Fidel Castro into our family of nations. It was a terrible mistake. Castro made you and our entire country look like fools throughout the entire episode.
- Any of our generals could have told you, if you had asked them, that your cockamamie plan to "penetrate" Latin America was ridiculous. On the contrary, Castro's attempts to export his violent revolution have already led us into conflict with the Latin American communist parties that we have labored long to establish and nurture. By refusing to rein in Castro, you ruined all that.
- The Soviet line must, in all instances also be the Cuban line. If Castro and his colleagues can't or won't play by these rules, then we must either abandon Cuba or replace Castro. Those are the only two viable alternatives.

Therefore, Nikita Sergei'ich Khrushchev, having failed to protect the interests of the Soviet Union, as you were sworn to do, you shall hereafter be known simply as "Pensioner Khrushchev." You are hereby stripped of all your positions and responsibilities in the Party and government of the Soviet Union. Have you anything to say?

NIKITA SERGEI'ICH: Yes. You have obviously gathered together to splatter shit on me. You've done a fine job of that. I thank you for that. [Khrushchev sneers and laughs simultaneously.] It seems that you are getting rid of me because I tried to achieve a stable peace—I tried to work toward a stable peace—with the Americans, with Kennedy, and this required dealing with Fidel Castro in a certain way. I made the decisions I had to make in a timely fashion to prevent a nuclear war. You know of course that many believe Kennedy was killed because he also tried to achieve peace in the Caribbean and around the world. Many people believe this. I believe this. So, I thank you for not killing me. And I wish you good luck, Comrade Brezhnev. You will need it. I am finished.[2] [Khrushchev looks defiant and resolute, as the lights grow dim.]

[*The stage goes dark for roughly fifteen seconds. When the lights return, we see Fidel Castro, now a very old man, with white hair and a white beard, sitting on a stool, leaning on a cane, his hands shaking. When he begins speaking, his voice is higher, squeakier, more forced than ever. He labors over every word.*]

FIDEL: I was in Varadero when I learned that Kennedy had been assassinated. Believe it or not, at that very moment I was discussing a secret message

Kennedy had sent to me, carried by the French journalist, Jean Daniel. Kennedy wanted to know if I understood how close the world came to total catastrophe in the October crisis, and would I be willing to work with him to prevent such an event from every occurring again. That was basically it.

When Daniel asked me that question, I exploded. Are you kidding? Is Kennedy kidding? During the October crisis we Cubans said 'goodbye' every night to our children and our country. Every night we felt that tomorrow, for us, for Cuba, would not exist. So did we know how dangerous the crisis was? Yes, we knew. We knew in spades. We felt it in our bones. We were convinced that we would be completely destroyed, and there was not one thing we could do about it. I told Daniel to tell Kennedy that I answer 'yes' to both questions: I know how dangerous the crisis was; and I am willing—if Kennedy is ready—to work toward a more stable arrangement. That is what I told Jean Daniel.

Then the message came. It was at 1:30 p.m., just before lunch, beside the beach at Varadero. Kennedy was dead. Later, our sources reached the conclusion that a right-wing conspiracy was behind the assassination. Maybe, maybe not. Anyway, Kennedy was gone. Then the next year, Khrushchev was gone. I spent the next forty years of my life fighting both superpowers. [Fidel's voice becomes conspiratorial.] Listen, every Cuban knows that history has yet to record whether Cuba has suffered more from U.S. hostility or Russian friendship. [Fidel breaks into a squeaky laughter.]

I hardly gave another thought to nuclear weapons until my illness. I almost died in 2006. I gave up all my positions. I thought my time was up. While I went in and out of a coma, I had nightmares about the October crisis. It was the most intense and memorable episode in my life, and in the life of my country. A lot has been made about my letter to Comrade Nikita of October 26/27, 1962—the letter in which I asked him to destroy the United States with a nuclear strike, if the U.S. attacked, invaded and destroyed our country. Let me tell you something about that letter. That letter was my last will and testament. That was my deathbed wish. That was the last letter I thought I would ever write. I thought Armageddon for Cuba would commence within hours, or even minutes. I thought we had no hope of surviving. Maybe that's why my coma nightmares were about the October crisis—what I thought was my deathbed in 2006 brought to mind my 'deathbed' of October 1962.

Anyway, the more I thought about it, the more I realized that it was a monumental mistake to accept Khrushchev's offer of the nuclear missiles. The missiles made us very important back then. But at the same time that the weapons made us important, we were about to be totally destroyed because of the weapons. When I finally recovered—well, partially recovered—in 2008 I resolved to do what I could to alert the world to the danger of living with nuclear weapons.

I have been blogging for the past couple of years about many things, but my main focus is the nuclear threat. That's right. At age 85, I have become a blogger—a revolutionary blogger, of course. In the Second Declaration of Havana, which appeared on February 4, 1962, I wrote: "*El deter de todo revolucionario es hacer la revolucion*" ("the duty of a revolutionary is to make the revolution"). I still believe that. If we can abolish nuclear weapons—well, that would be revolutionary. How revolutionary am I? I wrote this in my blog on October 15, 2010, on the forty-eighth anniversary of the October crisis [Fidel reads from a sheet of paper]: "In a nuclear war, the collateral damage would be the life of humankind. Let us have the courage to proclaim that all nuclear or conventional weapons, everything that is used to make war, must disappear." When my brother Raul, President Raul, heard about this he said, "Fidel this is unbelievable; you have lost your mind and become a pacifist."

[Fidel puts the paper away. He takes a deep breath, while staring out at the audience. He resumes speaking, but with considerable effort.]

My comrades, in October 1962, I knew nothing about nuclear weapons, nothing about the nuclear balance of power. Nothing at all. Comrade Nikita was right to ignore my letter asking for a nuclear strike on the United States if they should invade our country. It would have been the end of the world. It would have deprived us of the opportunity to pass on the world to our children and grandchildren in the hope that they might improve on our efforts. We must rid the world of these weapons before we destroy ourselves.

[Speaking in a halting voice.] You know I used to end my speeches with *"patria o muerte, venceremos"* (*"Fatherland or death, we will prevail"*). I don't apologize for that. Because we have this attitude in Cuba, our Revolution has survived for more than a half century, in spite of strenuous efforts to make us surrender or collapse. But my new revolution has a new motto. It is from the Old Testament book of Deuteronomy 30:19: "I have set before you life and death, a blessing and a curse: therefore choose life, that both thou and thy seed may live." I know: it's odd for a dialectical materialist to cite the Bible. I say: take your inspiration where you find it. I was trained by Jesuits. Maybe some of it stuck to my brain.

[Fidel tries unsuccessfully to stand up. He sits back down on his stool. He raises one fist in the air, as he holds firmly to his cane. He glares at the audience and says, "Elegir la vida, no la muerte. Venceremos!" ("Choose life, not death. We will prevail!")]

End of Theatrical Preview

* * *

#40

Nikita S. Khrushchev to John F. Kennedy

December 10, 1962[3]

> *"we and you were prepared to fight. . . a thermonuclear war"*

It is late on December 4, 1962. Nikita Sergei'ich is in his Kremlin office on the day following the first Presidium meeting since Anastas Ivan'ich Mikoyan's return from Havana. In that meeting, Nikita Sergei'ich led the praise for his old friend, who

talked Fidel into submission last month, permitting an end to the Cuban crisis. But
he also used the occasion to try out some ideas he intends to integrate into his De-
cember 12th speech to the Supreme Soviet, giving the official Soviet view of the cause,
conduct, resolution and lessons of the Cuban crisis. He thinks: of course, those 1500
flunkies in that rubber stamp body will clap and cheer and the transcript will have
all those stupid references in brackets to ["Applause in the hall"], and even a few
to his personal favorite, ["Stormy and prolonged applause in the hall"]. Normally,
Nikita Sergei'ich thinks these required performances in front of feckless functionaries
are a waste of time. But this time, he actually looks forward to it.

He asks himself, "Why am I looking forward to this?" He is surprised by the
extent of his excitement over this normally routine appearance before a body that
has not cast a single "no" vote in its entire history—since Stalin established it 1938.
His mind is awash with ideas. Foremost among them is this: he feels he has been
at the center of decisions and events as the world has passed a fundamental turning
point—away from confrontation between East and West, away from emphasis on
armaments and toward diplomacy, away from the brink of catastrophic nuclear war,
toward a sober rapprochement between the superpowers and their respective allies.
At the heart of his new understanding is the feeling that both sides, led by Kennedy
and himself, were scared to death that the world was about to be destroyed—that
the fatal step was just a move or two away. But somehow he and Kennedy had
miraculously stepped back just in time, in spite of the shenanigans of his impetuous
ally Fidel Castro. Nikita Sergei'ich feels that the caution displayed by Kennedy and
him allowed the world to survive intact.

Yet to Nikita Sergei'ich, what has survived does not, in one respect, resemble
the world as it appeared to him just a month and a half ago, on the eve of the
confrontation over missiles in Cuba. This new world is one in which crises must be
avoided. He quickly scribbles some rough notes about concrete actions he intends
to take that are consistent with this new appreciation of the fragility and precious-
ness of everything. He will not insist on getting U.S. forces out of West Berlin. He
wishes they would leave, but if they don't, he can live with it. He will no longer
send secret aid to the Pathet Lao insurgents in Laos, over which a nuclear crisis
nearly developed on several occasions over the previous year and a half. He will
explore with Kennedy what must be done to sign a Nuclear Test Ban Treaty some-
time in 1963. Nikita Sergei'ich is almost giddy with excitement as he goes over
this list. It occurs to him as he muses over these developments and aspirations that
what is new—to him, to Kennedy, to the world at large—is hope: *hope for peace,*
for a better world for his children and grandchildren.

Moreover, Nikita Sergei'ich is seized by the conviction that Kennedy feels the
same way. He is sure of it. He can sense it between the lines of Kennedy's letters
and public pronouncements. As he is musing, it suddenly happens yet again, as it
has now for many days, sometimes in the oddest circumstances. Nikita Sergei'ich
finds himself in a reverie in which one phrase is repeated over and over, until it
is almost musical: "six more years, six more years, six more years. . . ." Kennedy

will be reelected. He is certain of that. The latest polls show Kennedy's favorability rating at about 75 percent, which his aide for U.S. affairs, Oleg Alexand'rich Troyanovsky, has informed him is almost unprecedented. So there can be no doubt: he and Kennedy will be a team for the next half-dozen years.

At this point, almost overcome with all the possibilities that he now feels hopeful about, he catches himself. Wait a minute, he thinks: after all the sorrow and bloodshed and broken dreams I have seen in my life, after two world wars that killed millions of my own people, how can I believe that so much is now possible? I must be careful, he thinks. After all, I don't want the rest of the leadership to think that I have turned into the pie-eyed, drunken village idiot. Then again, the hell with them, he says to himself, just as his secretary informs him that his American visitor, Mr. Norman Cousins, the editor of the Saturday Review, *is waiting to see him. He tells her to show him in.*

Cousins arrives bearing personal messages from both Pope John XXIII and President Kennedy. The Pope, who is dying of cancer, has asked Cousins to tell Nikita Sergei'ich simply that, "nothing is impossible." After Cousins utters the phrase in English, the interpreter, Viktor Sukhodrev, repeats it in Russian. All three men are silent for some moments. Finally, Nikita Sergei'ich breaks the silence. "You know, Mr. Cousins," he says, "nobody will ever make a Catholic out of me, but if any man could, it would be Pope John."

Nikita Sergei'ich then asks to hear what message Kennedy has sent. Cousins answers: "The president wants to know, basically, whether you feel as he does— that you two, our countries, and the world have passed very near to the fiery furnace of nuclear war, and that you two must take the lead in walking the world back from the precipice. That is his message—fundamentally, it is a question."

Nikita Sergei'ich's response is brief: "Yes, absolutely. Kennedy and I were in the same trench together, with the same kinds of enemies."

After thanking Cousins for delivering the messages, Nikita Sergei'ich explains what he means. "There were those," he says, "who actually wanted to launch the war that might well have spelled doomsday for the human race. Take the Chinese, for example," Nikita Sergei'ich explains, "they say I was afraid to stand up to a paper tiger. It is all nonsense. What good would it have done me, Mr. Cousins, in the last hour of my life to know that though our two great nations were in ruins, the so-called 'sacred honor' of the Soviet Union was intact?" Nikita Sergei'ich pauses, as he recalls the confrontations he had during the Cuban crisis with his own military people, and of course, with Fidel and his people—who all seemed to Nikita Sergei'ich like a bunch of lemmings marching toward oblivion.

Just before Cousins leaves, Nikita Sergei'ich reaches into his desk, pulls out some stationery, and scribbles two Christmas greetings: one to Pope John XXIII, and one to President Kennedy. He asks Cousins to deliver them personally, and Cousins agrees to do so. He also asks Cousins if he is a Catholic, like Kennedy and the Pope.

Cousins responds that he is not, but is instead a Unitarian. Nikita Sergei'ich asks, "What does a Unitarian believe?"

Cousins replies: "Unitarians believe that we are all God's children. You know, Mr. Chairman, in light of this discussion of what you say you learned from the Cuban crisis, I think you would make a fine Unitarian."

Nikita Sergei'ich, laughing, responds: "If you can convince the Pope and Kennedy to become Unitarians, then count me in." Both men laugh as soon as the interpreter is finished translating the comment into English.

After saying goodbye to Norman Cousins, Nikita Sergei'ich returns to his desk and makes more notes for his December 12th speech, and for a letter he wants to write to Kennedy. Six years, six years, he thinks. Six years is a long time, but there is so much to do.

Dear Mr. President:

It would seem that you and we have come now to a final stage in the elimination of tension around Cuba. Our relations are already entering their normal course since all those means placed by us on the Cuban territory which you considered offensive are withdrawn …

That is good. We appreciate that you, just as we, approached not dogmatically the solution of the question of eliminating the tension which evolved and this enabled us under existing conditions to find a more flexible form of verification of the withdrawal of the above mentioned means. Understanding and flexibility displayed by you in this matter are highly appreciated by us though our criticism of American imperialism remains in force because that conflict was indeed created by the policy of the United States with regard to Cuba.

…

Within a short period of time we and you have lived through a rather acute crisis. The acuteness of it was that we and you were prepared to fight and this would lead to a thermonuclear war. Yes, to a thermonuclear war with all its dreadful consequences. We took it into account and, being convinced that mankind would never forgive the statesman who would not exhaust all possibilities to prevent catastrophe [and] agreed to a compromise.

…

We believe that the guarantees for non-invasion of Cuba given by you will be maintained and not only in the period of your stay in the White House, that, to use an expression, goes without saying. We believe that you will be able to receive a mandate at the next election too, that is that you will be the U.S. president for six years, which would appeal to us. In our time, six years in world politics is a long period of time and during that period we could create good conditions for peaceful coexistence on earth and this would be highly appreciated by the peoples of our countries as well as by all other peoples.

…

Please convey to your wife and your whole family wishes of good
health from myself, my wife and my entire family.

N.S. Khrushchev

* * *

#41

John F. Kennedy to Nikita S. Khrushchev

December 14, 1962[4]

"we should not permit others to stand in the way"

*Jack is preparing for a meeting with his speechwriter Ted Sorensen and his brother
Bobby. The two topics on the agenda: Jack's forthcoming State of the Union address, scheduled for January 14th, and his response to the most recent letter from
Khrushchev. While the State of the Union message must cover the whole range of
issues facing the nation, Jack wants to devote a substantial portion of it to some
positive lessons and actions deriving from the missile crisis. He senses that Americans were really scared during the crisis, to an unprecedented degree. They felt
vulnerable to total annihilation and the feeling made them deeply uncomfortable.
He wants to offer them a message of hope: that Americans and Soviets will take
concrete actions in the coming months and years to reduce the risk of anything like
the Cuban missile crisis ever occurring again.*

*Bobby and Ted arrive, and Jack begins by telling them he has now finished
reading a new and really scary book—scary to him, at least:* Seven Days in May,
*by Fletcher Knebel and Charles Bailey. "It's about an attempted coup in the U.S.
by a group of disgruntled military officers who think the president, Jordan Lyman,
is being insufficiently forceful in dealing with the Soviet communists. Jordan Lyman could be me," he says. He asks them if they know the book. Neither has read
it, though both are aware that it is controversial.*

*Jack goes on to outline the plot to them. The fictional Joint Chiefs are led by a
general who resembles Jack's own Air Force Chief, General Curtis LeMay, and for
good reason. As Knebel, a journalist by trade, told Jack just before the missile crisis, a
1961 interview of LeMay by Knebel scared the daylights out of him. Jack says Knebel
told him that LeMay, in the interview, strongly advocated a "splendid first strike"
capability against the Soviet Union. What LeMay meant by this shocked Knebel.
"According to the journalist," Jack says, "LeMay wants the U.S. to have the capacity
to attack all the known Soviet nuclear weapons and their launch vehicles and destroy
them on the ground (including both missiles and bombers), before the Soviets can
launch a second strike against the U.S. Of course, LeMay admitted to Knebel, it is
possible that a few Soviet missiles or bombers would escape the first strike and be
launched against the U.S. In that case, a few million Americans might be killed.*

This would be unfortunate but, as LeMay sees it, the deaths of so many Americans, while of course tragic, would be easily outweighed by the complete destruction of the Soviet Union, the victory of the U.S. in the Cold War, and the return of unchallenged, U.S. global supremacy." Jack tells Bobby and Ted, "Jesus Christ, he is mad, he is stark, raving mad, isn't he?" Bobby and Ted aren't sure whether Jack is referring to the real LeMay or his fictional representation, or both. But they share Jack's view of the actual LeMay, so both nod their agreement.

Jack says one detail of the plot of Seven Days in May *seems relevant at this particular moment.* "In the novel," he says, "the coup plotters are moved to try to remove the president because he and the leader of the Soviet Union have signed a disarmament treaty that, if ratified, will require both superpowers to destroy their nuclear arsenals. During the ratification process in the U.S., right-wing extremists, goaded by the LeMay types at the highest levels of the U.S. military, claim that the Soviets will cheat and that, after the U.S. has totally disarmed, Moscow will announce that it has hidden a lot of nuclear weapons, which they will use as leverage for the systematic nuclear blackmail of Washington. The Soviet goal, according to the coup plotters, is ultimately either to enslave or physically destroy America. Either way, Soviet global dominance will be assured, and the cause will be an agreement that a foolish and naïve president signs with the Soviet Union.*

"What a coincidence," Jack says. "This book comes out just as Khrushchev and I are feeling our way toward a Nuclear Test Ban Treaty. Having dealt with the real-life Curtis LeMay during the missile crisis, all three of us know that LeMay— and not only LeMay, but all the Chiefs—hate the very idea of an arms control treaty with the Soviets, for exactly the same reason attributed to LeMay's fictional representation in Seven Days in May. It's eerie, isn't it?"

Bobby, looking, as usual, slightly disheveled and in need of a haircut, reminds his brother that on November 20th—the very day Jack and Khrushchev basically declared an end to the missile crisis—the Joint chiefs sent Jack a memorandum via Bob McNamara that asserted the necessity and possibility of achieving a first-strike capability.

Jack responds: "Yeah, Bob said those guys didn't actually use the term 'first-strike,' but that is the only possible reason, according to Bob, why they want all the hardware they've asked for in the next Pentagon budget. Bob says he can't explain it any other way. Every day I ask myself: what in the hell would we do with those madmen if we didn't have Bob McNamara to hold the line against them? Sometimes I think that Bob is all that is standing between the Chiefs and . . . well . . . maybe something like what we have here in Seven Days in May. The thing is, Bob doesn't only have a steel spine. He's also smarter than the whole bunch of them together. He's also got some good spies working the territory all over the Pentagon. Thank God for McNamara across the river."

"Mr. President," Sorensen says after observing a respectful moment of silence, "I have been thinking about your wish to end the State of the Union address on a hopeful note—hopeful especially about avoiding Armageddon. I was thinking of a *naval metaphor along the following lines: you tell the American people that you wish to close on a note of hope for reducing the risk of another nuclear confrontation with the Soviet Union. You note the storm that has just passed, a storm in which we all nearly capsized and drowned. In the coming year, you say, "'We will steer our ship with hope,' as Thomas Jefferson said, 'leaving fear astern.' Something like that."*

"Yeah," Jack says to Sorensen and Bobby, "I like that. I like the hopeful conclusion and I like the maritime metaphor. And I especially like the reference to Jefferson. Now, all we have to do is draft a speech for which Ted has just supplied the conclusion." Sorensen nods his understanding and agreement.

"Oh," Jack says, "one more thing about Seven Days in May. *John Frankenheimer wants to make a movie based on the book. He says that he has already heard from some elements in the Pentagon that to make a movie from that book would be 'un-American.' That's total bullshit, but it gave me an idea. I told Frankenheimer that if he wants to shoot the White House scenes here at the White House, we just need to coordinate our schedules so that I am in Hyannis Port on a weekend when they want to shoot their scenes. Oh, and I hear that Rod Serling, the guy from* Twilight Zone, *is doing the screenplay. He's perfect. I sometimes feel like I'm living in a* Twilight Zone *episode these days."*

"We all do," Bobby says, as he leaves the oval office. "That's why you and Khrushchev have got to move fast on the Test Ban Treaty. Bob McNamara won't be able to control the Pentagon crazies forever. And the minute you and Khrushchev sign the thing, the real nut cases like General Edwin Walker down in Dallas will scream bloody murder."

"Right," Jack says. "Ted, let's get going on that response to Khrushchev right now." As Bobby leaves, Jack and Ted Sorensen begin discussing ideas for the letter to Khrushchev and the State of the Union address.

Dear Mr. Chairman:

I was glad to have your message of December 11 and to know that you believe, as we do, that we have come to the final stage of the Cuban affair between us, the settlement of which will have significance for our future relations and for our ability to overcome other difficulties. I wish to thank you for your expression of appreciation for the understanding and flexibility we have tried to display.

. . .

You refer to the importance of my statements on an invasion of Cuba and of our intention to fulfill them, so that no doubts are sown from the very start. I have already stated my position publicly in my press conference on November 20, and I am glad that this statement appears to have your understanding; we have never wanted to be driven by the acts of others into war in Cuba. The other side of the coin, however, is that we do need to have adequate assurances that all offensive weapons are removed from Cuba and are not re-introduced, and that Cuba itself commits no aggressive acts against any of the nations of the Western Hemisphere. As I understand you, you feel confident that Cuba will not in fact engage in such aggressive acts, and of course I already have your own assurances about the offensive weapons. So I myself should suppose that you could accept our position—but it is probably better to leave final discussion of these matters to our representatives in New York. I quite agree with you that the larger part of the crisis has now been ended and we should not permit others to stand in the way of promptly settling the rest without further acrimony.

...

Thank you for your expressions of good wishes to me and my family, and let me in turn send you and your wife and family our personal good wishes for the coming year.

John F. Kennedy

* * *

#42

Jacqueline Kennedy to Nikita S. Khrushchev

December 1, 1963[5]

"the world should not be blown up."

Jackie Kennedy, exhausted by a week of nonstop activity following her husband's murder in Dallas, has said goodnight to her children, Caroline and John, on what she knows will be one of her last nights in the White House. Indeed, she has spent most of the day working with the small army of people who will be moving her family's personal effects out of the White House a few days from now.

Although it is late, she is deeply disturbed by a conversation she had a few hours ago with her brother-in-law Bobby Kennedy and Ted Sorensen. Both told her that they have received word from various sources in the Soviet embassy in Washington that Soviet leader Khrushchev is devastated by the death of her husband. In fact, they told her, Khrushchev may already have given up on the many peace initiatives he intended to pursue in collaboration with Jack during what he and Jack hoped would be another six years of working together. The Soviets say their information on Lyndon Johnson does not make them optimistic about being able to work with him on issues of disarmament and world peace. Jackie sits alone, wondering what she can do to encourage the Soviet chairman. She understands his grief—she more than understands it. She has become, she feels, almost a bundle of pure grief since Dallas. She feels that if she can keep going, then Khrushchev can too. A way must be found to get Khrushchev to pick up the baton and run toward the finish line of nuclear disarmament and world peace—issues to which Jack and Khrushchev had a mutual and powerful commitment.

She has in front of her on her desk two items: a letter from Khrushchev dated November 23ʳᵈ; and a calendar—polished wood, inlaid with silver—of the month of October 1962, with thirteen contiguous days, October 16–October 28, in bold-face, to commemorate the event that more than any other set Jack and Khrushchev off on a common path. Jack gave identical calendars to the members of his Executive Committee that advised him during the crisis, and to her. She remembers that he presented it to her at the end of November 1962 on the same day he gave them to his advisers. He winked as he said, "By the way, it comes from Tiffany's, but I sort of designed it myself. I only give these to my most important advisers." She remembers feeling grateful for being included in the group. She also felt that she had earned it. Every evening during those thirteen days, Jack filled her in on the proceedings of the day just ended. Often he could not get to sleep. So they stayed up into the wee hours of the morning talking about the crisis, what to do, how dangerous it was, and how the crisis made both of them feel desperate about the future that their children would face, or whether there would be any future for them at all.

Jackie turns to the letter from Khrushchev and re-reads it:

WN150 VIA RCA
MOSCOW 1215 NOVEMBER 23 1963
MRS. JACQUELINE KENNEDY
WITH DEEP PERSONAL SORROW I LEARNED ABOUT THE TRAGIC
DEATH OF YOUR HUSBAND—THE PRESIDENT OF USA JOHN F.
KENNEDY. IN EVERYONE WHO KNEW HIM HE INSPIRED GREAT
RESPECT, AND MY MEETINGS WITH HIM WILL FOREVER REMAIN IN
MY MEMORY. PLEASE ACCEPT MY MOST SINCERE CONDOLENCES
AND EXPRESSIONS OF MY DEEPEST SYMPATHY ON THE DEEP SOR-
ROW THAT BEFELL YOU.
    N. KHRUSHCHEV
    23 OF NOVEMBER 1963[6]

Jackie finds the awkwardness of the English translation poignant and touching. It seems to come from the heart of the man who, in the Cuban missile crisis, was transformed from a bitter enemy of America into Jack's partner in searching for a way through the missile crisis and beyond the Cold War.

She decides to write a letter to Khrushchev. She has already discussed the pos-sibility with Mac Bundy. Mac has a plan for getting it to the Soviet leader. She will write it out in longhand. Mac will edit it and pass it through the State De-partment channels. And he will personally deliver it to the Soviet ambassador, to be forwarded directly to Khrushchev.

She will tell the Soviet leader what she told Anastas Mikoyan, who represented Khrushchev at Jack's funeral: "My husband is dead. Now peace is up to you." At least that is what she hopes she said. Truthfully, she has trouble recalling the events of that day. One thing she does remember is that in the receiving line at the White House, Mikoyan was weeping. Jackie did not know at that point that Mikoyan's wife had died around the time of the missile crisis, while he was in Cuba negotiating with Fidel Castro. Mac Bundy informed her of this when she asked Mac how to explain Mikoyan's emotional reaction at the funeral. She thinks she will never forget Mikoyan's show of empathy.

She picks up her pen and then puts it down immediately. She realizes that, along with explaining to Khrushchev what she thinks are the objectives he and Jack shared she will also have to say something about Lyndon Johnson. After all, Khrushchev can't achieve world peace on his own. He will need to work with Johnson. Jackie barely knows him. She is well aware that Bobby hates him, though she is not quite clear why Bobby's animosity toward Johnson is so intense, even for Bobby, who is well known for the strength of his passions—so completely unlike Jack, who tended to see irony and humor in everything, even Johnson. Once, with only the two of them present, for example, Jack attempted an impersonation of Johnson's deep, nasal Texas drawl, and failed so completely that both of them broke into hysterical laughter.

Jackie is aware that Bobby believes Johnson is not interested in carrying on Jack's commitment to world peace. Bobby says he is a hardliner, a dogmatic anticommunist who sees the world through slogans like "free world" and "enslaved world." She also recalls vividly Jack telling her late one night during the missile crisis, "If Lyndon was president, we'd already be at war." So she tends to think Bobby is probably right about Johnson. But she decides to lie about this to Khrushchev. She must give the man some basis to hope that he can bring Johnson around. Maybe Lyndon can learn on the job the way Jack did. Well, a person can hope, anyway, she thinks.

Once again, she picks up her pen. This time she is ready to write her letter to the Soviet leader.

Dear Mr. Chairman President:

I would like to thank you for sending Mr. Mikoyan as your representative to my husband's funeral. He looked so upset when he came through the line, and I was very moved.

I tried to give him a message for you that day—but as it was such a terrible day for me, I do not know if my words came out as I meant them to.

So now, in one of the last nights I will spend in the White House, in one of the last letters I will write on this paper at the White House, I would like to write you my message.

I send it only because I know how much my husband cared about peace, and how the relation between you and him was central to this care in his mind. He used to quote your words in some of his speeches—"In the next war the survivors will envy the dead."

You and he were adversaries, but you were allied in a determination that the world should not be blown up. You respected each other and could deal with each other. I know that President Johnson will make every effort to establish the same relationship with you.

The danger which troubled my husband was that war might be started not so much by the big men as by the little ones.

While big men know the needs for self-control and restraint—little men are sometimes moved by fear and pride. If only in the future the big men can continue to make the little ones sit down and talk, before they start to fight.

I know that President Johnson will continue the policy in which my husband so deeply believed—a policy of control and restraint—and he will need your help.

I send this letter because I know so deeply of the importance of the relationship which existed between you and my husband, and also because of your kindness, and that of Mrs. Khrushcheva in Vienna.

I read that she had tears in her eyes when she left the American embassy in Moscow, after signing the book of mourning. Please thank her for that.

Sincerely,
Jacqueline Kennedy

* * *

#43

Fidel Castro, YouTube Video Post, "Against Nuclear War"

October 15, 2010[7]

"In a nuclear war the 'collateral damage' would be humanity."

Fidel is in his study, going over what he hopes is the final draft of a message that will soon be filmed and posted on the web. The film crew has arrived and is setting up its equipment as quietly as possible, since it is obvious Fidel, his reading glasses perched on the end of his nose, pen in hand, is intensely involved with the material in front of him. To Cubans he will always be the comandante en jefe *(commander in chief)—so the film crew is respectful to a fault. Noticing this, Fidel waves his pen in the air and tells them not to worry about him, and that they should just do what they need to do. "It's not the first time I've been filmed, you* know," he says, laughing. "Really, I have been on camera before." Finally, loosened up, the crew drags their cameras, microphones, light bars and foil reflectors and the rest of their paraphernalia into position. Fidel tells them he will let them know when he is ready. Meanwhile, he tells them, they can go outside where some coffee and sweets await them on a table.

Fidel is nervous, very nervous. This moment has been a long time coming. When he was ill—when he nearly died, in 2006–2007—he relinquished all his official posts, though this was not publicized at the time. He decided that if he were given a little more time in this earthly existence, he would devote the bulk of whatever energy he had left to a single cause: the abolition of nuclear weapons from the face of the earth. It was sometime in 2008 or thereabouts, that he mentioned it to his brother (now Cuban President) Raul, and also to the perennial Cuban Vice President, Jose Ramon Fernandez (aka El Gallego, because his ancestors were from Galicia, in northwest Spain). They were both skeptical. In the first place, they and others pointed out, not many people care about the issue these days. "It's not like it was during the Cold War," El Gallego told him. "Nowadays, you hardly hear about the nukes at all. Besides, what do nuclear weapons have to do with Cuba, since the 1962 October crisis?" he asked rhetorically.

In general, the way Fidel remembers it, everyone around him was skeptical about his idea—everybody except Fidelito, his son the nuclear scientist, who thought it would be a very good idea. With Fidelito's help, Fidel has become a student of nuclear danger. He has invited experts on various aspects of nuclear weapons and their effects to come down to Cuba so he can interrogate them. He is trying to bring his own gut feeling that the weapons must be abolished into line with the empirical reality of the smartest people currently doing research and writing about the nuclear threat.

Just this past August (2010), for example, Fidel met for three days with Jeffrey Goldberg, a reporter for the U.S. magazine, The Atlantic, to discuss Goldberg's work on the Israeli security establishment and their apparent endorsement of preventive war against Iran. Goldberg was a provocateur. He asked Fidel how he squared his pursuit of nuclear abolition with his infamous— "infamous" was Goldberg's word, Fidel recalls—letter to Khrushchev asking the Soviet leader to blow the United States to smithereens. At one point in his discussion with Goldberg, Fidel showed the reporter a picture of himself taken recently, in which he was endeavoring to look as angry as possible—he can't remember why he posed for such a picture. When he showed the picture to Goldberg, he said, laughing, "Look at me; that's how angry I was at Khrushchev in the October crisis."

But that was almost fifty years ago. In August 2010 Fidel told Goldberg he had been wrong in October 1962. He also implied that Khrushchev had been right not to do as he asked, and he would have been right not to attack the U.S., even if the U.S. had invaded Cuba. "There was so much I didn't understand at that time," *he told Goldberg.*[8] *He also remembers thinking: what if the Israelis, Americans and Iranians now are like me in October 1962? What then?*

And just last month, he attended a lecture in Havana by the Rutgers climatologist, Alan Robock, on "nuclear winter." Fidel had invited Robock to Cuba specifically to give that lecture. He found Robock's talk disturbing, especially when Robock revealed that of the more than 22,000 nuclear weapons in the world, if only around two hundred were exploded in a war, nuclear winter could set in, due to the dust cover and other factors. With the onset of nuclear winter, humanity would die a slow, miserable, degrading death over years and decades, even if less than one percent of the current stock of nuclear weapons were detonated. Fidel found this absolutely shocking. Some of his acquaintances had told him, when he first began his one-man blogging campaign to abolish nuclear weapons, that with the demise of the Cold War, we no longer need to worry about a nuclear catastrophe such as might have occurred in the October crisis of 1962. A smallish nuclear war in the Middle East or South Asia or involving North Korea? Sure. But not an event that threatens to extinguish the human race. Listening to Robock, and discussing the issues with him over three days in Havana, Fidel feels vindicated in his choice of the abolition of nuclear weapons as his retirement obsession—absolutely vindicated.

He is waiting for Fidelito at the moment. He wants to go over one or two more things with him—especially his use of Albert Einstein in his message—whose work Fidelito of course knows intimately, while Fidel struggles with just the mere outline of what the great Einstein thought and wrote. Fidel doesn't remember thinking about Fidelito when he was mulling over what to focus on, if he were to recover enough to actually do some writing and speaking. But he should have realized, he thinks, that Fidelito would be a big help. Fidel thinks he has probably spent more time with Fidelito in the past two years than he had in the three previous decades.

As Fidel recalls it now, many of his recurring thoughts during his recovery from his near-fatal illness, were about the October crisis of 1962—especially about something that he discussed on several occasions with Robert McNamara, Kennedy's defense secretary, in Havana. It was this proposition: rational human beings, in a deep crisis, can make decisions leading to nuclear war even though that is not their intent. As McNamara pointed out to him on several occasions, this means a catastrophic nuclear war can occur even if none of the leaders of the involved countries seek one. Due to misunderstanding, misjudgment and the pressure of a crisis, rational leaders can make terrible decisions. Fidel told McNamara—in 1992 and 2002, at conferences in Havana on the thirtieth and fortieth anniversaries of the October crisis—that if the October crisis were to occur again, exactly as it did in 1962, he (Fidel) would react the same way. He would write the same letter to Khrushchev on October 26–27, asking him to launch Soviet nuclear missiles at the U.S., in the event of a U.S. invasion and occupation of the island. He made clear that he was talking about a situation devoid of hindsight. He would know no more, and no less, than he knew in October 1962. In that case: same decision, same letter. That is what he told McNamara at the time, and he believed it. Cuba was threatened with extinction via a U.S. attack. So it made sense to tell Khrushchev to martyr Cuba in the interest of destroying the capitalist enemy forever. In fact, he told McNamara that if McNamara had been in his position, he would have done the same thing.

Fidel remembers with a wry smile that McNamara was so horrified by that remark that he had trouble speaking clearly for a moment or two. And now Fidel has taken up the principal cause McNamara worked for over the last twenty-five years of his life: abolishing nuclear weapons. Fidel remembers, from time to time, the last words he and his former enemy ever spoke to each other, in 2002. As NcNamara was departing, Fidel invited him to participate in a conference in Havana ten years hence, in 2012, on the fiftieth anniversary of the crisis. McNamara responded by saying he would be dead by then and probably in hell. "On the contrary," Fidel remembers saying, "I think you will go to heaven, and I hope to meet you there." Fidel remembers thinking: poor McNamara, even in old age, the ghosts of Vietnam still haunted him. He was a good man, who was instrumental in helping Kennedy avoid an attack and invasion of Cuba that would have resulted in a nuclear catastrophe, possibly the extinction of the human race. Fidel thinks: McNamara never got enough credit for what he did in the October crisis. Even now, people would rather criticize a villain for committing the U.S. to a war in Vietnam, rather than praise him for playing a big role in preventing the destruction of human civilization.

Fidel is becoming impatient. "Where the hell is Fidelito, anyway?" he asks himself. Who does he think he is, making people wait? Does he think he is me? *Fidel laughs right out loud at this thought: that the mild-mannered, reclusive Fidelito could possibly become like his father. He is still smiling at this juxtaposition, when Fidelito comes striding through the door, looking, for all the world, like a portly, somewhat geeky version of himself about twenty-five years ago.*

Father and son go right to work, as the members of the film crew begin to drift back into the room. Fidelito asks his father if he really wants to be filmed making the statement in that red and black flannel shirt he is wearing. It looks, he says, like something a farmer or a lumberjack might wear during the winter in Russia to collect the milk from the cows. Fidelito, who was educated in Russia and speaks fluent Russian, reiterates his point: "Seriously Papa, you look like a Russian peasant."

Fidel laughs. "To hell with that," he responds. "Who cares what I am wearing?"

"Fair enough," says the son to his father. "Actually, on second thought you look ... I would say, interesting—eccentric, as befits a man on a mission, such as yourself." As Fidelito says this, he can barely suppress a giggle. "So, are you ready to go before the camera to talk about this subject?"

This is the nub of the problem for Fidel, the reason for his anxiety. While he has written voluminously in the past year and a half about the nuclear threat, he is nervous about how he will appear on camera. His hands shake. He can't see very well, even with his glasses. He is not the Maximum Leader anymore. In fact, he is not the maximum anything. Some Cuban journalists refer to him in the Cuban press as blogger en jefe *("blogger in chief"), which he both likes and doesn't like. At any rate, when he is blogging about the nuclear threat, he imagines that readers remember him as he was for so long: dominant, overpowering and inexhaustible. "And now." He thinks, "Fidelito tells me that I look like a Russian peasant fetching milk from the barn."*

Fidelito looks over the draft. He asks Fidel if he really wants to mention the danger of war in the Middle East, between Israel, the U.S. and Iran. "Wouldn't it be better," he says deferentially, "to keep your message on the highest plane, speaking to all humanity?"

"No, I want that reference in there," Fidel responds, "because that is where the danger is right now. That is where some nuclear catastrophe might begin—and it would affect all humanity, eventually. That is where the next October crisis might happen. Obama or Netanyahu or Ahmadinejad might screw up or get confused and then—who can believe that the war would not go nuclear, once the Israelis find out how hard the Iranians are going to hit them in retaliation?"

Fidel asks Fidelito to tell the camera crew he is ready. He feels his hands shaking. He simply cannot stop them from shaking no matter how hard he concentrates. And he cannot remember what he wants to say if he takes his eyes off the script for even a few seconds. He feels a panic attack coming when he recalls that he once led this nation of eleven million people, whereas now he is lucky to have his son as a research assistant and a few sturdy bodyguards to hold onto when he ventures out in public. The director shouts, "Listo?" ("Ready?"). Fidel holds up one finger and shakes it back and forth, signaling that he needs another minute to gather his thoughts.

At this moment, the idea comes to him full force, like an explosion. Suddenly, he has the kind of clarity of thought for which he was famous in the old days. He will stop resisting reality, stop pretending to be something he is not, and simply be what he is: the old man—like Hemingway's fisherman, Santiago, in The Old Man and the Sea, *who fought the sharks alone off the Cuban coast. He calls to the director of the camera crew and gruffly tells him to be sure to capture these images: Fidel's hands shaking, his eyes flinching, his difficulty in standing while he delivers the message. The director nods that he understands.*

This feels familiar to Fidel—being in charge, even though being in charge this time consists paradoxically of telling a film director that he, Fidel, isn't even fully in charge of his own bodily movements anymore. He wants his audience to know he is old and he is scared because of the threat of nuclear war. He remembers McNamara also looking a little bit crazy and a little bit scary. It was his eyes, Fidel thinks. They shone like an Old Testament prophet.

He is suddenly filled with the realization that at eighty-three years old, and having experienced the October crisis, he alone can speak about nuclear danger with the conviction and credibility of one who knows from his experience things no other living human being knows (now that McNamara is dead). I know what can happen, he thinks. I know everything could be lost forever, if we don't get rid of nuclear weapons. Kennedy was there and he knew this. Khrushchev was there and he knew this. McNamara was there and he knew this. Now it's up to me. I am the last survivor. I am the last witness. I am the last one who was there and know from my experience that we could lose everything. I know!

"Listo?" ("Ready?") asks the director a second time. "Listo y capaz!" ("Ready and able") Fidel answers. "El Viejo esta listo y capaz!" ("The old man is ready and able.")

The director, smiling, points at Fidel, and he begins reading his text. Fidelito, off-camera, watches his father and thinks my God, my father the Maximum Leader: he has become a nuclear age Jeremiah in a plaid flannel shirt. I think it suits him.

The use of nuclear weapons in a new war would mean the end of humanity. This was candidly foreseen by scientist Albert Einstein who was able to measure their destructive capability to generate millions of degrees of heat, which would vaporize everything within a wide radius of action. This brilliant researcher promoted the development of this weapon so that it would not become available to the genocidal Nazi regime.

Each and every government in the world has the obligation to respect the right to life of each and every nation and of the totality of all the peoples on the planet.

Today there is an imminent risk of war with the use of that kind of weapon and I don't harbor the least doubt that an attack by the United States and Israel against the Islamic Republic of Iran would inevitably evolve towards a global nuclear conflict.

The world's peoples have an obligation to demand of their political leaders their RIGHT TO LIVE. When the life of human kind, of your people and your most beloved human beings run such a risk, nobody can afford to be indifferent; not one minute can be lost in demanding respect for that right; tomorrow will be too late.

Albert Einstein stated: "I do not know with what weapons World War III will be fought, but World War IV will be fought with sticks and stones." We fully comprehend what he wanted to convey, and he was absolutely right, yet in the wake of a global nuclear war, there ultimately wouldn't be anybody around even to make use of sticks and stones.

There would be "collateral damage," as American political and military leaders always affirm, to justify the deaths of innocent people.

In a nuclear war the "collateral damage" would be all humanity.

Let us have the courage to proclaim that all nuclear or conventional weapons, everything that is used to make war, must disappear!

Fidel Castro Ruz
October 15, 2010

APPENDIX A

The Armageddon Time Machine/Text

Acquiring the Letters

A letter is a joy of earth—
It is denied the Gods—

—Emily Dickinson[1]

Labor well the minute particulars . . . and not in generalized demonstrations
of the rational power. General good is the plea of the hypocrite, the flatterer and
the scoundrel.

—William Blake[2]

This book represents the culmination of our nearly thirty-year quest for an Armageddon time machine for the nuclear age: some combination of credible oral testimony, declassified documentary evidence and scholarly analysis that might reveal what it was like for leaders in Washington, Moscow and Havana to look straight into the gun barrel of nuclear war during the October 1962 Cuban missile crisis.

Our objective at the outset of this quest, in the early 1980s, was to grasp what that crisis was *about*, and what it was *like* up close and personal for John F. Kennedy, Nikita Khrushchev, and Fidel Castro. If we could accomplish this, then it might be possible for others to achieve a vicarious experience of the horror felt by those leaders, bearing their huge responsibilities, when the world seemed to teeter on the brink of destruction. This historical objective seemed important to us because we believed it had the potential to provide a real-world foundation for the achievement of a second objective: to figuratively walk back from that imagined brink, identify why leaders came so close to Armageddon in October 1962, and apply our analysis to efforts to reduce the risk of such a catastrophic crisis ever happening again. We sought, in other words, *a policy-relevant history of the Cuban missile crisis.*

WHERE WE BEGAN: THE KENNEDY SCHOOL OF GOVERNMENT

It was at the Kennedy School, where we both were students in the early 1980s, that we encountered two issues for the first time. Issue number one was the belief—widespread in the 1980s—that risk of nuclear war between Russia and the West was substantial and growing, and that something had to be done to reverse the downward spiral toward a possible Armageddon.[3] Young people may find this difficult to believe. But it is true. Fear of nuclear war roughly thirty years ago was palpable, scary, and overwhelming to millions. The societies of the developed world during much of the 1980s were, in fact, virtually saturated with fear of a nuclear Armageddon.[4]

The second issue was: how dangerous, really, was the Cuban missile crisis? This was a much-discussed subject at the school of government bearing President Kennedy's name.[5] But it was also a subject of fascination throughout that portion of academia that devotes itself to international affairs, and includes historians, political scientists, economists and strategists. Back then scholars of international affairs endlessly debated a series of questions connected to the crisis of October 1962, such as:

- Was it really as *dangerous* as it seemed to some at the time?
- *How close* to war did the crisis get?
- If it was really dangerous, how close to *nuclear war* did the U.S. and USSR actually get?

If you were persuaded that nuclear war was quite unlikely in the missile crisis, then the conversation tended to stop right here. But for those who thought the crisis was very dangerous, other questions arose, such as the following:

- If a nuclear war had occurred, what kind of war would it have become—would it have been confined to Cuba, or to the Western Hemisphere, or would it likely have escalated into a global conflagration?
- If a nuclear war had occurred, what would have been the tipping point at which nuclear war would have been initiated—given that all concerned knew that even the use of one, or a few, nuclear weapons might escalate to the total destruction of their nations, perhaps all nations?

- What was it like, in October 1962, to bear responsibility for avoiding a nuclear war when the momentum toward Armageddon seemed to many to be almost irresistible?
- What might be some lessons from this deepest Cold War crisis that, if properly applied, might prevent sliding so close to nuclear Armageddon ever again?[6]

McNAMARA'S FIRST CHALLENGE: SHOW ME A NUCLEAR SCENARIO WITHOUT REGRET!

In the summer of 1984 these two issues—risk of nuclear war during the Reagan presidency, and risk of nuclear war in the Cuban missile crisis—began to fuse in our minds. The catalyst to the fusion was Robert McNamara, Kennedy's secretary of defense during the missile crisis. In 1984 we participated in a conference in which McNamara (whom we had never met) was a participant. The setting was as surreal as its name: the Big Sky resort, high in the Rocky Mountains, in southwestern Montana. The stated purpose of the conference was to identify the most likely paths to nuclear war between Washington and Moscow, and to suggest nuclear weapons deployments that would deter Soviet aggression in "hot spots" like the Middle East and the borderland between Eastern and Western Europe while, at the same time, not raising the risk of nuclear war to dangerous levels. At least that's what was in the printed agenda.[7]

But McNamara single-handedly changed the agenda of the conference in mid-course. In a decisive intervention, he made three points to the other participants: (1) nobody knows how to quantify the risk of nuclear war, thus nobody knows how to raise the risk of war to this or that level of nuclear risk; (2) in the event of a global nuclear war, human civilization would be put at risk, which meant to him that nuclear weapons should be eliminated, not deployed in ostensibly "safe" ways to deter the Russians; and (3) he said that in the depths of the Cuban missile crisis, he had realized once and for all that a nuclear war could occur in an unexpected crisis even though none of the involved parties to the conflict desired it, or even thought it possible, at the outset of the crisis. Thus, he challenged the participants in the conference to think harder about how to eliminate nuclear weapons, rather than "fiddling around with human destiny," as he put it.[8]

Then he issued a concrete challenge to the conference participants. He asked each of them to propose one or more scenarios in which initiation of the use of nuclear weapons in a crisis or conflict might, in their view, result in what McNamara called "a net gain to the initiator." Like a chess master playing many games simultaneously, he went around the conference table asking each participant, in turn, to propose a scenario, whereupon he proceeded to demonstrate, in each case, why in his estimation the initiator would have been better off—far better off, in fact—not using nuclear weapons at all.

We watched this in amazement—amazed partly by McNamara's mental agility and the sheer force of his personality. But we were also amazed as some of these bright people at the table seemed actually to believe the use of nuclear weapons would be a good idea under certain circumstances. One after another, the participants suggested scenarios in which they believed that the first use of nuclear weapons might result in a net gain to the initiator, and one after another (in our view), they failed to be convincing in the face of McNamara's withering analysis.

Wrapping up the session, with an intensity that brought to mind the prophet Jeremiah warning the clueless Israelites about their impending disaster, McNamara summed up his view of what had just occurred. In so doing, McNamara said something that was both surprising and credible to us. We were the note-takers. The following is reconstructed from our notes:

> Look, the reason I put the question to this group, and the reason I find your responses totally unconvincing, is that I have been there, I have done that—I have had the raw experience of trying to articulate these kinds of scenarios in the crucible of the Cuban missile crisis. I tried, but I failed to discover any use of nuclear weapons that was worth the risk of initiation or retaliation. President Kennedy tried, and he failed too. Bobby Kennedy tried and failed. Any of you who have read Khrushchev's long and rambling Friday [October 26 1962] letter to JFK can only conclude that Khrushchev also failed to see any sense at all in using nuclear weapons. Once the first one goes off, he said, we will begin to clash like blind moles and completely destroy each other. Reading his letter always reminds me that on that last Saturday of the crisis—I was walking in the White House Rose Garden at sunset on that beautiful Indian summer day—and I really wondered if I'd live to see another Saturday sunset.
>
> I know some of you think I am extreme—that the risk wasn't really as high as the president and I believed at the time. Maybe you also think that Kennedy should have ordered military action against the Soviet bases in Cuba. I've even read that some believe I was traumatized by this single event, the missile crisis. Well, you're damn right I was traumatized. So was the president. Call it what you want, but I want to say to you that in that situation, I learned the lesson of a lifetime, which is: that we were on the brink of the worst disaster in recorded history and that, somehow, we escaped. The mere possibility of military action by us leading to the use of nuclear weapons in Cuba or elsewhere against the United States totally deterred me, as it deterred the president, from ordering such an attack.
>
> I have no idea whether I'll ever be able to prove that our assessment of the risk—Kennedy's and mine—was correct. In order to prove it, we would need to compare notes with the Soviets and the Cubans, and I realize that this

seems unlikely to happen anytime soon. But what I discovered in the Cuban missile crisis is that nuclear "weapons" aren't weapons at all. They are the principal components of a global doomsday machine that very nearly ignited during the missile crisis. Nuclear weapons should never be used. Never! They are good only for deterrence, but whatever deterrent value they have is not worth the risk that they might be used. So we should get rid of them as soon and as safely as possible.

On this absolutely central issue, I believe my concrete experience trumps your abstract scenarios. I was there. I know. I know that we never want to come that close again, let alone start a nuclear war of our own volition. And I believe that if President Kennedy were sitting at this table, he would say the same thing.

This was a watershed moment for us in two respects:

- *A Policy-relevant Cuban Missile Crisis?* We had never heard anyone connect the Cuban missile crisis in such a direct and convincing way to what was, in the 1980s, the number one policy problem faced by the world's most powerful countries—how to avoid a nuclear war that might destroy human civilization.
- *Khrushchev in Synch with Kennedy?* His reference to Khrushchev's October 26, 1962, letter to Kennedy was revelatory. Most scholars who were aware of the letter dismissed it, or even mocked it, as the raving of a man who was possibly so overcome with stress that he was on the brink of a mental breakdown—neither of which tended to encourage retrospective admiration of either the letter or its author. Now McNamara claimed that the letter proved that the author of that letter was of one mind with his former boss, President Kennedy.

First, on the policy-relevance of the missile crisis: the power, conviction and messianic zeal of McNamara astounded us. He had, by 1984, already become the Jeremiah of the nuclear age.[9] But another literary analogue also occurred to us when we thought of Bob McNamara and the missile crisis. Like Charles Dickens' ghost of Jacob Marley updated for the nuclear age, McNamara seemed to have returned from his hellish experience of that crisis possessed by demons that goaded him relentlessly to do what he could to abolish nuclear weapons.

McNamara's highly charged conviction that all nuclear weapons must be eliminated stood in stark contrast to the cool, calculating scenarios put forward by others at the conference—members in good standing of what was sometimes called the "nuclear priesthood." (The comparison to priests was apt: these people were thought to know things about nuclear weapons and nuclear war that were unavailable to ordinary people—how to make nuclear weapons, how to deploy them, and how to use them advantageously, if it came to that.) If what McNamara said was true, then the nuclear "priests" were false prophets, theoreticians in love with their often-elegant hypothetical scenarios, but whose absence of experience bearing the burden of nuclear responsibility with the fate of the earth on the line, as it seemed to many to be in October 1962, rendered them irretrievably out of their depth, naïve and even dangerous. That was McNamara's view.

As McNamara later repeated to us many times, a nuclear war initiated without eventual regret is a "null set."[10]

Second, on the psychological convergence of Kennedy and Khrushchev: it was that single reference in McNamara's decisive intervention that provided us our first data point in what would become a major research program, eventually extending over more than twenty years and involving a multinational team of scholars and former officials on several continents. Nikita Khrushchev's letter to John F. Kennedy of Friday October 26, 1962, confirmed to McNamara that Khrushchev was looking down the same gun barrel of nuclear war that Kennedy and his advisers experienced during the crisis. If true, then in some sense Kennedy and Khrushchev somehow wound up in the same psychological space by the end of the crisis.

Our heads were spinning. Weren't Kennedy and Khrushchev bitter adversaries? Weren't Washington and Moscow the two nerve centers of the global Cold War? Weren't U.S. and Russian military forces arrayed specifically to threaten, and perhaps ultimately, to annihilate each other? Hadn't the crisis been portrayed by most scholars and Kennedy administration memoirists as an intense battle of nerves that had been "won" by Kennedy and "lost" by Khrushchev? "Yes" to all of the above. But now if McNamara's reference to Khrushchev's letter was to be credited, a paradigm shift in our thinking was necessary. According to McNamara, Kennedy also felt that events were getting out of control and that the fundamental objective eventually became simply finding an exit ramp out of the crisis, regardless of the political domestic consequences in Washington and Moscow, where the hawks on each side were bound to grumble that an opportunity had been lost to destroy, or at least to humiliate, its principal adversary. McNamara seemed to be saying that neither Kennedy nor Khrushchev backed *down* in the missile crisis. Instead, he claimed that both backed *off*, apparently in the nick of time.

Bob McNamara was way ahead of us and it would take some time for us to catch up. Once we began our collaboration with him roughly a year after the July 1984 Big Sky conference, we would discover that he had dramatically shifted the primary problem of the Cuban missile crisis from an obsession with crisis *management*, to an effort to use the missile crisis as a laboratory in which to learn crisis *prevention*. We hadn't noticed before our encounter with McNamara just how much of the analysis of the crisis was made up of speculation as to how Kennedy had pulled a rabbit out of hat—how his "coercive diplomacy" (in the jargon of 1984) forced Khrushchev to remove the missiles from Cuba without having to go to war. But if McNamara was right in his interpretation of Khrushchev's October 26, 1962, letter to Kennedy—that both leaders were on the same wavelength by that late point in the crisis—then the fundamental problem was no longer Kennedy's alleged powers of political prestidigitation. Instead, the essential question for us became: *how in the world did the two leaders get so far apart in the first place?* How do we account for the extraordinary degree of misunderstanding, misperception and misjudgment that led them to the brink of nuclear war, even though initiating such a war was unthinkable to both of them?

Due to this shift in emphasis, from crisis management to crisis prevention, we would in due course discover that the key question—why did Kennedy and Khrushchev misunderstand each other so comprehensively?—had a one-word answer: *Cuba!* Kennedy had no idea that the Cubans' would conclude after the April 1961 Bay of Pigs debacle that he would soon order a full-scale attack and invasion of the island by U.S. forces, and that such an attack would, the Cubans believed, involve the use of U.S. nuclear weapons. Yet Kennedy had actually reached the opposite conclusion: he wanted Cuba *off* his agenda; the last thing he wanted was a war involving Cuba, to say nothing of a *nuclear* war involving Cuba. Khrushchev, likewise, was essentially clueless about his Cuban ally. He had no idea that by deploying nuclear forces to Cuba, the Cubans would assume that the Soviet nuclear weapons on the island would be used in the face of any U.S. attempt to invade the island, nor did he imagine that the Cubans would use all of their powers of persuasion to convince the Soviet forces on the island to use their nuclear weapons against the Americans if they invaded the island, whether or not the U.S. used nuclear weapons first.

So: Kennedy thought Khrushchev had Castro and the Cubans under control, but he didn't; and Khrushchev thought he had Castro, et al. under control but, as he would learn to his horror, he didn't.[11] Cuba was the intervening variable, the "X-factor," the outlier, the loose cannon that nearly exploded in the faces of the superpowers in October 1962. But we are getting ahead of our story. It would be several years before the *Cuban* Cuban missile crisis came to center stage in our understanding of the apocalyptic drama of October 1962.

McNAMARA'S SECOND CHALLENGE: BUILD AN ARMAGEDDON TIME MACHINE!

On the coffee break following the conference session in Big Sky, Montana, we screwed up our courage and introduced ourselves to McNamara. Our exchange was not only a watershed event for us. It was also vividly surreal in ways that would justify our nickname for him during the more than twenty years of our collaboration—"Maximum Bob!" (This is a reference to a novel, *Maximum Bob*, by mystery writer, Elmore Leonard, about a Florida judge who is known for his severity in handing out sentences.)[12] After we introduced ourselves, he asked us what we did. We said that our original training was in psychology, adding that we were married, and that we had met in graduate school as aspiring psychologists. At this point, according to our notes, McNamara exploded, as follows:

> What? You are psychologists? Why are you here with all of those people [a reference to the nuclear strategists who made up the majority of the participants]? Wait a minute. Come on over here to this stairwell where we can talk. Sit down. [We sat down on the stairs, while he stood, gesticulating furiously and speaking in a loud, hoarse bark.]
>
> If you are psychologists, then you must be humanists, right? [We saw no point in splitting hairs, and so said "Yes."] Good. Good. Jesus Christ this field needs some humanists. All those damn strategists—they think they understand nuclear weapons, when to use them, how to deploy them. Hell, some of those people used to work for me in the Pentagon during the Kennedy and Johnson administrations. They didn't learn a damn thing from the Cuban missile crisis! Not a damn thing!
>
> These people think we're robots, think they can predict everything we do, and so know how to "manipulate nuclear risk"—do you believe they actually use that phrase? I'll tell you how to manipulate nuclear risk—manipulate it down to zero as fast as possible, before another missile crisis occurs and it's too late, because we're not going to be that lucky next time.
>
> Well, you're humanists so you must know the implications that follow from the fact that human beings are in charge of these awful weapons. We're fallible human beings! You know that, don't you? [Again, we simply nodded agreement, which was an accurate representation of our opinion, particularly when viewed through the "True-False" prism with which McNamara had framed this and nearly all other issues.] Then you know that sooner or later, fallible human beings and nuclear weapons are going to . . . to . . . destroy nations, whole damn nations. The missile crisis proves that.

Before we could muster even a meager reply, he bolted for the men's room, barking over his shoulder that he would talk to us later.

For the remainder of the conference, Bob McNamara badgered us, cajoled us and finally all but ordered us to find a way to learn more about the actual experience of the Cuban missile crisis—not just from him, but from the rest of those in Kennedy's cabinet who advised the president during the crisis. Once we had our act together, he said, we should test his "three missile crisis hypotheses," as he called them: (1) nuclear war in October 1962 was terrifyingly close; (2) using data from the missile crisis, show that escalation to nuclear catastrophe would have been a virtual certainty if an attack and invasion of Cuba had been initiated in those circumstances; and (3) figure out a way for people who had nothing to do with the missile crisis—especially young people—people who had not even been born at the time of the crisis, the leaders of the future—to grasp the overwhelming danger it involved, and to take steps to eliminate that danger by dedicating themselves to eliminating nuclear weapons.[13]

That night, we took stock of what had happened and what McNamara was urging us to do. As we understood him our assignment, if we agreed to undertake it, was as follows:

- *Measure* (somehow) the proximity to Armageddon.
- *Determine* (somehow) the probability of Armageddon if the U.S. had attacked and invaded Cuba.
- *Convey* (somehow) the existential dread that accompanied the burden of nuclear responsibility in the face of Armageddon to those not involved with it personally.

Point three was the ultimate objective, the payoff: build an Armageddon time machine in which vicarious time travelers to October 1962 might feel some portion of what Bob McNamara (and Kennedy and Khrushchev) felt when Cuba was the hinge of the world. Bob's feeling, which was eventually our own, was that people thus sobered would see more clearly than ever before that nuclear weapons make us supremely insecure and vulnerable to catastrophe, and thus should be abolished.

OUR EMBRACE OF "MISSION IMPROBABLE"

Measure *somehow*. Determine *somehow*. Convey *somehow*. This first encounter with McNamara resembled the opening set piece of an American TV show from the late 1960s and early 1970s (and later a series of movies), called *Mission Impossible*. At the beginning of each episode, the stars in the original series played a reel-to-reel tape recording outlining the mission of their "Impossible Missions Force," should they choose to accept it. After listening to the recorded message, the tape would spontaneously self-destruct.

There were differences, of course, between the *modus operandi* of the Impossible Missions Force and our own quest for an Armadeggon time machine. Whereas those in the TV series were given their instructions only once, and on tape, we received ours face-to-face, from McNamara himself. Not just once but dozens or maybe even hundreds of times. It was his magnificent obsession. Far from disappearing after proposing the mission, he would ultimately spend more than twenty years working with us on a variety of projects, including the construction of a comprehensive Armageddon time machine that included not only the view from Washington and Moscow, but also the view from Havana. In fact, the Cuban piece of the puzzle of October 1962, which we knew nothing about at the outset of our "mission," would soon become the Rosetta Stone of the Cuban missile crisis: once decoded, it would unlock the door to a much deeper understanding of why the crisis occurred in the first place and why it nearly spiraled into nuclear catastrophe.

McNamara pushed us at the July 1984 conference, and subsequently, to accept the "mission": connecting the Cuban missile crisis of 1962 with worry over nuclear risk in the present and future. He told us he was virtually certain that he was right about the sky-high risk of nuclear war in October 1962, but he had only his own recollections on which to base his view. After all, he admitted, there were hawks like Paul Nitze within the Kennedy administration who did not believe risk in the missile crisis was all that great, and who therefore pressed the president to order an attack on the missile sites in Cuba, follow up with an invasion of the island, and conclude by destroying the communist regime of Fidel Castro. In addition, McNamara was well aware that he had never had an opportunity to discuss the missile crisis with senior officials in Moscow, not to mention Havana. He wondered out loud whether they had the same sense he had (and, he was convinced, that Kennedy had) that they had been on the brink of Armageddon during the crisis, and very nearly over that brink. He said he realized it would be difficult to gain access to top-level Russians and Cubans. But he said if we found a way to get through to them, "I'll be on the first plane to Moscow or Havana, or wherever they are—as long as they are knowledgeable and open-minded."

This comment really did make McNamara's idea seem like an episode of "Mission Impossible." (*Havana?* We had no idea at that point whether it was even legal for Americans to travel to Cuba.) His proposal was fascinating and potentially important. But by the summer of 1984, U.S.-Soviet relations had hit rock bottom, and U.S.-Cuban relations were virtually non-existent, as they had been since the days of the Kennedy administration. McNamara was the first senior member of the Kennedy administration whom we had ever met. We knew of little declassified, real-time documentation from the Kennedy White House that might provide an empirical anchor for whatever discussions we might try to arrange, if we were lucky, with Kennedy administration officials. We had never met, nor at that point did we entertain even the possibility of meeting, with senior officials from the Soviet or Cuban governments who helped steer their nations through the abyss of October 1962. And we did not know whether relevant documentation even existed in Soviet and/or Cuban archives or, if it did, whether there was any chance the two would share it with us for the purpose of comparing their documentation with that of their former adversaries on the U.S. side. That was all on the one hand: the mission was at least daunting, and at worst bound to fail, as we were reminded regularly by many of our senior colleagues.

On the other hand, we had some advantages. We had potentially good access to the Kennedy administration's senior officials, via our connection with the Kennedy School, and via assistance from McNamara and others from the administration, especially Kennedy's national security adviser, McGeorge Bundy, who would eventually provide crucial assistance to us in our efforts to get in touch with many former colleagues from the administration. We had also made contact with The National Security Archive, an NGO in Washington devoted to using the Freedom of Information Act for the declassification and release of U.S. documents bearing on national security. The Archive would become our indispensible partner on the Cuban missile crisis project and all subsequent historical projects in which we have been involved.

And then there were those amazing letters between Kennedy and Khrushchev, the gold standard for vicarious entry at the highest level into the mindsets of the two leaders during the crisis. By the mid-1980s, it had become known that Kennedy and Khrushchev had corresponded regularly, on a wide variety of issues, although at the outset of our investigation of the missile crisis most of the correspondence was still classified and unavailable. We now know that Khrushchev first wrote to Kennedy just days after his election victory in November 1960 and that Kennedy reciprocated. They continued to write to each other until Kennedy's assassination on November 22, 1963. (The collected correspondence, available online via the State Department's Archives, would come to something on the order of 1,500 pages, if it were formatted in 8.5 in. × 11 in.)

The chronology of the declassification and release of these Armageddon letters written during the Cuban missile crisis had, by the mid-1980s, occurred in these phases:

- *October 1962*. Four letters—two by Kennedy, two by Khrushchev—which were exchanged between Friday October 26 and Sunday October 28 on what turned out to be the climactic weekend of the crisis. These messages were broadcast and the transcripts made available.[14]
- *Mid-1971*. Graham Allison, of the Kennedy School of Government, had published *Essence of Decision: Explaining the Cuban Missile Crisis*, in which he assembled, from various sources, what was known about the epochal October 26 letter from Khrushchev to Kennedy (the letter cited by McNamara at the 1984 Big Sky meeting). The letter, even in the partly summarized, truncated form presented by Allison was astounding in its anguished, urgent, almost poetical appeal to Kennedy to not let the world slide into nuclear catastrophe.[15]

- *February 1973*. The State Department published definitive versions of the ten letters between Kennedy and Khrushchev during the most intense phase of the crisis, October 22–28, 1962.[16]

It was something on which to build. Fools rush in, of course, where the wise fear to tread. Yet the possibility of building a historically accurate, Armageddon time machine that might vicariously deliver the look and feel of the imminent nuclear catastrophe of October 1962 seemed to us too important to resist. We ceased with the gallows humor of calling the project "mission impossible," and enthusiastically embraced it as "mission improbable."

Even so, we knew it would be an uphill struggle. We had no meaningful documentation even on U.S. decision-making from November 1962. This was a significant gap because pressure toward war over the Soviet deployment in Cuba continued until November 20, when Kennedy finally announced that he had ordered the U.S. military to return to a peacetime level of readiness. (U.S. forces all over the world had been ordered during the crisis to the highest level of readiness short of nuclear war.) We had the impression that bitter differences of opinion had arisen between the Cubans and Soviets over the Kennedy-Khrushchev agreement, according to which the U.S. publicly pledged not to invade Cuba (and privately assured the Soviets that land-based NATO missiles in Turkey would be removed in early 1963), and the Soviet Union pledged to withdraw its missiles from the island. In fact, as November 1962 wore on, the U.S. pressured the Soviets to remove not just its medium-range and intermediate-range ballistic missiles, but virtually everything else it deployed in Cuba: planes, boats, troops, and equipment of various sorts. Since the Cubans refused to allow UN inspectors onto the island to confirm the withdrawal of Soviet men and equipment, the U.S. Navy had to confirm the withdrawal via helicopter reconnaissance in international waters.

We had virtually nothing from the Cuban perspective—neither reliable oral testimony nor declassified documentation about what was going on during the crisis on the island of Cuba, and thus what it was like to be squarely in the crosshairs of the nuclear gun barrel.[17] Was it possible, we wondered, that Khrushchev had corresponded with Castro during the missile crisis as he had with Kennedy and, if he had, what might the exchanges between Havana and Moscow reveal about the key questions first posed by McNamara:

- How dangerous was the crisis?
- How might it have escalated to war?
- And if it had escalated to war, what were the likely paths to a catastrophic nuclear war?

We toted up what we did not have, but certainly would need, if we were to build the kind of policy-relevant time machine that stood a chance of transporting people back to October 1962 in a credible fashion—a fact-based bit of vicarious time travel to Washington, Havana and Moscow in October 1962. Here is a list of four important constituents of "mission improbable."

- *Access to people close to Khrushchev*, who had died in September 1971. (What people? Were they alive? Were they allowed to talk to us? If so, how would we locate them?)
- *The November letters between Kennedy and Khrushchev.* (We had been led to believe these letters existed, but did they? Would both governments agree to declassify them? Had the Soviet Union ever declassified *anything?*)
- *Access to Fidel Castro.* (Of the three principal leaders in the crisis, Castro was the only one still living, but how would we reach him? What obstacles might the U.S. government throw at us if we attempted to reach Castro in Cuba? Even if we actually were able to arrange a meeting, could we trust his memory or his veracity? Would this famously loquacious leader even allow us to ask our own questions?)
- *Access to any Castro-Khrushchev letters exchanged during the crisis.* (Did they exist? Had Cuba ever declassified anything? Had Castro ever authorized documents in his personal archive to be released to the public? Would the Cuban and Soviet governments both have to agree to release of such documentation as existed?)

Despite these improbabilities, we received strategic, financial and moral support from mentors and colleagues at the Kennedy School of Government, as we launched into "mission improbable." We decided to begin modestly by organizing a conference in March 1987 that dealt strictly with U.S. decision-making during the crisis.[18] We also decided that following the first conference, and following each subsequent conference (if a follow-up seemed worth organizing), we would decide either to terminate the project if we weren't achieving our objectives, or to plan the next step if we believed we were making progress sufficient to justify the work and expense involved.

WHY "MISSION IMPROBABLE" (IMPROBABLY) SUCCEEDED: U.S. INTEREST, SOVIET RECONCILIATION, CUBAN ANGER

Recasting our mission "impossible" as mission "improbable" involved a lot of wishful thinking. We were in way over our heads. Even with the assistance of the brilliant and energetic international team of collaborators we had assembled, we had no chance of pulling this off under anything like the conditions in which the "mission" had been conceived. We were, in a word, delusionary. But spurred on by Bob McNamara's stirring and insistent advocacy, and in light of the potential importance of the project, we decided to (as we now see it) leap before we looked.

Yet "mission improbable" improbably succeeded. Pasteur famously claimed that in the pursuit of scientific discovery, chance favors the prepared mind. In our pursuit of a time machine composed in part of the Armageddon letters, chance did far more than rearrange a laboratory or unearth some relics at a research site. In our case, chance seemed to have unexpectedly but comprehensively rearranged the entire international system, seemingly on our behalf.

On November 9, 1989, the Berlin Wall began to crack. Subsequent events, stretching into the mid-1990s, accomplished several things, none of which had been predicted by anyone who was sane and sober before November 9, 1989: a unified Germany; a collapsed Soviet Union and an emergent Russia; and the peaceful end of the Cold War. The crack in the world that began in earnest in 1989 also created the ideal conditions for building our time machine.

Our good fortune had three principal components:

1. *Our Method.* We developed a new research method, *critical oral history*, which former officials and scholars found attractive, and which also enhanced our team's efforts to obtain declassified documents on the crisis. We first field-tested the method at a conference on the Cuban missile crisis in March 1987.[19]

2. *End of the Cold War.* Astonishingly, in November 1989 the Soviet Union and its empire began to collapse—peacefully, but comprehensively. As the Cold War ended, high-level decision-makers in key Cold War events suddenly were approachable (since their governments, and ours, no longer officially considered each other's enemies). And more than a few were suddenly and totally available (since the day jobs of many of them had ceased to exist). Suddenly, the prospect of access to declassified documents on a pivotal and controversial topic like the Cuban missile crisis was no longer a pipe dream. Instead, we could scarcely buy our plane tickets fast enough to keep pace with the opening up of Cold War archives, especially in Russia and Eastern Europe.[20]

3. *The Simultaneity of (1) and (2).* Unanticipated by us, our method, which we cobbled together initially for use in a conference with an all U.S. cast of characters, turned out to be a psychological magnet that attracted not only Americans, but Russians (née Soviets) and Cubans,

eager to get their stories on the record. The journalist and historian Frances FitzGerald described the discussions at a critical oral history conference as "part confessional, part group therapy and part reconciliation—a brew that often produces a cascade of revelations."[21] In a surreal atmosphere, tough former cold warriors now sat across from their opposite numbers, some wearing sneakers, golf shirts and blue jeans. Typically, participants on each side respond as fully as their knowledge and experience allows, so that the participants have the uncanny feeling that they are learning things they had always wanted to know but, before the end of the Cold War, had no one to ask.

By the late 1980s and early 1990s, we found ourselves suddenly able to begin to vicariously crawl back *into* that gun barrel of nuclear war alongside Kennedy, Castro and Khrushchev.

A brief word is in order about the mechanics of critical oral history: we created the method to address the dilemma described long ago by the Danish philosopher, Søren Kierkegaard. He pointed out that we live life forward, groping in the dark, unaware of the outcome of our actions, yet we are forced to understand events in reverse, working our way retrospectively backward to their supposed causes. This creates a profound disconnect between lived experience and our understanding of that experience. Caught in the moment, decision-makers often feel confused, unsure, and sometimes even afraid. But the scholarly (after the fact) study of decision-making usually removes the confusion and fear, focusing simply on explanations of outcomes.[22]

We developed critical oral history to build a bridge between the confusion of lived experience and the relatively cut and dried after-the-fact rendering of that experience. It does so by combining, in structured conferences, (1) decision-makers, (2) declassified documents (which provide added accuracy and authenticity to the conversation), and (3) scholars.[23] As we discovered during the Cuban missile crisis project, critical oral history can yield rich and surprising insights into what it was really like for decision-makers, then and there, thus yielding more accurate analyses and applicable lessons for decision-making here and now.

Who knew that critical oral history would be the right method at the right time for the three locales that mattered most in the examination of the Cuban missile crisis: Washington, Havana and Moscow? Not us, at least not at first. Who could have predicted that the Russians, eager to mend fences and share secrets with their former Cold War nemesis, the U.S., would depart so radically from the old Soviet script of surly silence and gush forth with oral testimony and (eventually) documentary evidence that repeatedly astonished the American participants? The phenomenon was called *glasnost* (openness) and, with regard to the missile crisis, it was simply amazing to be present when, for example, longtime Soviet Foreign Minister Andrei Gromyko told Moscow conference participants in January 1989 the details of the Soviet plan to systematically lie to the U.S. about the missile deployment in Cuba.[24] There were dozens of such moments over the life of the project, 1987–2002.

Equally, who knew that the Cubans, who in the late 1980s and early 1990s were being abandoned by the collapsing Soviet Union, would draw a parallel between what they believed was their abandonment by Khrushchev during the Cuban missile crisis and their abandonment by Mikhail Gorbachev and his successors, from 1989 onward. Not us, certainly. Initially, we had no idea how angry Fidel Castro and his colleagues had been in October and November 1962 at what they saw as Khrushchev's unnecessary, cowardly, humiliating capitulation to Kennedy. Cuba had been neither consulted, nor had it even been adequately informed, when Khrushchev and Kennedy reached the agreement to end the crisis: with Kennedy pledging not to invade Cuba, and Khrushchev pledging to remove Soviet missiles from the island.

Castro's view, as we would hear from him personally, and at length, on several occasions, was that the Soviets had arrogantly refused to listen to the Cubans at any stage of the crisis and, during the peak of tension and danger at the end of October 1962, the Soviets basically threw the Cubans overboard and wished them luck with their U.S. adversary. Castro's anger was palpable. Hell hath no fury, we would learn, like that of a Cuban revolutionary who feels taken for granted and betrayed by his Soviet patron. And we got the point: the Cuban story mattered and only the Cubans, not the former Russian leaders in Moscow, were qualified to tell the story of events on the island of Cuba connected with the Cuban missile crisis.[25]

CRITICAL ORAL HISTORY: ACQUIRING THE REMAINING ARMAGEDDON LETTERS

The late 1980s and early 1990s remain a blur to us. In a little over three years, we traveled to Moscow on six occasions and to Havana ten times. These were in addition to even more frequent visits to Washington and New York to speak with former Kennedy administration officials. We were, in effect, amateur shuttle diplomats trying to encourage, reassure, challenge, and in other ways play the role of honest brokers in an effort to organize critical oral history conferences on the Cuban missile crisis—meetings at which representatives of all three involved countries participated. In the context of these exercises—in the U.S., Russia, the

Caribbean island of Antigua, and Cuba—we realized that these meetings were not only of interest to former and present officials who wanted to tell their own stories, but they were also occasions which gave us and our colleagues at the National Security Archive considerable leverage in requesting declassified documentation from all three relevant parties. And at the top of our list of desired documents were what we call in this book the Armageddon letters.

It is important to understand why the method of critical oral history has been, in effect, an intellectual force multiplier in our efforts to pry loose secret documents and revelations from oral testimony. Even with the end of the Cold War and its loosening effect on the archives and vocal chords of former high-ranking officials from the former East Bloc, we doubt we would have had much success in acquiring the Armageddon letters if we had approached each official and each archive individually. The instinct is almost always to withhold rather than reveal. This is particularly true among the national security officials with whom we typically deal.

But this instinct was overcome on many occasions due to the presence of an ongoing and productive project in which documents and oral testimony were not given away free of charge but, so to speak, with the expectation of getting a substantial return on the participants' informational investment. It was as if each participant from every side was saying: I will tell you what we were thinking, expecting and doing, as long as you reciprocate. There were important national differences in motivation to participate. The Americans—led by Bob McNamara, McGeorge Bundy and Ted Sorensen—were intensely curious about all aspects of the crisis, since in 1962 they didn't anticipate its onset, its level of danger or its abrupt conclusion. The Russians were also curious, of course, but many were also eager to show the Americans and the world that they could play by the rules of openness and transparency that characterize the method.

The Cubans, finally, were determined to use the opportunities provided by critical oral history to tell their story to the Americans *and the Russians*— which had the effect of focusing us on events that mattered to Cuba, many of which the Americans and Soviets had overlooked. Their wish to be heard was typically urgent and intense. Often, this involved highly confrontational tactics by the Cubans, several of which nearly caused conferences to be scuttled in mid-course. The reason became clear once we familiarized ourselves with the Cuban point of view: they felt they had been ignored and marginalized in the events of October 1962, and they were determined not to let this happen in the critical oral history of the event several decades after the fact.[26]

Here are the principal milestones in the acquisition of the previously classified Armageddon letters:

- *November 23, 1990.* Castro-Khrushchev letters are released. Cuba declassifies and releases five letters between Fidel Castro and Nikita Khrushchev written at the height of the Cuban missile crisis. The timing of the declassification and release of these letters is carefully chosen by the Cubans. It occurs a month and a half prior to our critical oral history conference in Antigua, whose participants will include a Cuban delegation hand-picked by Fidel Castro, former high-ranking Russian officials, and an American group led by McNamara and Kennedy White House aide and historian, Arthur Schlesinger, Jr. The letters took center stage at the Antigua conference—a conversation that was instrumental in convincing the Americans to accept an invitation to come to Havana one year later for a conference in which Fidel Castro himself would lead the Cuban team. Castro's October 26, 1962, letter to Khrushchev is especially revealing. He tells Khrushchev that the Americans are definitely going to launch a massive airstrike on Cuban targets, and they will probably attempt to invade as well. If the invasion occurs, Castro requests that Khrushchev order a massive nuclear strike on the U.S. He further tells Khrushchev that Cuba is prepared for martyrdom if the ultimate triumph of socialism requires it. At the Antigua conference Arthur Schlesinger commented, in the understatement of the meeting: "It is difficult to get one's mind wrapped around a request to destroy the world as we know it, however contingent that request may have been."[27]
- *January 6, 1992.* Kennedy-Khrushchev November letters are released. Seventy-two hours before the scheduled follow-up conference in Havana, the U.S. State Department releases the November-December 1962 correspondence between Kennedy and Khrushchev. Members of our team in Washington from the National Security Archive immediately retrieve the documents and deliver them to Cuban diplomats, who send them straightaway to Havana via diplomatic pouch. In Havana, the letters are immediately given to Fidel Castro, who has never seen them. Castro spends all night reading them (in English, his level of interest being such that he doesn't want to take the time to have them translated into Spanish). He tells us in Havana that while reading the Kennedy-Khrushchev letters he became furious with the Russians all over again. Castro said the letters confirmed his hunch at the time: the Russians had colluded with the Americans, against Cuba, to remove from Cuba virtually all the elements of the Soviet deployment—missiles, planes, boats, guns, equipment of all sorts, leaving Cuba exposed and vulnerable to the aggressive whims of its U.S. adversary. As Castro told us in the conference and also privately, you expect to be betrayed by an adversary, but not an ally. Castro

decides, after reading the letters, to participate fully in the entire four-day conference.[28]

- *January 9, 1992*. Details of the Soviet deployment are made available. Russian General Anatoly Gribkov reveals for the first time that warheads for Soviet strategic and tactical nuclear weapons had reached Cuba in 1962, and were ready for use by Soviet personnel on the island. In his carefully prepared opening statement to the Havana critical oral history conference, Gribkov makes the single most astounding revelation of the entire project on the Cuban missile crisis. He reveals that: (a) nuclear warheads had reached the island of Cuba during the crisis and could have been used against American targets (the CIA guessed at the time that the warheads had not arrived, but wasn't sure); and (b) that *tactical* nuclear weapons were ready for use against an American invading force (the U.S. intelligence community never seriously considered the possibility that the Soviets would deploy nuclear war-fighting weapons in Cuba). Moreover, the Soviet field commander in Cuba, in Gribkov's judgment, would have used them if the U.S. invasion had occurred. Gribkov, a former head of the Warsaw Pact, was also the mastermind of the entire deployment, which was code-named "Operation ANADYR." We would eventually learn many intimate details of the deployment, including the type and location of the 162 nuclear weapons on the island at the time of the crisis. Bob McNamara listens to Gribkov in agitated, retrospective horror. He knows that he would have been the one to implement a U.S. air attack and invasion if Kennedy had ordered one, and that thousands of American Marines would probably and unexpectedly have been incinerated on the beaches in Cuba as a result. And that would have been just the beginning of a process that would likely have escalated and resulted in Armageddon.[29]
- *January 9-12, 1992*. Castro gives Cuba's version of events. Fidel Castro, in a series of lengthy interventions, provides the Cuban context for our understanding of the crisis. Castro gives Cuba's analysis of the genesis, evolution and conclusion of the crisis. Cuba, he says, went to the Soviets following the Bay of Pigs invasion of April 1961 and discussed how the Soviets might be able to help the revolutionary government deter a full-scale U.S. invasion, which the Cuban leadership was certain would occur as soon as the Kennedy administration got its forces into place around Cuba. That, according to Castro, is where the *October crisis* began, with the Bay of Pigs operation. Castro made no attempt to disguise his residual bitterness at the way the Soviet leadership in Moscow had (as the Cuban leadership saw it) cavalierly and arrogantly refused to listen to the Cubans' views on key aspects of the

deployment of nuclear weapons. When Khrushchev raised the possibility of sending nuclear weapons to Cuba, the leadership in Havana recommended deploying the weapons publicly, as the U.S and NATO had done in Italy and Turkey. Castro said he told the Soviets that the U.S. would react to a surprise deployment aggressively. But the Soviets demanded secrecy and deception. After the crisis broke, according to Castro, Cuba was calmly awaiting the U.S. invasion, as it stated its conditions, which included the cessation of U.S. over-flights, return of the Guantanamo naval base to Cuba and other demands. But instead of consulting with the Cubans, Castro told the conference that the Soviets panicked in the face of the expected U.S. attack and left Cuba to fend for itself. He said that having deployed the nuclear weapons and having thus rendered Cuba a prime target for U.S. aggression, Khrushchev then immediately removed the principal means of deterring or defeating the Americans, and he did so without even requiring the Americans to acknowledge the demands of the Cubans. In his most provocative statement, given in response to a question from McNamara, Castro told us that if he had been given control of the nuclear weapons by the Soviets, he would absolutely have used them. He said that was how he felt in October 1962 and that was how he felt now, thirty years later. Cuba, he assured us, was prepared for martyrdom.[30]

- *1995–2005.* Release of November documents from the Mikoyan channel. The declassification and release of Soviet Deputy Premier Anastas Mikoyan's cables to Khrushchev from Cuba in November 1962 provide the final missing chapter in the Armageddon letters. While Kennedy and Khrushchev have agreed that Cuban weapons sites will be monitored under UN supervision, Castro steadfastly refuses admission to inspectors no matter where they are from. In this Gandhi-like maneuver of passive resistance, the Cubans demonstrate their supreme displeasure over all aspects of the Kennedy-Khrushchev deal. When this Cuban tactic threatens to scuttle the superpower agreement and send Washington and Moscow back to the brink of nuclear war, Khrushchev hurriedly sends his deputy, Mikoyan, to explain the facts of life to Castro and his colleagues. Castro and Khrushchev continue their conversation, mediated by Mikoyan and his cables to Moscow. In Cuba, Mikoyan is met with stony silence punctuated by Cuban hostility and a nearly week-long period during which Castro refuses even to meet with him. Then matters get worse, as the Soviets cave into the U.S. demand that the Soviets remove all their weapons systems, including IL-28 bombers, Komar patrol boats and the tactical weapons systems and almost all Soviet troops—essentially stripping the island of every sort of Soviet presence. Ultimately, a verification scheme is worked out by Washington and Moscow, according to which U.S. helicopters identify Soviet cargo in international waters, as the ships head back to the Soviet Union. The Russians are astonished that the Cubans are angry. They are blatantly condescending in their character-ization of the Cubans as "hot-headed Latins." And they are absolutely mystified at the absence of Cuban gratitude for (as the Soviets see it) rescuing the Cubans from nuclear annihilation. The Cubans, on the other hand, see the Soviets as spineless pseudo-revolutionaries.[31]

By 2005 or thereabouts, we had the unexpurgated text of Kennedy/ Khrushchev/Castro in the Cuban missile crisis. We had the Armageddon letters.

APPENDIX B

The Armageddon Time Machine/Context

Bringing the Letters Back to Life

[Do not] keep the corpse of history unburied and refrigerated, on a cold mortuary slab, for anatomical demonstration.

—H.R. Trevor-Roper[1]

This is Radio Nowhere—
Is there anybody alive out there?

—Bruce Springsteen[2]

The Armageddon time machine has two components. Both parts must be present and functioning properly, or the time machine won't work—it will be incapable of vicariously transporting us accurately back to the relevant times and places involved in the Cuban missile crisis. This distinction between the two parts can be expressed in various ways: the text, versus the context; the substance versus the atmospherics; what the documents actually say, versus what the documents probably mean; what is within the lines versus what seems to be between the lines; what is independent of the conditions under which it originated and was received, versus what cannot be grasped apart from those conditions. We like *text/context*. "Context" literally means "with the text." Once we have a text—such as one of the forty-three Armageddon letters—we want to know as much as possible about what went "with" it, which is conveniently summarized by the "W5" cluster sought by all good journalists: who, what, when, where and why.

TEXT ONLY: ARMAGEDDON AT
THE DEAD LETTER OFFICE

The forty-three Armageddon letters in this book constitute our *text* of history's closest brush with total annihilation. They were written, dictated, recorded, read over the radio, received from messengers, read from Teletype printouts, translated sometimes informally and quickly over the telephone, and other times formally and slowly in embassy cubicles. A few, which became public immediately after they were drafted, were read by tens of millions of incredulous people on the front pages (above the fold) of newspapers in the U.S., the Soviet Union, Cuba and around the world. They existed then, and they exist today, in a printed reality, typically black type on white background, the unchanged and unchanging textual account of the words of Kennedy, Khrushchev and Castro on the eve of destruction.

The search for a *text*—for declassified written documents like the Armageddon letters—has a beginning, often a long tug-of-war in the middle with government bureaucracies that hold the documents, and (with luck and effort) a successful conclusion. Someone hands you a document. You read it. Or if you can't read the language in which it is written, you have it translated and then you read it. You share it with colleagues. You've done your job. It is often difficult and frustrating, but it is also often gratifying. There is nothing like the feeling—you never quite get used to it—that this time, against all odds, you may just have stumbled onto the Cold War equivalent of King Tut's tomb. As you hold a copy of the newly declassified document in your hand for the first time, you may be unable to resist the thought: maybe this document explains *everything!* In fact, the "critical" in critical oral history is enhanced to the degree that interesting, relevant, surprising, declassified documentation is available prior to, and throughout the execution of, a critical oral history conference. Once the participants absorb the material, the documents tend to place useful empirical constraints on both the memories of the former officials and the tendency of scholars toward theoretical abstractions.

Yet documents do not supply their own context. Documents are inanimate and lifeless in and of themselves. They can suggest life; they can remind us of life. But they truly come to life for us only in proportion to the extent to which we bring *context* to our understanding of them. Otherwise, all documents—even documents deriving from this most dangerous crisis in recorded history—are at risk of lying dead on the page, as British historian H.R. Trevor-Roper put it: "the corpse of history unburied and refrigerated, on a cold mortuary slab, for anatomical demonstration."[3]

This is alas more or less what has happened to the analysis of the Cuban missile crisis over the past half-century. As the basic chronology of events has been filled in, the crisis is milked for lessons and made to fit into various theoretical schemes such as "coercive diplomacy" and "rational choice." Leaders have been psychoanalyzed and their experience marginalized, as the uncertainty, fear and near panic that was key to the crisis in real time has gotten siphoned off. The crisis remains interesting, but it is no longer scary. It no longer evokes retrospectively anything like the fear and trembling that characterized the original October 1962 version. There are a few exceptions. But not many, and even those that emphasize the close proximity to Armageddon merely say it or write it, but they typically don't show it—they don't make us feel it. Consequently, we feel free to ignore its potential importance. There are still more than 22,000 nuclear weapons on planet earth, for example. If we were made to feel the way Kennedy, Khrushchev and Castro felt in late October 1962, the way would be clear for a dash toward nuclear abolition. Otherwise, our text alone, the Armageddon letters, would continue to gather psychological dust in history's dead letter office.

TEXT IN CONTEXT: RESUSCITATING THE ARMAGEDDON LETTERS

Every text lay in the literary equivalent of a coma until its *context* is supplied. With context, it can be brought retrospectively back to life. We can begin to appreciate the breadth and depth of the human beings who produced the texts, and the situations they faced. Perhaps the most important single feature of resuscitating texts from history's dead letter office is that we begin to understand what it was like to go through what the historical figures went through *without knowing the eventual outcome*. Fact number one in any textual investigation of the Cuban missile crisis is: it ended peacefully. But fact number one emerging from the context we have discovered over the years is: the key figures, at various points, believed they were on a downbound train to oblivion, and that if this occurred, they would bear a good deal of the responsibility for the catastrophe. To the extent that contextualizing the crisis reproduces some portion of the experience of what it was like to believe that we are indeed on the eve of nuclear destruction—to the extent the crisis can be brought back to life—it can leave a lasting impression, even some gnawing fear that something like it might happen again. This is what Kennedy, Khrushchev and Castro believed in the aftermath of the actual crisis.

Fiction writing succeeds or fails based on the author's ability to build a time and space machine. The difference between the enterprise of fiction and our purpose in this work of history is that we have reconstructed the relevant contexts according to the facts as we understand them—all sorts of facts, derived from hundreds of sources, written documentation and especially oral testimony. We have used all of these sources in our effort to transport you vicariously back to moments and events that actually took place, more or less as we describe them in this book. We have invented no characters, no situations, and no conversations that have not been described to us in detail by people whom we believe have special knowledge and/or insight regarding the many contexts in which the Armageddon letters were written, sent, received and responded to. We have written a story that, to the best of our ability, is consistent with the facts as they are known.

DISCOVERING THE CONTEXT:
KEEP LISTENING, KEEP TALKING

The contextual material preceding each of the forty-three Armageddon letters derives mostly from our conversations over the years with people at, or near, the center of decision-making in Washington, Moscow or Havana. To state what is both obvious but also, we believe, profound: the process of gathering data this way—by listening, talking, interrupting, taking notes or remembering some portion of the conversation after the fact—operates by rules bearing no resemblance to filing a Freedom of Information Act request. In fact, it is often unclear whether there are any rules at all. Some people lie. Most don't. Most try to tell their own version of the truth, but everyone forgets, invents, enhances, and otherwise constructs a version of the past that they put forward with the confidence of one who is simply repeating what is playing on a CD player in his or her brain. No interview is taken at face value. But together, dozens or hundreds of interviews begin to form a mosaic that can be understood and described. The process is not ideal, but you will not discover by any other means what the context was like: was he angry? Was he exhausted? Did he know that so and so had already decided that the preferred action was impossible? No? Why not? On and on it goes.

A big problem is that our brains seem to prefer linear paths to knowledge about the past, such as is provided by texts like declassified documents. That's just too bad for the historian looking for the context in which events occurred. Human conversation is almost completely nonlinear. Typically, about a nanosecond after you hear yourself say "huh, so that's what was going on," you have already heard something else, possibly from the same source, or someone else present, that refines, refutes or redirects your line of inquiry.

In theory, recording conversations would have somewhat ameliorated at least the verbal chaos of multidimensional human conversation (though it would not help with issues like lying, failing memory, or spurious enhancement of the storyteller's proximity to power and authority). But we almost never taped the conversations that are the principal basis for our efforts to reconstruct the context of the Armageddon letters. Most of our sources were very uncomfortable having informal conversations recorded. Many simply said they would refuse to say anything into a microphone. The paradox never ceased to amaze us. We were trying to put together a deal that would bring these people to a conference table for a *recorded*, and eventually transcribed and published, conversation with their adversaries and allies—something they were keen to do. Yet at the mere mention of recording our private conversations, they suddenly claimed to remember hardly anything at all. Early on, we ceased carrying a recorder to the interviews.

Many people wanted the conversations to involve others: aides, colleagues, even family members or anyone else who might help them jog their memories. What this meant in practice was that conversations tended to be long and exceptionally nonlinear, bordering sometimes on crazy. Everyone's story needed to be told. People became argumentative and emotional because accounts of "the same" events by different people were often contradictory. We coped with this polyphonic proclivity as best we could, trying to participate in several semi-related conversations simultaneously, all the while scribbling shorthand notes on pads of paper propped up on our knees.

It was hard work. We took a lot of notes—reams of notes, scribbled in shorthand, while staring into the eyes of our interlocutors. Later we wrote out our notes—or whatever portion that was legible. Journalists are familiar with this problem, historians less so. We often felt as if we were living out a nightmare in which we were embedded in some giant multi-dimensional kaleidoscope that is being shaken by a hyperactive demon. One moment something seems to have happened on this day, in that building, then the next minute the "same" event is occurring somewhere else, then not at all. Or were they talking about the same events? And so on. So the context kept pouring out of the mouths of our interlocutors—reiterated, refined, and ultimately, if with luck and effort, integrated meaningfully into what we were hearing from all the others.[4]

"GETTING THE BUTTS IN THE SEATS": WHY EVERYONE KEPT TALKING TO US, FOR YEARS

If these sorts of interviews had been one-shot deals—like most interviews with senior officials—nearly all of them would have been a total waste of our time and the time of our interlocutors. Limited to a single session, we would hardly have gotten to know each other. Inconsistencies would have arisen and we would have had no way to reconcile them. We would never have gotten into the deeper texture of their recollections of the Cuban missile crisis. Follow-up was essential to making the enterprise work. To eventually transform material that is interesting but confusing, into interesting and somewhat comprehensible contextual material, we had to be able to pursue our sources again and again, until at least some of the big wrinkles were ironed out, and competing versions of events were compared and contrasted with each other. We kept badgering them until our sources had, usually with us as mediators, either convinced one another of the historical truth or falsehood of their respective memories of events, or given up the effort. In short, we had to be royal pains to our sources, and our sources had to find the process sufficiently interesting to keep inviting us back for still more painful interrogations.

Why, then, did they keep inviting us back—to Washington, Moscow, Havana? Did they just want to shoot the breeze with us yet one more time? Did they have nothing else to do? No. In nearly every case, they submitted willingly to our reiterated badgering because these conversations were in the service of a greater purpose: to organize a critical oral history conference. All sides needed to probe whether they could trust one another, and the currency of trust was twofold: first, the willingness to address seriously the many questions we posed on behalf of the senior officials from one or another of the other two parties (the *context*); and second, to acquire declassified documents in advance of the planned critical oral history conference.

The run-up to a critical oral history conference typically involves hundreds of hours of such discussions. Putting a few senior former (or occasionally, as in Fidel Castro's case, *current*) officials at a table for a few days is very labor intensive. Here, just to illustrate the point, are some of our own ballpark numbers. Between 1986, when our exploration of the missile crisis began, until January 1992, when the breakthrough Havana conference occurred, we spent over 350 days on the road: mainly in Washington, Moscow and Havana. Each trip, and each interview or other discussion that occurred on each trip, was preceded by drafting and sending (by fax or diplomatic pouch in those days; emails came later) long, detailed memoranda regarding: first, what we took at that point to be the current state of our understanding; and second, a request to explain to us where we were wrong, and to provide some documentation and/or oral corroboration to buttress their critiques. The precise number of trips, interviews and memoranda doesn't matter. As always, we did what we had to do. Between ourselves, we discussed our task in terms of a phrase we borrowed from the late George Steinbrenner (the longtime owner of the New York Yankees): we "put the butts in the seats" at a critical oral history conference—in this case, American, Russian and Cuban butts belonging to the most significant living former and present officials involved in the Cuban missile crisis.

In the beginning, we spent most of our time grilling former U.S. officials, as we tried to discover whether the human and financial resources required by this particular research enterprise would be justified by its probable outcome. And first we needed to know who might be willing to participate, and what "price" each would charge for admission—typically, authoritative information regarding how key decisions were made. As the Russians got involved at the highest levels, due to Mikhail Gorbachev's personal interest, we began spending a larger proportion of our time in Moscow. When, finally, Fidel Castro got word to us that he and Cuba wanted in, the majority of our travel time was spent in Cuba, trying to familiarize ourselves with a narrative that was almost completely at variance with anything we had heard in either the U.S. or Russia. Our home institution (beginning January 2, 1990), Brown University's Watson Institute for International Studies, relieved us of teaching duties for much of the period, 1986–1992. This activity continued, though at a less frenetic pace, until around 2005 or so, by which time the law of diminishing returns asserted itself, as senior figures died or became incapacitated, fewer relevant documents were released, and/or we began to hear repetitions of stories we had heard previously.

Our strategy amounted to an informational war of attrition: snuff out the mistrust of decades by accumulating from credible sources thousands and thousands of facts—purported facts, possible facts, maybe even questionable facts, but facts nonetheless according to people we ourselves were learning to trust, insofar as we believed that, for their reasons, they wanted the next planned critical oral history conference to occur just as we did. Not only we, but also they, wanted to put the butts in the seats.

Bob Woodward said recently that the first principle of investigative journalism is this: people tell their lies during the daylight hours; but at night, when the conditions are right, they will tell you the truth.[5] In our own experience, we have encountered relatively few people we have caught telling us outright falsehoods. (Of course, this could mean they were good liars or that we were easy marks, but we don't think so.) Still, Woodward's distinction is a useful one and, adapted to the nonlinear process of gathering the context for the Armageddon letters, we would rephrase Woodward's point this way: during the day, you get official, occasionally stuffy, by-the-book, cautious responses. But at night, vodka after mojito after Diet Coke, you are more likely to get information that is personal, eye opening, atmospheric and animated. In this way the Cuban missile crisis gradually comes alive. Bruce Springsteen is right. We had a little faith and, often, there was contextual magic in the night.[6] The next morning—that's another story. But the nights were fruitful.

Notes[*]

EPIGRAPH

1. As rendered by the *New King James Bible*.

2. Kurt Vonnegut, Jr., *Slaughterhouse Five (Or The Children's Crusade): A Duty-Dance With Death* (New York: Dell, 1969), pp. 193; 10. On the title page of the first edition of the book, Vonnegut appended the following to his name, all in caps, and formatted as follows:

A FOURTH GENERATION GERMAN-AMERICAN
NOW LIVING IN EASY CIRCUMSTANCES
ON CAPE COD
[AND SMOKING TOO MUCH],
WHO, AS AN AMERICAN INFANTRY SCOUT *HORS DE COMBAT*, WITNESSED
THE FIRE-BOMBING
OF DRESDEN, GERMANY,
"THE FLORENCE OF THE ELBE,"
A LONG TIME AGO,
AND SURVIVED TO TELL THE TALE.
THIS IS A NOVEL SOMEWHAT IN THE TELEGRAPHIC SCHIZOPHRENIC
MANNER OF TALES
OF THE PLANET TRALFAMADORE,
WHERE THE FLYING SAUCERS
COME FROM.
PEACE

---

*Unless otherwise specified, all websites listed in the endnotes were checked for accessibility on May 28, 2012.

INTRODUCTION

1. Cormac McCarthy, *The Road* (New York: Random House, 2006), pp. 278–279.

2. For a point of entry into the vast literature on the Cuban missile crisis, see Appendix A, The Armageddon Time Machine/Text: Acquiring the Letters and Appendix B, The Armageddon Time Machine/Context: Bringing the Letters Back to Life.

3. Robert S. McNamara, from "The Fog of War," a 2003 Errol Morris film, distributed by Sony Pictures Classics. The quotation from McNamara may be found in our book, which is based on the film: James G. Blight and janet M. Lang, *The Fog of War: Lessons From the Life of Robert S. McNamara* (Lanham, MD: Rowman & Littlefield, 2005), p. 59.

4. This is our formulation of Robert McNamara's own conclusion from his experience of the missile crisis: "the indefinite combination of nuclear weapons and human fallibility will result in the destruction of nations."

5. "Show Don't Tell." Track one on *Presto*, the thirteenth studio album of the Toronto-based rock band, Rush (Atlantic Records, 1989). Appropriately for a book focused on how we "lucked out" in escaping Armageddon in the Cuban missile crisis, the cover of *Presto* is filled with rabbits that have evidently emerged from a top hat that levitates above a mountain top.

6. McCarthy, *The Road*, pp. 278–279. McCarthy uses idiosyncratic spelling and punctuation, which we follow in this passage.

PRELUDE: SLEEPWALK

1. The letters between Kennedy and Khrushchev—120 of them, covering 170 dense pages in a very small font—are conveniently available online at the U.S. State Department's website. The first entry is this one, Khrushchev's congratulatory message sent on the day after Kennedy was elected president: www.state.gov/www/about_state/history/volume_vi/exchanges.html, p.1.

2. Ibid., pp. 1–2.

3. Ibid., pp. 3–4.

4. Ibid., pp. 4–5.

5. Ibid., pp. 5–6.

6. Ibid., pp. 6–9.

7. http://lanic.utexas.edu/project/castro/db/1961/19610423.html.

8. www.walterlippmann.com/fc-02-04-1962.html. This website reprints a shortened version of the epochal Second Declaration, which embodies the young Fidel Castro at his rhetorical zenith, a document full of optimism about the future of the socialist movement, and Cuba's pivotal role in it. The full text can be found at www.walterlippmann.com/fc-02-04-1962.pdf.

9. Available on the website of the University of Texas' Latin American Network Information Center at http://lanic.utexas.edu/project/castro/db/1962/19620726.html.

10. www.mtholyoke.edu/acad/intrel/jfkstate.htm. This website, built and maintained by Mt. Holyoke College international relations scholar Vincent Ferraro, is whimsically called "Cogito, Ergo, IR." It is one of the most valuable websites we

have encountered for instructors and students of recent U.S. foreign policy. Its document collection is not only large, but also well organized.

11. Released by *TASS*, carried in the New York Times.

12. www.mtholyoke.edu/acad/intrel/precrisis.htm.

ACT I: COLLISION

1. John F. Kennedy to Nikita S. Khrushchev, October 22, 1962. In Laurence Chang and Peter Kornbluh, eds., *The Cuban Missile Crisis, 1962* (New York: The New Press, 1998), pp.158–59. Most (though not all) of the Cuban missile crisis correspondence between Kennedy and Khrushchev can be found in this very useful volume, which every student of the Cuban missile crisis should have on the shelf, at the ready.

2. Nikita S. Khrushchev to John F. Kennedy, October 23, 1962. In Ibid., p. 166.

3. Fidel Castro, interview on Cuban television, October 23, 1962. Available in an English translation on the website of the University of Texas' Latin American Network Information Center, at: http://lanic.utexas.edu/project/castro/db/1962/19621024 .html. This speech of Castro's, like the others on this website, is reprinted from the CIA's translation over its Foreign Broadcast Information Service (FBIS, pronounced "Fibbus" by Cold War aficionados).

ACT II: SPIRAL

1. Jules Verne, *20,000 Leagues Under the Sea*. Trans. by Thomas A. Barron (New York: MacMillan, 1995). (1870)

2. John F. Kennedy to Nikita S. Khrushchev, October 23, 1962. In Chang and Kornbluh, eds., *Cuban Missile Crisis*, pp. 171–72.

3. Nikita S. Khrushchev to John F. Kennedy, October 24, 1962. In Ibid., pp. 173–74.

4. John F. Kennedy to Nikita S. Khrushchev, October 25, 1962. In Ibid., p. 183.

5. Nikita S. Khrushchev to John F. Kennedy, October 26, 1962. In Ibid., pp. 195–98.

6. Nikita S. Khrushchev to John F. Kennedy, October 27, 1962. In Ibid., pp. 207–9.

7. Fidel Castro to Nikita S. Khrushchev, October 26, 1962. In Ibid., p. 199. This letter, along with the other four letters exchanged during the crisis between Khrushchev and Castro, may also be found in Appendix 2 of James G. Blight, Bruce J. Allyn, and David A. Welch, *Cuba on the Brink: Castro, the Missile Crisis and the Soviet Collapse*, expanded second ed. (Lanham, MD: Rowman & Littlefield, 2002), pp. 502–19. Castro's letter of October 26 is on pp. 509–10. The collection in *Cuba on the Brink* also reprints the valuable introduction to the correspondence just as it appeared when the letters were first published by the Cuban government in November 1990 in a special issue of *Granma*, the Cuban Communist Party daily. Although the long introduction is unsigned, it is understood to have been written by Fidel Castro himself.

8. Nikita S. Khrushchev to Fidel Castro, October 28, 1962. In Chang and Kornbluh, *Cuban Missile Crisis*, p. 249; and Blight et al., *Cuba on the Brink*, pp. 510–11.

ACT III: ESCAPE

1. John F. Kennedy to Nikita S. Khrushchev, October 27, 1962. In Chang and Kornbluh, *Cuban Missile Crisis*, pp. 233–35.
2. The flash bulletin is reprinted in Michael Dobbs, *One Minute to Midnight: Kennedy, Khrushchev and Castro on the Brink of Nuclear War* (New York: Knopf, 2008), p. 231.
3. Nikita S. Khrushchev to John F. Kennedy, October 28, 1962. In Chang and Kornbluh, *Cuban Missile Crisis*, pp. 236–39.
4. John F. Kennedy to Nikita S. Khrushchev, October 28, 1962. In Chang and Kornbluh, *Cuban Missile Crisis*, pp. 240–42.
5. This Teletype announcement is reprinted in Dobbs, *One Minute to Midnight*, p. 334.
6. Fidel Castro to U Thant, October 28, 1962. In Chang and Kornbluh, *Cuban Missile Crisis*, pp. 251–52.
7. Fidel Castro to Nikita S. Khrushchev, October 28, 1962. In Ibid., p. 250.
8. Nikita S. Khrushchev to Fidel Castro, October 30, 1962. In Ibid., p. 253.
9. Fidel Castro to Nikita S. Khrushchev, October 31, 1962. In Ibid., p. 254.

ACT IV: SQUEEZE

1. Nikita S. Khrushchev to John F. Kennedy, October 30, 1962. In *Problems of Communism*, special issue (Spring 1992), "Back From the Brink: The Correspondence Between President John F. Kennedy and Chairman Nikita S. Khrushchev on the Cuban Missile Crisis of Autumn 1962, pp. 62–73. This remarkable volume contains all of the correspondence between Kennedy and Khrushchev in October, November, and December 1962. All the letters are presented in both Russian and English. And on pp. 28–29, the letters are summarized in brief statements and arranged in a chronological grid that is extremely helpful in putting all this prose into an understandable narrative framework. The volume begins with statements by the U.S. Secretary of State James A. Baker III and the Russian Foreign Minister Andrey Kozyrev. This letter from Khrushchev to Kennedy is omitted from Laurence Chang and Peter Kornbluh, *The Cuban Missile Crisis, 1962*, rev. ed., foreword by Robert S. McNamara (New York: New Press, 1998).
2. John F. Kennedy to Nikita S. Khrushchev, November 3, 1962. In *Problems of Communism*, pp. 73–74; and Chang and Kornbluh, *Cuban Missile Crisis*, pp. 270–71.
3. Nikita S. Khrushchev to John F. Kennedy, November, 4 1962. In *Problems of Communism*, pp. 75–76; and Chang and Kornbluh, *Cuban Missile Crisis*, p. 274.
4. John F. Kennedy to Nikita S. Khrushchev, November 6, 1962. In *Problems of Communism*, pp. 77–81; and Chang and Kornbluh, *Cuban Missile Crisis*, pp. 275–76.
5. Nikita S. Khrushchev to John F. Kennedy, November 11, 1962. In *Problems of Communism*, pp. 82–88; and Chang and Kornbluh, *Cuban Missile Crisis*, pp. 280–82.
6. Memorandum of Conversation between Anastas I. Mikoyan, Oswaldo Dorticos, Ernesto ("Che") Guevara, and Carlos Rafael Rodriguez. Evening, November 5, 1962, Havana, Cuba. Available from the National Security Archive: www .gwu.edu/%7Ensarchiv/nsa/cuba_mis_cri/621105%20MemCon%20Mikoyan%20 (evening).pdf.

7. Ciphered telegram from Anastas I. Mikoyan to the Central Committee of the Communist Party of the Soviet Union, November 6, 1962 (Top Secret/No copies). Source: The Archive of the President of the Russian Federation, special declassification, April 2002. Translated by Svetlana Savranskaya and Andrea Hendrickson. Available from the National Security Archive: www.gwu.edu/%7Ensarchiv/nsa/ cuba_mis_cri/621105%20MemCon%20Mikoyan%20(evening).pdfhttp://www .gwu.edu/%7Ensarchiv/nsa/cuba_mis_cri/621105%20MemCon%20Mikoyan%20 (evening).pdf.

8. John F. Kennedy to Nikita S. Khrushchev, November 12, 1962. In *Problems of Communism*, p. 88; and Chang and Kornbluh, *Cuban Missile Crisis*, p. 283.

9. Nikita S. Khrushchev to John F. Kennedy, November 13, 1962. In *Problems of Communism*, pp. 88–92; and Chang and Kornbluh, *Cuban Missile Crisis*, pp. 284–85. The letter was dated November 14; it was sent from Moscow and arrived on November 13 in Washington, which is situated eight time zones earlier than Moscow.

10. Fidel Castro to U Thant, November 15, 1962. We are using the UN translation from Spanish into English. Reprinted as Appendix B in James G. Blight and Philip Brenner, *Sad and Luminous Days: Castro's Struggle With the Superpowers After the Missile Crisis* (Lanham, MD: Rowman & Littlefield, 2002), pp. 210–13. The FBIS translation of the letter, which is less felicitous but conveys the same information as the UN translation, is available online from the Latin American Network Information Center at: http://lanic.utexas.edu/project/castro/db/1962/19621116.html. The letter is remarkably defiant, even by Fidel Castro's lofty standard of defiance, in that he thumbs his nose not just at the U.S.—which had become commonplace by this point in the fractured U.S.-Cuban relationship—but also at the Soviet Union, only slightly less directly. Castro essentially tells U Thant that the Cubans have certain demands and conditions, which the Soviets in their cowardice failed to put on the table in their negotiations with the U.S., but which, for the Cuban government, are still fundamental conditions which must be met as prerequisites to Cuban participation in any deal the Americans and Soviets work out.

11. John F. Kennedy to Nikita S. Khrushchev, November 15 1962. In *Problems of Communism*, pp. 92-96; and Chang and Kornbluh, *Cuban Missile Crisis*, pp. 286-289.

12. Nikita S. Khrushchev to John F. Kennedy, November 19, 1862. In *Problems of Communism*, pp. 96–106; and Chang and Kornbluh, *Cuban Missile Crisis*, pp. 300–3.

13. John F. Kennedy to Nikita S. Khrushchev, November 20, 1962. In *Problems of Communism*, p. 106. The message is not included in Chang and Kornbluh, *Cuban Missile Crisis*.

14. John F. Kennedy, *Public Papers of the President, 1962* (Washington, DC: U.S. Government Printing Office, 1963), p. 830.

15. John F. Kennedy, *Public Papers of the President, 1962*, p. 835.

POSTSCRIPT: HOPE

1. John F. Kennedy, American University commencement address, delivered June 10, 1963, in Washington, DC. The entire text is available on the website of the Kennedy Library: www.jfklibrary.org/Research/Ready-Reference/JFK-Speeches/ Commencement-Address-at-American-University-June-10-1963.aspx.

2. Many of these charges against Khrushchev were drafted by Dmitri Polyansky, a Presidium member, whom Leonid Brezhnev promoted to first deputy chairman of the Council of Ministers (Brezhnev's top aide) in 1965, shortly after the coup that brought down Khrushchev. See Aleksandr Fursenko and Timothy Naftali, *"One Hell of a Gamble": The Secret History of the Cuban Missile Crisis—Khrushchev, Castro & Kennedy, 1958-1964* (New York: Norton, 1997), pp. 353–54.

3. Nikita Khrushchev to John F. Kennedy, December 10, 1962. In *Problems of Communism*, pp. 110–17. (Chang and Kornbluh, *Cuban Missile Crisis*, does not include the Kennedy-Khrushchev correspondence beyond November 1962.)

4. John F. Kennedy to Nikita S. Khrushchev, December 14, 1962. In *Problems of Communism*, pp. 117–20.

5. Jacqueline Kennedy to Nikita S. Khrushchev, December 1, 1963. The letter is the final entry in the State Department's compilation of the "Kennedy-Khrushchev Exchanges." It is available at www.state.gov/www/about_state/history/volume_vi/exchanges.html. The letter was, according to Kennedy biographer William Manchester, written out by Jacqueline Kennedy in longhand and given to National Security Adviser McGeorge Bundy, who made several minor changes, and then sent it on to Khrushchev.

6. The complete text of the letter from Nikita Khrushchev to Jacqueline Kennedy is in Jay Mulvaney and Paul De Angelis, *Dear Mrs. Kennedy: The World Shares Its Grief, Letters November 1963* (New York: St. Martin's Press), p. 179.

7. Fidel Castro, televised message on the danger of nuclear war: www.youtube.com/watch?v=1f_UPdbOIH8. Fidel Castro reads the statement, in Spanish (with English subtitles). The piece concludes with footage of Fidel Castro's March 2002 visit to Hiroshima, where he laid a wreath in honor of the victims of the atomic bombing of August 6, 1945. Fidel Castro continues to write about nuclear danger. A convenient source, which catalogues English translations of Fidel's blog is: www.globalresearch.ca/index.php?context=listByAuthor&authorFirst=Fidel&authorName=Castro%20Ruz. This website contains Fidel's articles from 2007 to the present. An especially interesting posting occurred on January 6, 2012, when Fidel noted that 2012 is the 50th anniversary year of the October crisis and—in his view—the year that a war in the Middle East, probably a nuclear war, will occur. See "the March Towards the Abyss": www.globalresearch.ca/index.php?context=va&aid=28549.

8. Jeffrey Goldberg, "Castro: No One Has Been Slandered More Than the Jews." *The Atlantic Online* edition: www.theatlantic.com/international/archive/2010/09/castro-no-one-has-been-slandered-more-than-the-jews/62566/. See also James Fallows: "Castro: I Was Wrong During Cuban Missile Crisis, at: www.theatlantic.com/international/archive/2010/09/castro-i-was-wrong-during-cuban-missile-crisis/62580/. Both were originally posted on September 7, 2010.

APPENDIX A

1. Emily Dickinson, poem number 1672 (dated 1885). In R. W. Franklin (Ed.), *The Poems of Emily Dickinson* (Cambridge, MA: Harvard University Press, 2005), p. 604.

2. William Blake, *Jerusalem*, chapter 3, plate 55. http://www.thefourzoas.com/jerusalem/chap_3_plate_55.html.

3. The Kennedy School became the hub of a good deal of policy-oriented discussion of nuclear issues with the publication of a 1983 book written by several of its faculty (in collaboration with other faculty members from Harvard's Government Department): see Albert Carnesale, Paul Doty, Stanley Hoffmann, Samuel P. Huntington, Joseph S. Nye, Jr. and Scott D. Sagan, *Living With Nuclear Weapons*, foreword by Derek Bok (New York: Bantam, 1983). The book was praised by some for its acceptance that we must live under a nuclear cloud virtually forever—given the risks involved in attempting to disarm—and criticized by others who repudiated what they took to be its fatalism. A Harvard colleague, Abram Chayes, said for example that the book explained everything we need to know about the nuclear threat, "from L to M." A discussion of the book's impact and possible resonance with the Cuban missile crisis may be found in James G. Blight, *The Shattered Crystal Ball: Fear and Learning in the Cuban Missile Crisis* (Lanham, MD: Rowman & Littlefield, 1992), pp. 3–10.

4. In looking back to the era of the first Reagan administration, the discussions of the risk of nuclear war seem almost surreal. The air we breathed seemed to carry a whiff of something Khrushchev noted in December 1962, with respect to the last week of October 1962, namely, that "the smell of scorching hung in the air." The most seminal text—the book that lit the fuse of fear of Armageddon for millions—was Jonathan Schell's *The Fate of the Earth* (New York: Knopf, 1982). After reading his chapter, "A Republic of Insects and Grass" (a scientifically informed portrait of a post-nuclear war America), we were stunned. See also Spencer R. Weart, *Nuclear Fear: A History of Images* (Cambridge, MA: Harvard University Press, 1988) for a compelling history of the waxing and waning of fear of nuclear war, from the Second World War through the end of the Reagan years.

5. At the Kennedy School, discussions of the Cuban missile crisis always began with a consideration of a book by the (then) dean of the school, Graham T. Allison, *Essence of Decision: Explaining the Cuban Missile Crisis* (Boston: Little, Brown, 1971). The book was revised in 1999 by Allison and Philip Zelikow (New York: Addison-Wesley-Longman). The book grew out a seminar attended by Allison at the school throughout the 1960s on the Cuban missile crisis, at which various members of the Kennedy administration appeared regularly to answer questions about their roles in the event.

6. All such questions were essentially unanswerable in the early 1980s because little or nothing was known about decision-making in Moscow or the situation on the ground in Cuba. The CIA had told Kennedy that there *probably* weren't any nuclear warheads in Cuba during the crisis, for example, so how dangerous could it have been (to the United States)? As we later learned, 162 nuclear warheads had reached the island and were ready to be used in the event of a war.

7. In fact, the conference was to chart the course for the Kennedy School's Project on Avoiding Nuclear War, as it emerged from reactions to *Living with Nuclear Weapons* the previous year.

8. A feature of this unexpected focus of the conference was that many of the people around the table had been "whiz kids" in the McNamara Pentagon during the Kennedy and Johnson administrations. Most had not dealt with McNamara for

the past fifteen years or so, since his departure from the Pentagon when he became president of the World Bank in March 1968. Sensing our amazement on a coffee break at the proceedings, Ted Warner, an alumnus of the McNamara Pentagon, winked at us and said, "Just like old times."

9. McNamara was not alone in this pursuit. He had already helped assemble a team that was dubbed by Alexander Haig, "The Gang of Four": McGeorge Bundy, George Kennan, McNamara and Gerard Smith—all distinguished former national security officials, who wrote and spoke regularly on U.S. and NATO nuclear policy. Much of what they wrote stood in direct opposition to policies favored by the Reagan administration. See, for example, their advocacy of a NATO No First Use doctrine: McGeorge Bundy, George F. Kennan, Robert S. McNamara and Gerard Smith, "Nuclear Weapons and the Atlantic Alliance," *Foreign Affairs*, vol. 60, no. 4 (Spring 1982), pp. 753–68; and Bundy, Kennan, McNamara and Smith, "The President's Choice: Star Wars or Arms Control," *Foreign Affairs*, vol. 63, no. 2 (Winter 1984), pp. 264–78. Bundy wrote the final drafts of these and related pieces, following long face-to-face discussions between the members of the "Gang of Four." Bundy once told us, "Bob McNamara always thinks the really good stuff always falls on the cutting room floor"—a reference to McNamara's more radical stance than his three partners.

10. In fact, those initiating a nuclear war, should they survive for a time after the war, would in McNamara's view experience *nothing but regret* for having gone nuclear. The nuclear strategist Herman Kahn (upon whom filmmaker Stanley Kubrick modeled the character of Dr. Strangelove in his 1964 film, *Dr. Strangelove*, one of the greatest films ever made about the nuclear threat) had said back in the 1950s that after a nuclear war, "the living will envy the dead." Most of the people around the conference table in Big Sky, Montana in July 1984 were dedicating their lives to suggesting ways in which one should amend, or even outright retract, Kahn's prophecy. But Bob McNamara was saying, in effect, "You guys are wasting your time—worse, you are guilty of self-delusion if you think initiating a nuclear war will produce anything other than unmitigated catastrophe."

11. We are reminded of an equally pathetic and tragic situation that arose during the U.S. war in Vietnam. A few people in McNamara's Pentagon, led by McNamara, had concluded by mid-1965 that the only possible end to the war would involve a negotiated agreement between Washington and Hanoi. The Johnson administration, instead of pursuing Hanoi directly, delivered their invitation to begin negotiations to the Soviet Foreign Ministry in Moscow, and never got an answer, never understood how little leverage the Soviets had over Ho Chi Minh's government. The missile crisis ended less tragically but not because Kennedy chose to negotiate with Castro. He didn't. It ended peacefully because, in large part, Kennedy didn't push his luck, which he sensed was running out, by ordering an attack on Cuba.

12. Elmore Leonard, *Maximum Bob* (New York: HarperCollins, 1991).

13. It is unclear to us in retrospect whether all, most, or merely some of this three-part breakdown of the Cuban missile crisis was imparted to us by Bob McNamara during that first encounter in 1984. We do remember, however, McNamara's emphasis on finding a way to get to Soviet and Cuban decision-makers during the crisis. We told him at one point about a comment made by his former deputy, Paul Nitze, who said the Cuban missile crisis was "in Bob McNamara's brain." He meant

that McNamara was terrified by an irrational fear of nuclear war during the crisis and that, if Nitze had been secretary, he would have persuaded the president that nuclear risk was essentially non-existent and recommended that Kennedy authorize an attack and invasion of Cuba. In the mid-1980s, McNamara knew that he could not respond effectively to statements like Nitze's because he had no idea what the Soviets would have done in response to a U.S. attack. Less than ten years after our first encounter with McNamara, we would have an answer: the probability was alarmingly high that in the event of U.S. military action against Cuba, nuclear war would have erupted in and around the island, escalating far beyond the Caribbean, possibly destroying human civilization. McNamara's instincts in this case were right, as were Kennedy's. The Cuban missile crisis was not just in Bob McNamara's brain, after all.

14. All the Kennedy-Khrushchev correspondence is now available online at the U.S. State Department's website: http://www.state.gov/www/about_state/history/volume_vi/exchanges.html. The annotations often contain useful details regarding the history of the individual letters.

15. Allison, *Essence of Decision*, pp. 220–23.

16. Portions of the letters had been leaking out all through the 1960s and into the early 1970s. When Khrushchev died in September 1971, the time seemed right to release the documents—that is, the official versions of Kennedy's letters to Khrushchev, and the U.S. State Department's official English translations of Khrushchev's original Russian letters.

17. One reason why we didn't know anything about the Cuban perspective is that few in our immediate environment at the time thought it mattered one way or the other what the Cubans thought, or how they may have acted. The basic principle was: the United States responded to a deployment of *Soviet* missiles; the United States forced the removal of *Soviet* missiles; end of story. If the way the event was referred to in the United States had been an accurate reflection of its underlying assumptions, it would have been called the *Soviet* missile crisis. See James G. Blight and David A. Welch, foreword by McGeorge Bundy, *On the Brink: Americans and Soviets Reexamine the Cuban Missile Crisis*, 2nd ed. (New York: Hill and Wang/Noonday, 1990), pp. 291–316, for an account of the shift in focus as sources in the Soviet Union and Cuba began to open up to us.

18. The conference was held March 5–8 1987 at the Hawk's Cay Conference Center, in Marathon, Florida. The edited and annotated transcript of that conference occupies most of Blight and Welch, *On the Brink*.

19. On the method of critical history see the following: Len Scott and Steve Smith, "Lessons of October: Historians, Political Scientists, Policy-makers and the Cuban Missile Crisis," *International Affairs*, vol. 70 (October 1994), pp. 659–84; James G. Blight and janet M. Lang, *The Fog of War: Lessons From the Life of Robert S. McNamara* (Lanham, MD: Rowman & Littlefield, 2005), pp. 3–25; and James G. Blight and janet M. Lang, "When Empathy Failed: Using Critical Oral History to Reassess the Collapse of U.S.-Soviet Détente in the Carter-Brezhnev Years," *Journal of Cold War Studies*, vol. 12, no. 2 (Spring 2010), pp. 29–74.

20. The "we" of whom we write in regard to chasing after Cold War documents includes many people. All have some sort of connection to what is quite possibly the greatest nongovernmental organization ever conceived, George Washington

University's National Security Archive. For the Cuban missile crisis project, "we" includes the Archive's founder, Scott Armstrong, its longtime director Tom Blanton, its research director Malcolm Byrne, its Russian studies maven Svetlana Savranskaya, and the Archive's ace Cubanologist, Peter Kornbluh. In addition, many others not directly employed by the Archive have been devoted to its cause of getting key documents released. Chief among these colleagues are Philip Brenner, long-time Cuba specialist at American University who first sparked our interest in the Cuban experience of the Cuban missile crisis, Christian Ostermann, director of the History and Public Policy Program at the Woodrow Wilson International Centers for Scholars, who translated many pages of transcripts of meetings between Fidel Castro and Erich Honecker, and the irrepressible, human document dynamo, James G. Hershberg of George Washington University's History Department who found documents in the far corners of the planet. We have all been in the thick of things together. We send our group's salutation, *Documentos o Muerte*, to one and all.

21. Frances FitzGerald to James Blight and janet Lang, personal communication, November 13, 1998.

22. For a book-length argument that familiarity with Kierkegaard's *The Concept of Anxiety* should be a prerequisite for anyone trying to understand the psychology of leaders in a nuclear crisis, see James G. Blight, *The Shattered Crystal Ball: Fear and Learning in the Cuban Missile Crisis* (Lanham, MD: Rowman & Littlefield, 1992). In the book, the process of contextualizing the Cuban missile crisis is referred to as "recovering the psychological life of the crisis" (p. 10). Kierkegaard pointed out why this is so difficult, yet necessary. "Eternity is a very radical thought. Whenever it is posited, the present becomes something entirely different from what it was apart from it . . . a person will think it, and he dares not to think it" (quoted in Blight, *Shattered Crystal Ball*, p. 10). This is difficult because those of us who attempt to analyze and understand what it was like must enter the psychological terrain as aliens—we will likely never have any such experience as the one we are trying to grasp. Therefore, failing to recover the psychological life of the crisis raises the odds that someone, somewhere, may have the experience of trying to lead a country out of its next date with Armageddon. It is not difficult to imagine Kierkegaard, the skeptical Lutheran, shaking his finger at us as if to say, "Don't count on getting out by luck next time."

23. In the execution of critical oral history projects with which we have been involved, the division of labor works like this. Decision-makers: we do most (though far from all) of the recruiting of former officials involved with whatever events we are investigating. Documents: our colleagues at George Washington University's National Security Archive take the lead in identifying and acquiring classified documents. For U.S. documents, this may involve filing one or more Freedom of Information Act (FOIA) requests and following up with the U.S. government. In other countries—none of which has a FOIA law—the process is often difficult and not easy to categorize. Someone remembers writing something. Someone else may have seen it and thinks it may be in this or that repository and volunteers to have a look if given access. Yet another person makes a few phone calls to people in the government who will have to approve access to classified material. Recruiting scholars—the third element in critical oral history—is usually easy. In fact, usually

too many scholars want to participate because (in many cases) they want to be in a position to ask questions they have wanted to ask for years, but could not gain access to the people who might know the answers.

24. See Bruce J. Allyn, James G. Blight and David A. Welch, eds., *Back to the Brink: Proceedings of the Moscow Conference on the Cuban Missile Crisis, January 27–28, 1989,* foreword by Georgy Shakhnazarov (Lanham, MD: UPA, 1992). Gromyko, known in the Western diplomatic corps as "Old Stone Face," due to his demeanor and general refusal to divulge information, seemed at this conference to be a completely different person. For instance, most participants who had dealt with Gromyko in the old days (whether Americans, Russians or Cubans) could scarcely believe they were witnessing the following exchange at the Moscow conference between Gromyko and former Russian Ambassador to the United States, Anatoly Dobrynin:

Dobrynin: I was not informed to the very last moment about the missiles in Cuba.

Gromyko: What, Anatoly Fyodorovich? Do you mean that I did not tell you, the ambassador, about the nuclear missiles in Cuba?

Dobrynin: No, you did not tell me.

Gromyko: That means it must have been a very big secret!
[General laughter] (pp. 145–46).

25. Fidel Castro has expressed his reactions to the Soviet collapse and (as he sees it) betrayal of Cuba on three principal occasions: first in October 1962, in the three Armageddon letters to Khrushchev included in this book. These are letters #20 (in Act II, "Spiral") and #26 and #28 (in Act III, "Escape"). Fidel Castro also expounded at length at a meeting of the Central Committee of the Cuban communist party in January 1968, in a twelve-hour speech over two days. Most of the people in the room had not been part of the leadership in October 1962, and he wanted them to know, basically, that the Soviets had been arrogant and cowardly in the crisis. The complete and annotated text of that remarkable speech is in James G. Blight and Philip Brenner, *Sad and Luminous Days: Cuba's Struggle with the Superpowers after the Missile Crisis* (Lanham, MD: Rowman & Littlefield, 2002), pp. 33–72. Castro covered the same ground yet a third time in January 1992 at a critical oral history conference in Havana, which he hosted and which our team organized. See James G. Blight, Bruce J. Allyn and David A. Welch, *Cuba on the Brink: Castro, the Missile Crisis and the Soviet Collapse,* revised and expanded ed. (Lanham, MD: Rowman & Littlefield, 2002).

26. Occasionally, Cuban sensitivity to being ignored by the superpowers has its comic side. It is January 1992 and Russian General Anatoly Gribkov has just given his initial presentation revealing, for the first time to Westerners, that tactical nuclear warheads had reached Cuba in 1962, and would probably have been used to repel a U.S. invasion of the island, had Kennedy ordered it. Bob McNamara has taken off his headset and is waving his hands. He wants to speak. He has never heard anything like this before. Finally, the Cuban chair for the session, Jorge Risquet, recognizes McNamara.

McNamara: May I suggest that, rather than try to clarify the issue now, we agree that General [William] Smith and Ambassador [Raymond] Garthoff meet with General Gribkov at his convenience and discuss the matter further?

Castro: I wonder why only the American general and the general of the armed forces of the former Soviet Union should meet? I think if we are going to clarify these things, at least a Cuban general or a civilian should be at the meeting.

Risquet: It seems that there is a certain persistence here of the superpowers' past tendency to ignore other parties. I think we should accept Mr. McNamara's suggestion, as amended by the Commander-in-Chief. (Blight, Allyn and Welch, *Cuba on the Brink*, pp. 65–66.)

The meeting never occurred. Gribkov refused to meet with any of the Americans, in part because he thought (incorrectly) that McNamara had accused him of lying. More than two-and-a-half years later, in 1994, McNamara and Gribkov held their long-postponed meeting at a conference in Washington—alas, without a Cuban representative present. Old habits die hard.

27. The complete text of all five letters, in their official English translations, may be found in Appendix 2 to Blight, Allyn and Welch, *Cuba on the Brink*, pp. 502–19. The section includes an interesting historical introduction to the letters that also appeared when they were first published in Cuba, "With the Historical Truth and Morale of Baragua," thought to have been written by Fidel Castro, though it appeared as an unsigned editorial. It is a remarkably concise history of Cuba's foreign relations told through the metaphor of the nineteenth-century Cuban patriot Antonio Maceo's refusal to capitulate to the Spanish. In other words, what Maceo courageously refused to do in 1878 was more or less exactly what the Soviets did in October 1962: they agreed to humiliating terms rather than insist on their rights.

28. Philip Brenner, of American University, acting on behalf of and in concert with the National Security Archive, was largely responsible for the release of these documents. Fidel Castro's access to the November letters between Kennedy and Khrushchev was central to Castro's decision to participate fully in the conference.

Here is what happened. On the afternoon before the conference was to begin, we were touring a Cuban biotechnology plant near Havana. Toward the end of the tour, a Cuban official came up to us and asked us to step aside and follow him to a nearby office. He looked nervous. He said that Fidel Castro, having read the November letters between Kennedy and Khrushchev in the middle of the previous night, had changed his plans. Formerly, he was to give an opening statement, disappear for the duration of the conference, then return at the end to answer questions. Now, we were told, he wanted to participate personally in every minute of the conference, "if that is agreeable to the American delegation." Agreeable? Was he kidding? We responded, "Yes, it is agreeable, so long as the president keeps in mind the advanced age of some of our participants, and keeps his interventions relatively short and concise." Castro did give a welcome to the participants that lasted exactly seven minutes, following which he glanced at his watch, then looked in our direction and said, "Seven minutes; was that short enough?" This remark sent all the Cubans in the room into hysterical laughter. We speculated that some of them might have spent decades waiting for a moment to suggest to Fidel that he "keep it short," and they had just lived out their fantasies through us.

29. Gribkov's initial presentation at the 1992 Havana conference was the single most dramatic revelation of the conference—or any conference we have ever been associated with. His entire intervention is in Blight, Allyn and Welch, *Cuba on the Brink*, pp. 56–63. In the aftermath of his comments, it became obvious that Gribkov thought we on the U.S. side already knew most of the details he was presenting. But we didn't—not even our military and intelligence people had any notion of what Gribkov would reveal, not in October 1962 and not in January 1992.

30. Fidel Castro at the height of his rhetorical powers is on display in the official record of his presentation of the Cuban view of the events. See Blight, Allyn and Welch, *Cuba on the Brink*, pp. 53–317.

31. The cables from Mikoyan to the Soviet leadership are very important. We are especially grateful to two colleagues for making them available to us, and to the public: the late Sergo Mikoyan, son of Anastas Mikoyan, a Russian specialist on Latin America and former executive secretary to his father. Sergo Mikoyan had in his possession for many years his father's journals, which included copies of many of the communications he sent to Moscow from Havana in November 1962. We also owe a big debt of gratitude to Dr. Svetlana Savranskaya, director of Russian Studies at the National Security Archive, for her work with Sergo Mikoyan to get the documents released, and for her careful editing and translating of the Mikoyan materials.

APPENDIX B

1. H.R. Trevor-Roper, "The Lost Moments of History," *New York Review of Books*, Vol. 35, No. 16 (October 27, 1987), pp. 61-67, p. 61.

2. Bruce Springsteen, "Radio Nowhere," the lead track on his 2007 album, *Magic*, issued by Columbia Records.

3. Trevor-Roper, "Lost Moments of History," p. 61.

4. Not all of the contextual material in this book is derived from our multi-decade dangling conversations with officials in Washington, Moscow, and Havana. We also want to acknowledge a significant debt to the authors of a number of books that we found to be exceptions to the general rule that printed sources yield the basic chronology, while context comes from reiterated face-to-face conversation.

Several books proved to be essential to us, across a wide range of events and decisions in all three involved countries. They are:

- Laurence Chang and Peter Kornbluh, eds., *The Cuban Missile Crisis, 1962*, revised ed., foreword by Robert S. McNamara (New York: New Press 1998). Brilliantly organized, generously annotated by two scholars from the National Security Archive, this book is a hybrid: part chronology, part declassified documentation, part behind the scenes reporting. No one with any interest in the Cuban missile crisis should be without this book.
- Aleksandr Fursenko and Timothy Naftali, *"One Hell of a Gamble": The Secret History of the Cuban Missile Crisis—Khrushchev, Castro and Kennedy, 1958-1964*

(New York: Norton, 1997). This book is based largely on previously unavailable sources in the Russian archives. Fortunately, the authors are as conversant with the available documentation and oral testimony from the U.S. and Cuban sides as they are on Russian decision-making. They make especially good use of memoirs by former Soviet officials. They tell a complex tale, full of rich detail, and they tell it well.

- Michael Dobbs, *One Minute to Midnight: Kennedy, Khrushchev and Castro on the Brink of Nuclear War* (New York, Knopf, 2008). Prodigiously researched by a talented and relentless investigative journalist, every page contains previously unknown or overlooked information. In addition to commentary on decision-making at the highest levels, the book draws on the author's path breaking research into ship logs and many miles of previously unknown photographic film taken by U.S. reconnaissance aircraft over Cuba and much else.

Two books that we found illuminating about the atmosphere in the White House during the Cuban missile crisis are:

- Robert F. Kennedy, *Thirteen Days: A Memoir of the Cuban Missile Crisis*, with an Afterword by Richard E. Neustadt and Graham T. Allison (New York: Norton, 1971). For White House atmospherics in print, there is still nothing like it. The more details we learn about October 1962, the more RFK's prose seems simply descriptive, rather than overheated. For example, he says on the first page that he will describe an event "which brought the world to the abyss of nuclear destruction and the end of mankind." In light of what we now know, that seems to be a statement of fact.
- Arthur Schlesinger, Jr., *A Thousand Days: John F. Kennedy in the White House* (Boston: Houghton Mifflin, 1965). Schlesinger seems to have been everywhere at once, full of insider information, and gifted with a supremely self-confident writing style that Kennedy would have appreciated. It's biggest fault, according to many critics, is Schlesinger's uncritical embrace of everything Kennedy seems to have done or thought as president, and his tendency to discredit Kennedy's critics with a cutting edge that is very sharp indeed. It is the chronicle of a very great, nearly perfect man, cut down in the summer of his years by an assassin in Dallas. Yet these very features of *A Thousand Days*—the combination of love for Kennedy and extraordinary access to him—is what gives readers the feeling of proximity to Kennedy—his habits, his absurdist sense of humor, his high intelligence. This is the history of the American Camelot. It is partial, not the whole story. But it is also deeply personal, and it grabs you if you let it, right from the epigraph from Hemingway with which is begins: "If people bring so much courage to this world the world has to kill them to break them, so of course it kills them." Bring a handkerchief, but bring a pen and notepad as well.

An extraordinary resource for probing the depths of Khrushchev's mind, and the machinations of Kremlin maneuvering is due to the work of his son, Sergei Khrushchev. See especially:

- Sergei N. Khrushchev, *Nikita Khrushchev and the Making of a Superpower*, trans. by Shirley Benson, foreword by William Taubman, annotations by William

Wohlforth (University Park, Pennsylvania: The Pennsylvania State University Press, 2000). This book is part scholarly history, part memoir, by the Soviet chairman's son and biographer. The long penultimate section on the Cuban missile crisis is overflowing with personal details and is more or less Nikita Khrushchev's own story, had he told it himself.

For an up close and personal look at Havana during the crisis, we found useful two scholarly memoirs by writers who had unusual access to the Cuban ethos of October 1962, including Cuban decision-makers:

- Maurice Halperin, *The Rise and Decline of Fidel Castro: An Essay in Contemporary History* (Berkeley: University of California Press, 1972). Halperin was hounded out of the U.S. during the McCarthy period and wound up in Moscow, working for the Soviet government as a translator. By chance, he met Che Guevara in early 1962 in Moscow. Guevara, finding that Halperin was fluent in Spanish, invited him to Cuba to work for him. Halperin accepted the invitation. He lived in Havana from 1962 to 1968, and was in Havana during the crisis. His book combines first-person observations and references to obscure Cuban publications that, by now, have ceased to exist for decades. His close analysis of Castro's speeches, along with his interviews with ordinary Cubans on the streets of Havana, combine seamlessly in this unique contribution to understanding the Cuban perspective on the crisis.
- K.S. Karol, *Guerrillas in Power: The Course of the Cuban Revolution*, trans. from the French by Arnold Pomerans (New York: Hill and Wang, 1970). Karol, a Polish-born journalist who lived in Paris, visited Cuba many times in the 1960s. Like Maurice Halperin, he was in Havana during the Cuban missile crisis. Karol combines genuine affection for the Cuban Revolution with an absurdist sense of humor that he feels is a necessary prerequisite to appreciating the overheated, paranoid atmosphere of Cuba in the 1960s. Karol is also conversant with developments occurring simultaneously in the Soviet Union and he is eloquent on the ways Fidel Castro kept trying to "square the circle" by protecting Cuba's interests, while not offending the Soviets.

Two other sources for what was happening in Cuba before, during and after the crisis are books with which we have been associated. They are:

- James G. Blight and Philip Brenner, *Sad and Luminous Days: Cuba's Struggle with the Superpowers after the Missile Crisis* (Lanham, MD: Rowman & Littlefield, 2002). This book focuses on a previously unknown, twelve-hour speech, given by Fidel Castro over two days in January 1968. Using an array of declassified documents, Castro gives the Cuban Central Committee his view of what happened in October 1962, and why. The bulk of the document is given over to a bitter, often darkly funny characterization of the Russians in terms still heard in Cuba: i.e., the Russians are like bowling pins: white, shiny, and they tip over easily.
- James G. Blight, Bruce J. Allyn and David A. Welch, *Cuba on the Brink: Castro, the Missile Crisis and the Soviet Collapse*, revised and expanded edition (Lanham, MD: Rowman & Littlefield, 2002). This is the complete, annotated record of the

January 1992 Havana conference on the Cuban missile crisis. It contains Fidel Castro's most extensive statement on the crisis, along with his retrospective views of Kennedy and Khrushchev. The five Khrushchev-Castro Armageddon letters are also included in an appendix to the volume.

5. Bob Woodward, Lecture at the Poynter Institute, St. Petersburg, Florida, March 2011: www.poynter.org/latest-news/top-stories/123587/bob-woodward-you-get -the-truth-at-night-the-lies-during-the-day/. (Accessed May 17, 2012).

6. The reference is to Bruce Springsteen's "Thunder Road," the first track on the album, *Born to Run*, issued by Columbia Records in August 1975.

Acknowledgments

S oren Kierkegaard wrote in 1844: "That dread makes its appearance, is the pivot upon which everything turns." The Great Dane was referring to each individual's confrontation with finitude, with death, with the end. In this book we are concerned with an event that very nearly resulted in the end of the entire world as we know it. It is our attempt to reinsert some dread into our understanding of the October 1962 Cuban missile crisis. Not sci-fi dread; not dread elicited falsely, just for effect. We mean dread commensurate with the dread felt by leaders at the time, and the dread we need to feel now if we are to grasp its momentous implications. We mean data-based, empirically grounded dread—the kind of dread that seemed to Kennedy, Khrushchev and Castro to prefigure Armageddon.

Now, a half-century after this nearest miss to nuclear Armageddon, it has become difficult to focus on the momentary experience of the nearness and to deemphasize a half century of explanations of the miss. The event is still interesting, but it seems less scary—much less scary than it did in October 1962. With the death of Robert McNamara in July 2009, and with Fidel Castro elderly, infirm and essentially retired, those at the highest levels in Washington, Moscow and Havana with living memories of the imminence of Armageddon are almost gone. After Castro dies, there will literally be no one to ask: what was it *about*, and what was it *like*, when the fate of the world hung by a thread, in part because of your own decisions?

In this book we attempt to begin to redress the imbalance between interest and fear. Beginning with the remarkable Armageddon letters between these leaders, we fill in some of the contextual material that is missing from the written record. Some is derived from published memoirs. But most of the material is culled from our own discussions over many years with the key decision-makers in Washington, Moscow and Havana.

We began discussing the book you have in front of you in the late 1990s with our publisher, Rowman & Littlefield, with an eye toward publication by October 2002, on the fortieth anniversary of the crisis. That didn't happen, though two other R&L books on the crisis did happen by October 2002. Our conversations about this book continued in a desultory way until, in February 2010, we moved to our present institution, the Balsillie School of International Affairs at the University of Waterloo, in Waterloo, Ontario, after twenty years at Brown University's Watson Institute for International Studies. At that point, with the approach of the fiftieth anniversary of the crisis in October 2012, we knew it was time to put up or shut up. The result is in front of you.

We wanted to say something new about the crisis and to say it in new ways. Fortunately, our new environment proved to be the perfect place to adapt our ideas to the possibilities presented by a trans-media approach for which this book is the anchor. The book literally would not exist were it not for the hospitality and support of our colleagues here in Waterloo. So we'd like to begin the kudos by acknowledging them.

This book is dedicated to the other three members of the *Armageddon Letters* team: Koji Masutani, Don Morrison and Dave Welch. They have been absolutely essential to the enterprise. If we may be forgiven for taking liberties with a lyric from Joni Mitchell's "A Case of You":

I drew a map of Canada,
O Canada—
With your three faces sketched on it—

We had heard Canada is nice. It is. But our little patch of it here in southern Ontario has also provided a creative and challenging environment in which to work.

Other colleagues here in Canada have eased our transition here north of the border. They are, in alphabetical order: Greg Brennan, Gary Bruce, Ken Coates, William Coleman, Alison DeMuy, David Dewitt, John English, Colleen Fitzpatrick, Frances Hannigan, Robert Harvey, Lauren Judge, Fred Kuntz, Annie Monteiro, Douglas Peers, Neve Peric, Alexandra Stephenson, Andrew Thompson, Ramesh Thakur, April Wettig, and Kristopher Young.

We also wish to thank members of our new community who do not have an affiliation with our school, think tank, or university. They literally made it possible for us to carry this book through to conclusion, when it looked as though we might have to abandon it due to ill health. Our gratitude to Julie Maidment, MD, Robert Stevens, MD, Kathy Sawyer, RN, and the entire team of nurses in the chemotherapy unit at the Grand River Regional

Cancer Center is boundless. Together they make the strongest imaginable case for the Canadian healthcare system.

To understand why the Cuban missile crisis was so dangerous we must grasp the reality on the island of Cuba, a reality that eluded both super-powers in October 1962. We have made it our business, over the past two decades, to learn everything we can about what actually happened in Cuba between the April 1961 Bay of Pigs invasion and the October 1962 missile crisis. Specialists on Cuba have been very generous with their time and knowledge over the years, going all the way back to the 1980s, when our home base was Harvard's Kennedy School of Government. We are grateful to all of them, from the island, from the USSR, and from the U.S., includ-ing: the late Aleksander Alexseev, Jose Antonio Arbesu, the late Enrique Baloyra, Philip Brenner, Fidel Castro, Raul Castro, Oleg Darusenkov, Jorge Dominguez, Alfredo Duran, Lino Fernandez, Rafael Hernandez, Milagros Martinez, Jose Miyar, Robert Pastor, Jorge Pollo, Fernando Remirez, Dago-berto Rodriguez, Wayne Smith, Juanita Vera and Josefina Vidal. Thanks to one and all for rubbing our noses in the complexities of Cuba until we were able (we think) to appreciate really good plantain soup, whether from La Bodeguita del Medio in Habana Viejo or the Versailles in La Pequena Habana.

Our research method, critical oral history, involves the simultaneous interaction of memories of decision-makers, declassified documents and scholarly analysis. Without exception, we have always outsourced the acquisition of declassified documentation to one of the greatest non-governmental organizations ever created, George Washington University's National Security Archive. Thus has it always been for us, going back to the founding of the Archive in the mid-1980s, simultaneous with the begin-ning of our joint project on the Cuban missile crisis. Our dream team at the Archive has included: Scott Armstrong, Sue Bechtel, Thomas Blanton, Malcolm Byrne, Laurence Chang, Michael Dobbs, Barbara Elias, James Her-shberg, Peter Kornbluh, Christian Ostermann, and Svetlana Savranskaya. Never have so few spoken so much truth to power, with such powerful results. Keep up the good work, docu-hounds!

We published our first book with Jonathan Sisk and Rowman & Little-field almost twenty-five years ago. We are proud to have published half a dozen books with them in the interim, including this one, also with our friend Jon Sisk. It has been a pleasure once again to work with Jon, and with his deputy, Darcy Evans. production editor Elaine McGarraugh, typesetter Andrea Reider, and cover designer Meredith Nelson. Everyone at Rowman & Littlefield went the extra mile for us to meet the very tight deadlines we all had. We thank them for this and for agreeing to play a central role in this effort to embed a book about the 20th century's most dangerous crisis in a cutting edge, 21st century, transmedia context.

We thank Peter Almond for the foreword to this book, and for (along with Koji Masutani) introducing us to the possibilities of a transmedia approach to the Cuban missile crisis, anchored by, but by no means limited to this book. We hope we have been somewhat educable.

In the summer of 2011, we were invited by a group of filmmakers in Boston to advise them on a documentary film they said they wanted to produce on the Cuban missile crisis. Over the course of approximately eighteen hours of conversation, packed into two days and nights, we told them what we knew. But during these conversations something almost magical happened: we suddenly knew exactly what kind of book we wanted to write—more or less the book you now have in your hands, focused on the Armageddon letters and the context within which they were written and received. The film team apologized repeatedly for taking advantage of us. But in retrospect, it seems we took advantage of them. We are deeply grateful to Team Boston: Peter Frumkin, Heather Merrill, Bob Nesson, and Ben Reichman—true colleagues and friends.

We are indebted to some people who defy categorization. We don't thank them "for" any particular thing. We express our gratitude, instead, simply for having had the opportunity to work with and around them, to learn from them, and be mentored by them. We thank, in this context, Thomas J. Biersteker, the former director of the Watson Institute for International Studies, for his steadfast and creative support for our unorthodox "Blight-Lang Enterprises" during his directorship.

In the same spirit of comprehensive gratitude, we thank Mark Garrison. Likewise, we also remember Elizabeth Garrison who, alas, was unable to read the final draft. Betty and Mark have touched us profoundly and in so many ways. The Garrisons gave us a professional home, the Center for Foreign Policy Development at Brown University, where the project that produced this book grew and flourished. Our debt to them is something we do not know how to repay.

James G. Blight and janet M. Lang
Balsillie School of International Affairs and Department of History
University of Waterloo

Index

About the Authors

James G. Blight and **janet M. Lang** are on the faculty of the Balsillie School of International Affairs and the Department of History at the University of Waterloo, in Waterloo, Ontario, Canada. They have spent more than twenty-five years investigating the Cuban missile crisis, interviewing and recruiting former and current decision-makers in Washington, Moscow, and Havana; unearthing and poring over declassified documents related to the crisis; as well as organizing dialogues among top decision-makers in the crisis from the U.S., Russia, and Cuba. They are the authors or co-authors of a half-dozen previous books on the crisis and dozens of articles on the events of October 1962. They are the authors of *Virtual JFK: Vietnam if Kennedy Had Lived* (Rowman & Littlefield, 2009), and most recently, *Becoming Enemies: U.S.-Iran Relations and the Iran-Iraq War, 1979–1988* (Rowman & Littlefield, 2012).

AUTHORS OF THE ARMAGEDDON LETTERS

John F. Kennedy was president of the United States of America from his inauguration on January 20, 1961, until his murder in Dallas, Texas, on November 22, 1963. He recalled the Cuban missile crisis as the moment when the odds of war with the Soviet Union were "between one out of three and even."

Nikita S. Khrushchev was named first secretary of the Communist Party of the Soviet Union in 1953, and chairman of the Council of Ministers in

1958. He served in these positions until his removal from both in a coup on October 14, 1964. He remembered the Cuban missile crisis as a time "when the smell of scorching hung in the air."

Fidel Castro Ruz was prime minister of Cuba from 1959 to 1976 and president of the Council of State from 1976 to 2008. When he retired from the affairs of state due to illness, his brother Raul Castro assumed the presidency of Cuba. He recalled the Cuban missile crisis as the moment when the world came "this close [holding up thumb and forefinger until they almost touch] to nuclear war."